SUBMISSION: IMPOSSIBLE

THE CONTROVERSY
THE CRITERIA
THE COUNTERFEITS
AND THE CLOUT

BY
LAURA HARRIS SMITH

The double-dog-dare-ya digest on the non-gender related issue of submission in *THE SIX MAIN RELATIONSHIPS OF LIFE*

Copyright © 2002 by Laura Harris Smith

Submission: Impossible
by Laura Harris Smith

Printed in the United States of America
Library of Congress Control Number: 2002106304
ISBN 1-591601-25-8

All rights reserved. No part of this publication may be reproduced or transmitted in any form or by any means without written permission of the publisher.

Unless otherwise indicated, Bible quotations are taken from The Possibility Thinkers Bible (New King James Version), ©1984, Thomas Nelson Publishers, or The Life Application Study Bible (New Living Translation), ©1996 Tyndale House Publishers, Inc., or The Holy Bible: New International Version, ©1984, The International Bible Society.

Xulon Press
11350 Random Hills Road
Suite 800
Fairfax, VA 22030
(703) 279-6511
XulonPress.com

To order additional copies, call 1-866-381-BOOK (2665).

If submission makes you panic
makes your insides feel volcanic
Take a deep breath, maybe two
Then dive in, this book's for you!

TABLE OF CONTENTS

ACKNOWLEDGMENTS .... vi - viii
PREFACE ....ix - x

SUBMISSION: THE CONTROVERSY 1-2

CHAPTER ONE: GROUNDS FOR SUBMISSION............. 3-10
CHAPTER TWO: DRY SUBMARINES........................ 11-17
CHAPTER THREE: THE LOST UMBRELLA 18-29

SUBMISSION: THE CRITERIA
(THE SIX MAIN RELATIONSHIPS OF LIFE)........ 30-31

CHAPTER FOUR: PARENTAL......................................32-44
CHAPTER FIVE: MARITAL 45-71
CHAPTER SIX: MUTUAL... 72-87
CHAPTER SEVEN: OCCUPATIONAL......................... 88-100
CHAPTER EIGHT: GOVERNMENTAL....................... 101-117
CHAPTER NINE: PASTORAL 118-155

SUBMISSION: THE COUNTERFEITS 156-157

CHAPTER TEN: RELUCTANT SUBMISSION.............158-164

CHAPTER ELEVEN: POUTY-FACE SUBMISSION....... 165-173

CHAPTER TWELVE: DOORMAT SUBMISSION 174-185

CHAPTER THIRTEEN: DECEITFUL SUBMISSION......186-199

CHAPTER FOURTEEN:
LET'S MAKE A DEAL SUBMISSION.......................200-207

CHAPTER FIFTEEN:
JUNE CLEAVER SUBMISSION...............................208-219

CHAPTER SIXTEEN:
SARCASTIC SUBMISSION.................................... 220-228

CHAPTER SEVENTEEN:
MURMURING SUBMISSION 229-243

SUBMISSION: THE CLOUT 244

CHAPTER EIGHTEEN:
FEARLESS SUBMISSION.......................................245-254

CHAPTER NINETEEN:
BEING WORTHY TO BE SUBMITTED TO 255-278

CHAPTER 20: FREQUENT TRYER MILES
(THE TROPHIES OF TRYING SUBMISSION) 279-325

ACKNOWLEDGEMENTS

To the **Holy Spirit** who has
baptized me, qualified me
crushed and reconstructed me,
visited with and spoken to me,
and Groomed me as Bride...
Thank You, and You are welcome.

To my husband, **Chris**, who has
fallen in love with me,
stayed in love with me for 20 years,
cared for me in sickness and in health,
and forced me to learn how to slow down...
I love you so much!
Here comes the "better", "richer", "in health" part!

To my children at present,
Jessica, Julian, Jhason, Jeorgi, Jude, and Jenesis
who have made me rich
made me laugh
made me tired
but then made me thankful...
You are still the one thing that sets me apart and makes me
famous, and I can't wait to see what you each become.

To my **Parents**, all four of you, thank you
for my life

for your support in 1984
and for taking me to Sunday School as a kid.
Although you would have wished to rely less on God's grace and more on better circumstances, I am living proof that you did everything just right! Thank you for letting God do the rest and for sharing me with Him these days.

To Apostle, Pastor, Buddy **Brad Watson**, thank you for asking questions when I came to you for answers.
I bless you for evoking, invoking and even provoking me at times! Save family, you have impacted the course of my life more than any other mortal thus far, and I love you.

To Pastor **Sheila Watson**, you are too good to be true! You laugh, you preach, you prophesy, you console, and you even know how to kick up your heels!
We were in our mothers' wombs at the same time for a reason, and although you got an 8-day jumpstart on me, I'm going to catch-up with you one day, my forerunner friend!

To **Cynthia Anderson**, who sees
to **Susan Frost**, who hears
and to **Nancy Sharpes**, who speaks
you're a ministry team worthy of million dollar paychecks.
Thank you for your hearts and your hands this season!

To **Melinda** who understands without words.
You are my confidant, my accomplice and somehow my biggest fan through thick and thin.
Little did we know 30 years ago...
Barbie and Ken would have nothin' on us, sister!

To the **Praying Women** on my prayer shield who spoke this book and its publication into existence, I am eternally grateful to you. You were chosen specifically, not because you sit around and have nothing better to do than pray for me, but because you are enterprising women of faith who despite your busy schedules choose to! God bless you!

To my **Harvest** family...there are no words.
Just tears of joy; memoirs of carpet time; visions of destiny.
You're a people of vision of whom the world is not worthy.

To **Jacqueline Curtis**, my mother-n-love,
thank you for modeling submission to me.
You are a beautiful run-way model!

To **Sandy Smith**,
for reading, editing, encouraging,
and for offering to buy lunches you knew I couldn't cover.
You are the most steadfast person I know and I love you.

To **Bill Collier**
for cover design...
Thanks for dropping the cover idea about the lady feeding the man grapes and fanning him with a palm branch.
You've come a long way brother! I am forever indebted to you for your enthusiasm on this project.

and finally, to my **Adversary**:
Your resistance has made my muscles strong,
and so for that I have to say, thank you.
God used you! Ha! *Didn't I tell you He would?!*

"Let the weakling say, 'I am strong!'" Joel 3:10

"Behold I give you the authority to trample on serpents and scorpions, and over all the power of the enemy, and nothing shall by any means harm you. However, do not rejoice that the spirits SUBMIT to you, but rejoice that your names are written in heaven." Luke 10:19-20

PREFACE

Most prefaces are written after a book is complete. I never understood that. Shouldn't a preface be written before? It sort of says what you really wanted to say in the first place, right? So by the time you are holding this book in your hands it will be completed, but to capture today's emotion, let me put it to you like this as I sit here at the genesis of this book without one word yet penned: I do not want to write a book on submission. The fear of God is all over me that I am going to write it and then be seen in public arguing with my husband over whether the kids should have beef or chicken on their tacos. It is not my nature to submit!

But despite that irrelevant tidbit, after listening to my constant evaluations and revelations of the relationships between men and women, parents and children, employers and employees and even pastors and congregants, it was actually my husband who suggested to me that I write a book on submission. My deeply spiritual answer was, *"Do I have to?"*. When he told me he saw evidence in my life that I had some revolutionary ideas on submission, I shrieked, "How can you say that? You know me better than anyone!" Sheepishly he replied, "I didn't say you were walking in all of them... I just said you had them!". His funny response made me want to cast off every weight and run towards the mark of excellent submission. Although he has had many opportunities, my husband has never been heavy handed, and like God, it is his kindness that has led me to repentance. Why? Because they both understand that it is impossible to expect submission unless you are worthy to be submitted to. Case closed.

With that said, I now urge you to also understand that marital submission is just a first base of sorts in the game of submission. There is parental submission, mutual submission, occupational, governmental and even pastoral submission. It is possible to be covered on all fronts of your life, and that protection will ensure the success and speed of your destiny. Simply put, submission breeds authority. So how much authority do you want? If you do not want submission, then you have misunderstood it.

My goal with SUBMISSION: IMPOSSIBLE? What Tiger Woods did for golf, and what Charlotte Church did for opera, may I be granted the honor of doing for submission.

So that is where this book begins. I really, really really, pray that by the time we both get to the end of it, we will have gained new insight and new ground in understanding this God given, tailor-made, stay-invisible-to-your-enemy-weapon called submission. Give us understanding Lord.

I hear - I forget
I see - I remember
I do - I understand

~Chinese Proverb

Section One ~

SUBMISSION: THE CONTROVERSY

Tell me why it's so innate
The age-old self-control debate
Aren't there better things to hate
Like pride and hate itself?

Different hairdo, same dispute
Two main players, Deaf and Mute
Searching for a substitute
to save them from submission

Futile quarrels, endless words
Compromises left unheard
Happy endings all deferred
for the drug of choice called ego

Why the fear of giving in?
Lose the battle. Gain a friend!
Conquer war, which in the end
Is the fight that's really worth winning

Chapter 1

GROUNDS FOR SUBMISSION

> Why on earth should I come under?
> Yield, and let them steal my thunder
> They've no right to take my plunder
> Just to make themselves rotunder
>
> If I trust them but they blunder
> Will my world be torn asunder?
> Or will God, the great refunder
> See my faith, and bless?...I wonder.

WHY CAN'T WE SUBMIT?

There is always someone older or wiser than us. Always someone standing by ready to spill their years into our ears and make us more sensible. *So then why are we all so stupid?* Specifically, why are we wasting years of our lives on lessons that we must learn ourselves -- "the hard way"?

Most people don't have a problem sitting at the feet of a seasoned philosopher. In all of us is a God-size hole placed there by God Himself to initiate the search for divine counsel, and we chase after that counsel again and again in our lives no matter what the cost. The problem arises and the objection occurs when that wisdom is being offered for free, and by someone who lives under our own roof, sits in our same pew, or lives on some other beaten path of our lives. Disregarded as familiar, we often mistake God's wisdom through another person as cheap advice. Even Jesus said a prophet isn't welcome in his own hometown.

Rather than believing that God could divinely plant, in our ordinary midst, someone with extraordinary wisdom tailor-made just for us and our future, we want the wise one to be someone we search out and choose for ourselves. In the end, our hearts are revealed: we will submit to what we can control. If we cannot control it, we will not submit to it.

SIGN ON THE DOTTED LINE

If you can make it through this section, section one, you will make it through the rest of the book. Pouring concrete isn't entertaining, but it is vital to the foundation we are trying to build upon; the house gets prettier as we go along. In fact, we're after more than just a house here. Let it be said that you are welcome at any point during the four sections of this book to bow out, walk off-site and end construction. If you can make it through section one, you will have a humble abode. If you can stomach sections two and three you'll have the makings of a mansion. But if you'll hang in there 'til the end of section four, you will get the fully furnished palatial estate.

I remember clearly on January 13, 1996, while in prayer one night the Lord asked me, "Are you willing to make the sacrifices to build an empire?" I had no idea what He was talking about, but "empire" sounded so good that I couldn't say no. It was a word that was not normally in my vocabulary and so I knew this was the query of the Lord. If only He'd stressed the "sacrifices" part with a bit more inflection in His voice. But a vow is a vow and so I tried to keep it. More honestly, I was scared to not keep it due to Solomon's words in Ecclesiastes. 5:4-5: "When you make a vow to God, do not delay in fulfilling it. He has no pleasure in fools; fulfill your vow. It is better not to vow than to make a vow and not fulfill it". I was stuck. I couldn't renege on the vow, and God didn't seem to be budging on my idea of removing this passage from Scripture, and so when the sacrifices seemed too uncomfortable over the years I would simply rewind to my favorite part of His offer and concentrate on the empire. I would try to imagine what I was building. I picked out wallpaper before there were walls. Every time I wanted to stop construction, sell the plot and turn it into a landfill, I remembered a contractor friend of mine and the setbacks he suffered when several of his sub-contractors walked out on a job and left a project unfinished. What had started out as an exciting million dollar project ended up as a pile of rocks for all to see on that busy intersection because certain men did not keep their vows. My friend recovered because he was a man of integrity, and he probably never realized how that pile of rocks inspired me to keep building my empire, but it did. I am, in fact, still on-site. So are you! Stick with me.

WHAT IS SUBMISSION?

Submission, in its simplest form, is the ability to trust God through other people. Yes, it's a valiant thing to submit to God directly, but whether we like it or not, God Himself, through Scripture, has ordained certain institutions through which our submission to Him is tested. The six main relationships of life. Those six institutions will be examined and cross-examined in this book, and hopefully every man, woman and child reading it will judge them – and themselves. Therefore, submission is not a gender related issue, meaning it is not required of women any more than men because God levies it from us all. This book will hopefully help realign your view of submission with God's. Some people don't even know how to spell it, while others know every letter of the law and have given it a bad name. We all need some realigning on the matter whether we steer too far to the left or too far to the right. Thankfully we have a source to go to whether that alignment is for our front end, or if necessary, our rear end (pun intended). That source is a collection of 66 books that God has conveniently placed into one encyclopedia -- the Bible. Think of it as your 66-chapter atlas. In each chapter's road maps we find stories of men and women, the roads they traveled down and the right and wrong turns they made. Submission crossroads. As we read through stories where they ran red lights or fearfully ignored green lights, we see their history repeating itself in our lives. Hopefully, we learn from it. The Bible is sacredly inspired and is much more than just another book. In Hebrews, chapter 4 verse 12, it says, "For the word of God is living and active. Sharper than any double-edged sword, it penetrates even to dividing soul and spirit, joints and marrow; it judges the thoughts and attitudes of the heart." For now let's just do the math and see how that all applies to us today: Inspired writing + inspiring characters = inspiration for you and your life. Ready for a creative infusion?

The complete answer to the question "What is Submission" will be answered creatively in the following chapters herein. You'll see what it looks like, and from the chapters on counterfeits, you'll learn what submission does not look like. Submission is not slavery, it is freedom, and until we clear that one up no one in their right mind will value it. In a day and age where there seems to be no trustworthy person left to submit to, the world has seemingly thrown the baby out with the bath water and labeled submission an antiquated enslavement. How sad. In the wake of this evacuation we find ourselves in a rebellious generation that takes advice from no one. The only difference in the old and the young is that the young are more honest and rebel overtly. The middle aged nod their heads and pretend to take the advice, but then expel it in their independence. Either way, everyone remains on their islands. The result is we have reaped the whirlwind and given birth to a generation of lone rangers.

THE TROUBLE WITH TRUST

We are all born into this world with a desire to trust. It is survival for infants, and very early in life our ability to rely on our care givers shapes our expectancy of ever being cared for. Trust must be earned. We will find it hard to submit where we cannot trust. Yes, submission is scriptural, but so is laying down our lives for those who submit to us. Control, executed with a heavy hand, will produce temporary submission with unceasing enmity. The truth is, if we rule with a heavy hand we will never have a hand to hold. If we constantly look down on others, we will never have anyone looking up to us. We should tenderly lead others by serving them with open palms and not closed fists.

Personally, I think submission would sound a lot more appealing if we just changed its name to "trust". The problem with this is it would do away with over 600 Scripture references on submission, obedience and "following". But in the end, a person who has trouble submitting does not have an issue with man, but with God, for true submission is the ability to trust God enough to let Him speak through others into your life. He can speak through anyone, wise and unwise, kings and children. In fact, one of my favorite Bible stories is in the book of Numbers, chapter 22, where a donkey speaks an instructional, timely word from the Lord to a hard-headed man named Balaam.

If you find it difficult to understand why you need submission in your life, or if you see a pattern of running whenever the opportunity presents itself to make decisions requiring pledge or real commitment, you probably have some trust issues. You can deny it over and over, and if you've ordered your life to where you rarely come face to face with this fact, then chances are that you won't. Not for a while. But be warned that when you finally do, and we all will, you'll discover that your house has been built on a flimsy foundation of fear. You can face it now, or you can face it later, but you will face it at some point in your life.

If submission is difficult for you, especially in any of the six main relationships of life we will examine in this book, it is most likely because you had your trust abused at an early age. This book will not deal with the wrongs that were committed against you, but with what you will now choose to do with them. We have all been wronged. There are not enough books in the entire world to house all the wrongs that we feel we have suffered. Unfortunately, many of us build a library and pull up a chair. We invite our friends inside in hopes of having someone to visit with as we review the volumes. When they decide not to stay, we become even more rejected, write another pity publication, heighten the walls and enlarge the library. At some point, we come to the crossroad of deciding to forgive and forget. Not an easy task. Forgiveness is hard work. I have found that those who have suffered the greatest wrongs are those whom God has his finger on as key players on His chess board, thereby drafting them as prime targets by their enemy, Satan. And yes, if you are a child of God, His enemy is now your enemy, even if you never picked the fight.

If you have taken a lone-ranger oath, then don't worry, you will never have to submit to anyone. You'll never have to partner with another person, or experience the joy of having to come into agreement with them. In the end, you'll eat the fruit of a 100% risk-free life that is defined by logic and dominated by doubt. No faith, trust or unity required. If that seems like Utopia to you, you may want to keep reading.

I BEG YOUR PARDON

If you can take one last look at the pain in your life and those who inflicted it, take the leap of faith across the chasm of unforgiveness and not look back, you will find it sweet on the other side. You will find yourself able to trust others again, and yes, even submit to them fearlessly when necessary. <u>The freedom of forgiveness is not a gift given to the other person, but to yourself.</u> The effects it has on the other person, however, is a whole other cherry on top. The decision is up to you. Forgiveness is not a feeling, it is a choice. You can enlarge the lamenting library, or you can torch it and start over, and those who start over make up for lost time by God's grace and discover their lives supernaturally blossoming at warp speed. Why? Because mercy triumphs over justice, and <u>we are never more like God than when we choose to forgive the unforgivable and pardon the unpardonable.</u>

If struggle is your middle name and heartache is your friend
If burden is your brother, and adversity's your twin
If calamity jane calls twice a day and let's herself right in
Unpacks her bags with 20 hags that are her next of kin.

If mishap is your mother and disaster was your dad
If all the good you ever did was somehow seen as bad
Rejoice dear friend and laugh out loud, your heart can now be glad!
That one time foe, and all his woe, was just a passing fad

<u>Remember:</u>
Better a blank piece of paper and pen, than a pity portfolio.
Better a virgin journal than archives of simmering soot.

<u>"Love keeps no records of wrongs." 1 Corinthians 13:5</u>

Chapter 2

DRY SUBMARINES

Let me make this loud and clear:
Please don't leave me stationed here!
I will go where You command
As long as it is on dry land

As long as I am in control
And living on a grassy knoll
Where I maintain my domination
In full sight of vegetation

Take an offering, sing a hymn,
But please oh God, don't make me swim!
For what's to say if I descend
That I'll come up for air again?

DUCK FOR COVER

Submarines have always scared me. Claustrophobic, cage-like, cramped and restrictive. Sort of reminds you of submission -- or at least, our distorted view of it. My husband, Chris, has actually been on a submarine before, and seeing how I wasn't interested in doing the same any time soon, I asked him to give me a detailed virtual tour of what he experienced. As he described it, I saw some interesting similarities between submarines and true submission. Submission to all types of authority involves coming under the leadership of something or someone in order to help expedite unified teamwork. As children, we practiced the concept in the game, "follow the leader". As adults, we comply to the requests of our bosses and supervisors. As residents of a country, for instance the United States, we have an unspoken allegiance to the Constitution and other laws of the land. And in marriage, we should subject ourselves to our vows made in public on the day of our union. Unity. World peace. Fidelity between men and women, parents and children, and even between nations. Just think of the harmony that could come from just an ounce of surrender! These are just a few of the six areas we will "dive" into as we take a look at the synergy of submission. Knowing God's sense of humor, He will probably require it of me to dive even deeper and visit a submarine one day. I'd prefer a dream or a vision but we'll see what happens...

First, Chris noted that while on the submarine you had to duck constantly. He said if you didn't watch your head and bow before going into each doorway, you would run right into steel or some other immovable object. He recalled the walkways were very narrow, and that you often had to turn sideways to shimmy through tight turns. No windows, paths that led precisely where you needed to go and nowhere else, very space-efficient quarters, and hard metal everywhere -- over, under and beside you at every turn. He kept reminding himself this was protective and not restrictive. He mentioned one girl on the tour that kept smacking her head because of not ducking at each entryway.

I first began comparing submarines to submission during a season of my life when God was requiring a greater trust of me towards my husband. There is a joke in our family that since our first three children have green eyes, like me, and the next three have blue eyes, like Chris, that my genes must have finally started submitting to Chris' sometime in between babies number three and four. The sad part is it's probably the truth. I sincerely married with the intention of wanting my husband to be the spiritual head of our home, knowing that if you have two heads you have a monster -- two steering wheels and you've got a wreck. Even though marriage is a co-laboring adventure in which the husband serves and submits to the wife as he lays down his life for her, it makes perfect sense that if every business has a president and every nation has a commander in chief, then every marriage should have a designated driver. Considering I was honestly moving in the revelation of submission I had at the time as a young bride, I guess I was right on track. The problem is that God kept requiring more revelation of me. I suddenly saw I had a choice to make. Keep viewing submission as an abominable chore required of me in during conflict resolution, or take the leap and begin to look for ways to trust Chris more in every area of our life together. At that point, I got excited about what I called, my "mission to come under", or my "sub-mission".

THE ARMED FORCES

Submarines are hidden, and thereby, an intricate part of any nation's Armed Forces. However, if I were to choose which military branch I desired to be a part of, it would probably be the Air Force or some other highly visible role. And despite all the perks I hear that come with being a Secret Service Agent for the U.S. Government, I would never want to do that because, well, it's too secret. I like to be on the front lines. Always up front and always very visible. Growing up I was told that I just liked being the center of attention. I used to think, "yeh, who wouldn't?", but then I married someone who outright hates it. People are so different! As I began to lay this truth about me at God's feet over and over again as an adult, expecting to see it disappear and yet continuing to have opportunities chase me down to lead and rally people, I slowly began to realize that what I was experiencing was a God-given mantle of leadership. I also realized that it was not a bad thing that I preferred being in front of people, and began to hear the Lord say that if I would cooperate with the training He had for me, He would entrust me with many people to lead. I had no sooner hollered "yippee", when He added, "He among you who desires to be great, let him first be a servant" (Mark 10:43). I knew right then that the way in which God would prepare me for visibility would be to test my character when hidden. Before flying high in His air force, He was going to require me to come under on a sub mission.

A submarine is a fearfully and wonderfully made thing, so to speak. Most people have incorrect information on them, as they do on submission, and view the ships as dormant and dull. The truth is, submarines are designed for war, and there are two types: attack submarines and ballistic missile submarines. Attack subs are complex warships that are used mainly to seek and destroy enemy submarines and other ships. Ballistic missile subs hide in the very depths of the ocean until the most strategic time to attack, and then they are able to target entire cities and enemy military bases, releasing multiple bombs to many locations at one time.

HOW LOW CAN YOU GO?

Subs usually attack from beneath the water's surface, and must remain in this hidden place to be effective. Early submarines could not do this for long periods. They had to come up for air for the crew every few hours, and in doing so made themselves vulnerable to attacks from enemy planes and ships. Today's subs, however, are much more developed and mature in their missions. Thanks to nuclear power which generates its own oxygen, submarines can stay submerged and hidden for months at a time, and they spend little time above water.

How does a submarine submerge to such depths? It dives by flooding its ballast tanks with water which increases the weight of the sub and causes it to sink. It glides downward smoothly after losing its positive buoyancy, or its ability to stay afloat. How do subs advance once submerged? By letting off steam! It seems their engines are part nuclear reactor and part steam generator and when put together, they produce intense heat. Large pipes carry water from the steam generator to the reactor where the water is heated to 600 degrees Fahrenheit. But because it is under intense pressure it cannot boil, therefore the water returns to the generator and eventually produces steam that propels the ship.

In case you've not noted the obvious comparisons between submarines and submission thus far, here are some cliff notes to chew on: Submission, like a submarine, requires the temporary hiddenness of individual agenda for the good of the whole crew's strategic mission during battle. It produces severe pressure when generators and reactors come together, then necessitates letting off steam in order to move forward. It requires deep humility and the ability to see bowing down as protection and not restriction. The internal torpedoes of submarines can be compared to prayer, and have honing devices that hunt down specific targets and assure precise success. Like the Holy Spirit, subs have internal navigation systems by which information is fed into a guidance system to ensure infallible direction. Plain and simple, submission makes unity and teamwork possible in the midst of any battle, and although it may require the temporary hiddenness of your own personal ambitions, in the end you will see your mission accomplished due to your ability to come under and stay there. Remember: Some of us are generators and some of us are reactors, but none of us should heat to boiling -- just let off a little steam and move forward!

HIGH AND DRY

Finally, try and imagine a grandiose navy submarine flying through the air (the Good Year Blimp doesn't count). It doesn't work, because it wasn't made for that mission. Now try to picture a perfectly crafted submarine, armed and ready for battle with the best honing devices, the best internal navigation system and top of the line sonar detectors -- and picture it shipwrecked on sand or even on the peak of a mountaintop, never submerging in the water in which it was made to rule. A dry submarine. Suddenly that million dollar ammo becomes a wasted investment.

Just in case you're still skeptical about taking the plunge and testing the waters of submission, keep in mind that the journey of every attack submarine is called a "cruise". Bon voyage!

"Faith without works is like a song you can't sing
It's about as useless as a screen door on a submarine"

~Rich Mullins   1949-1994

Chapter 3

THE LOST UMBRELLA

I'm cold, I'm lost, I'm sopping wet
But still I'm playing hard to get
'Cause last time when I used your tool
It broke and I was left, the fool

I lost my head, I lost my mind
All for the lie of "high and dry"
But now I see that's just a dream
There's no such shelter with that theme

So you won't find me underneath
I'd rather drown and grit my teeth
I'll stand my ground and stand right here
And perish in my liquid fear

MY LOST UMBRELLA

In the fall of 2000 while in Boston, Massachusetts, I had the opportunity to go on board the U.S. Constitution, the oldest warship in America. It was an unusually rainy, cold day, but several of my fellow state coordinators from the United States Strategic Prayer Network, along with Mike and Cindy Jacobs who spearhead the national network, trudged through the deluge and winds just for the opportunity to step foot on that boat and pray on-site for our nation's history and future. Once on deck, our dutiful tour guide was trying hard to shout above the storm and give us instructions, but it was all I could do to stay focused on my rebellious umbrella in my right hand, my infant daughter who was on my left hip, and my soaking wet open-toed shoes which were now under two inches of water. I was ever so thankful as we climbed down, down, down the tiny, narrow steps that led us into the dry hull of the boat. In the belly of that warship we warred for America to indeed be one nation under God again. Warmed only by prayer and the memoirs of resounding cannons that lined each wall, we completed our task only to once again resurface and take on the weather above deck. It was in the middle of the steep, narrow stairway with a line of people in front of me and another stream in back, that I caught my first glimpse of the tempestuous sky and realized that I no longer had my umbrella with me. Too late to turn back and with the next tour group waiting to descend, I wrapped one arm around baby Jenesis, one arm around my teenage daughter, Jessica, and the three of us took off through the storm. Having been told all our lives that we were so skinny we could stand still in the rain and not get wet, Jessica and I learned that day it wasn't true. By the time we found our car and other companions, we were soaking wet and chilled to the bone. This time, however, I was warmed along the way with some valuable revelations about umbrellas and authority, and the similarities between them during a storm.

Many people today are afraid of authority. Many of them have good reason to be. They have been abused, exploited, violated and wounded to the point of no return, short of supernatural intervention. Clinging tightly to the last thing in their lives that they *can* control, their power to forgive or not forgive, they often go down with the ship out of their fear of letting go. As described in the opening poem of this chapter, they'd rather drown in a deluge than risk the embarrassment of another leaky umbrella. If they do get drenched, at least they were in control of the decision. And while the results may devastate them, at least they were predictable and didn't require getting their hopes up. Sounds extreme, but you'd be surprised at how true it is.

In case you still can't see the link between umbrellas and authority, here's the idea: They are both coverings. Seeing submission to authority as an enemy is just as ridiculous as seeing an umbrella as the enemy during a storm. And holding the opinion that you don't need to be covered by any governing authorities in your life is just as absurd as believing you can stand still in the rain and not get wet!

James Bond knew the importance of being under cover. Most of us watched the infallible 007 and coveted the glamour and fame that came with the job, but few of us realized who was on the other end of that ticker-tape readout wrist watch. Headquarters. And it was headquarters who called all the shots, made all the plays and warned Bond of impending danger. He always complied and was always undefeated as a result. It was never mentioned in the script, but what would have become of Bond, James Bond, if he wasn't under cover?

"COVER FOR ME"

Retail employees trading shifts and army soldiers running toward battle lines understand the expression, "cover for me". It implies that one person will watch out for the other, or if necessary, trade places with them altogether. Ultimately, that is exactly what Christ did for each of us as He took our place on the cross, dying so that we might live. And while many of us find it easy to spiritually place our trust in God once we come to the startling realization of how He covered for us through His only Son -- the perfect sacrifice -- many of us stop there and are not willing to trust in His physical coverings which He has set in place for us through His earthly institutions. They are each laid out in Scripture, and we will dissect each one of them in Section 2, "Submission: The Criteria (The Six Main Relationships of Life).

"Everyone must submit himself to the governing authorities, for there is no authority except that which God has established. The authorities that exist have been established by God. Consequently, he who rebels against the authority is rebelling against what God has instituted, and those who do so will bring judgment on themselves." Romans 13:1

Perhaps you are someone who is under the delusion that you can cover for yourself. And perhaps that is true to a certain extent. But you would have to plot out your life with an unerring itinerary that no human can compose (unless of course, that human is someone sent from above to cover for you). In my years of ministering in local churches, I have met many people who overestimated themselves. While we can never overestimate God and all the gigantic feats He wants to do through us, we can never reach our fullest potential in Him if we underestimate His guidelines, one of which is submission. I have met many gifted people in my more than 25 years serving the Lord, but it has saddened my heart at how many of them are as lacking in humility and submission as they are rich in talent and know-how. They recognize how broad their shoulders are in the spirit, and yet fail to see the need that brings about to come under an even broader authority. "For everyone to whom much is given, from him much will be required." Luke 12:48 The picture comes to mind of a 300-lb. man trying to stay dry under a portable Handy-totes™ umbrella. And while many seek the lateral prayer coverage of dozens of "accountability prayer partners", many times this is just a very religious crutch used to avoid submission. If you carry much on your shoulders in any or every area of your life, it is urgent for you to be covered by a sizable authority. Not someone that you merely walk with and take advice from, but someone whom you trust enough to *obey*. Someone wiser, maybe older in the Spirit, who is further up by a few rungs on the ladder than you are and has a bit of a clearer view of things than you do. Not only do you need it, but you deserve it, for the Lord cannot promote you further until He knows He has you protected. He loves you that much. The greater your understanding of the benefits of authority, the more your desire will be to submit to it. We wonder why we are often under attack and constantly coming up against such struggle in our lives, and yet never seem to understand that we have run out from under our umbrellas in the midst of flash flooding. Either that or we run from umbrella to umbrella in search of the perfect covering, and then the typhoon hits, and having criticized every possible candidate we find ourselves caught in a torrential downpour.

"Can you raise your voice to the clouds and cover yourself

with a flood of water? Do you send the lightning bolts on their way? Do they report to you, 'Here we are'? Who endowed the heart with wisdom or gave understanding to the mind? Who has the wisdom to count the clouds? Who can tip over the water jars of the heavens when the dust becomes hard and the clods of earth stick together?" Job 38:34-38

THE CENTURION SANDWICH

Luke 7 describes a man who was not intimidated by submission. He was a Roman Centurion who was asking Jesus to heal his servant. The image of the strong, stalwart soldier needing anything from Jesus is enough to touch the heart, but then add to the mix his humility in saying, "Hey, you don't even have to come to the house, Jesus; just say the word from here and it will be done", and it shows just how well he understood Jesus' authority over spirits of infirmity. He said, "For I myself am a man under authority, with soldiers under me. I tell this one, 'Go,' and he goes; and that one, 'Come,' and he comes. I say to my servant, 'Do this,' and he does it", and so we see that he was a man of authority and yet a man under it. He was sandwiched in authority, brave enough to both administer it and submit to it, and thus he secured miracles. "When Jesus heard this, he was amazed at him, and turning to the crowd following him, he said, "I tell you, I have not found such great faith even in Israel." Luke 7:9

Joshua was another man sandwiched in authority, as was Moses. At the conclusion of the book of Deuteronomy and the beginning of the book of Joshua we see how Moses' service to the Jewish people came to an end as one who led God's people out of Egyptian bondage, through the desert and on towards their rightful destinies in a land all their own. However, Joshua was the successor with the important task of actually taking them into the Promise Land and establishing life for them there. Due to the rebellion and faithlessness of the people after leaving Egypt, God turned their eleven day journey to Canaan into a forty year trek through the wilderness in an attempt to do away with that defiant generation and subdue the land with a more faithful, pure one. Out of over one million Jews that had left Egypt, Caleb and Joshua were the only two left from the original group. Tells you a little something about Joshua, eh? Still, Joshua 11:15 reads, "As the Lord had commanded Moses his servant, so Moses commanded Joshua, and so Joshua did. He left nothing undone of all that the Lord had commanded Moses." I find it interesting that it doesn't say that Joshua obeyed God, but that Joshua obeyed Moses. Many people would have a hard time with that today. Although Joshua had watched Moses for years, we see in those transitional days how Joshua was really like a disciple of Moses', gleaning every last thing from him before stepping over the great divide and into the weighty role of commander in chief. We read in Deuteronomy 34:9 that "Joshua son of Nun was full of the spirit of wisdom, for Moses had laid his hands on him. So the people of Israel obeyed him and did everything just as the Lord had commanded Moses." In other words, for that season, the people submitted to Joshua, Joshua submitted to Moses, and Moses submitted to God. Moses also submitted to Jethro, his father-in-law when he gave him advice on how to govern God's people (Exodus 18:13-27). Ultimately, everyone was covered and was a covering for someone else. Even those people at the "bottom" of the chain who submitted to Joshua still had homes in which they were leaders. And if we went all the way to the "top", to Moses, we would see a man who was a servant to his people. When they sinned treacherously against God he would step between them and heaven and intercede for God to stay His hand of judgment. Full honor, yet full humility. At last there was order and unity in the land which could purchase them promotion and promise. When Moses died, the transition was a smooth one and the people said to Joshua, "We will obey you just as we obeyed Moses. And may the Lord your God be with you as he was with Moses. Anyone who rebels against your word and does not obey your every command will be put to death. So be strong and courageous!" Joshua 1:17-18 Can you imagine what we could accomplish today in our homes, schools, workplaces, and congresses with that kind of joyful order and submission?

PATCH THE HOLES

The Lord, nor I, could end this chapter without directly addressing the umbrellas. If you are a parent, a pastor, a politician or anything in between, then you are somebody's umbrella. Yes, Hebrews 13:17 commands those under you to "obey your leaders and submit to their authority", but it also commands you to keep watch over those you lead and give an account before God for them. Makes you want to patch the holes and sew your seams, eh?

God takes very seriously the task of caring for those under us. Always remember that you yourself are in need of covering, and must look for ways to submit to your governing authorities too. In the end, you will find yourself fully sandwiched in the protection of God, and a prime candidate for His blessings. If you choose not to submit yourself to God's guidelines for leaders, you will find yourself in the path of His fury. He may continue to work through you and mercifully allow you to stay in your post just as he allowed water to flow from the rock even after Moses disobeyed Him and struck it. To provide for His people, God allowed the water to flow, but remember that Moses was not allowed to enter the Promised Land afterwards.

In the book of Romans, Chapter 12 verse 8, the Apostle Paul says, "If God has given you leadership ability, take the responsibility seriously." In his second letter to the church at Corinth where he needs to visit and deal harshly with some situations there (13:10), Paul confesses that he hopes all is settled before he comes, then adds, "For I want to use the authority the Lord has given me to build you up, not to tear you down." He essentially says the same thing in his letter to Philemon by noting, "I could demand it in the name of Christ because it is the right thing for you to do, but because of our love, I prefer just to ask you." The same sobering message is conveyed to fathers in Ephesians 6:4, which says, "Fathers, do not exasperate your children; instead, bring them up in the training and instruction of the Lord". Jeremiah had harsh words for the spiritual leaders of Israel, the shepherds, who had been cruel to the people and scattered the sheep. In essence God promised to scatter *them* and prosper and increase those they had not attended to. In Psalm 58:1, David, one of Israel's greatest kings, angrily addresses some men in authority who had twisted God's justice and says, "Justice -- do you rulers know the meaning of the word? Do you judge the people fairly?" However, just a few chapters later he himself humbly cries out to the Lord and says, "O God, you know how foolish I am; my sins cannot be hidden from you. Don't let those who trust in you stumble because of me, O Sovereign Lord Almighty." (69:5-6). The Apostle Paul seems to echo this serious charge to leaders when he says to Timothy, "But some teachers have missed the whole point". (1 Timothy 1:6), and in the book of James, there is a warning to them, declaring, "My brethren, let not many of you become teachers, knowing that we shall receive a stricter judgment." (3:1).

THE SHEPHERD SHORTAGE

When the leaders in Israel began caring more for themselves then for the people God had put in their care, He was angry with them for not strengthening the weak and healing the sick. He called His prophet Ezekiel in to give them a startling message. "Son of man, prophesy against the shepherds of Israel; prophesy and say to them: 'This is what the Sovereign LORD says: Woe to the shepherds of Israel who only take care of themselves! Should not shepherds take care of the flock? You eat the curds, clothe yourselves with the wool and slaughter the choice animals, but you do not take care of the flock. You have not strengthened the weak or healed the sick or bound up the injured. You have not brought back the strays or searched for the lost. You have ruled them harshly and brutally. So they were scattered because there was no shepherd, and when they were scattered they became food for all the wild animals. My sheep wandered over all the mountains and on every high hill. They were scattered over the whole earth, and no one searched or looked for them. "'Therefore, you shepherds, hear the word of the LORD: As surely as I live, declares the Sovereign LORD, because my flock lacks a shepherd and so has been plundered and has become food for all the wild animals, and because my shepherds did not search for my flock but cared for themselves rather than for my flock, therefore, O shepherds, hear the word of the

LORD: This is what the Sovereign LORD says: I am against the shepherds and will hold them accountable for my flock. I will remove them from tending the flock so that the shepherds can no longer feed themselves. I will rescue my flock from their mouths, and it will no longer be food for them." Ezekiel 34:2-10

In Philippians 2:5-8 we are told, "Your attitude should be the same that Christ Jesus had. Though he was God, He did not demand and cling to the rights as God. He made himself nothing; He took the humble position of a slave and appeared in human form. And in human form He obediently humbled Himself even further by dying a criminal's death on a cross."

As a pastor or pastoral leader in any area of service, if you find yourself unable to purely carry out the call of the Lord due to a pattern of personal sin or wounding that needs to be taken care of, then be humble enough to step down for a season and submit to God's heart. There are warning signs along the way. 1 Timothy 3:12 speaks to church leaders and says that a man must manage his children and household well before being entrusted with more. As you allow God to heal your heart and life, look for ways to submit to the leadership in authority over you, and if you don't know who those men and women are who can speak into your life with influence, ask God to place them on your path, and He will.

"He will cover you with his feathers, and under his wings you will find refuge; his faithfulness will be your shield and rampart." Psalm 91:4

If you are a leader, a teacher, or an authority in any field,

God will require a greater accountability from you. More humility, more obedience and more submission. If you will serve those you lead in the fear of the Lord, perhaps one day we will have less people walking around with so many trust issues. Minus the woundings, they will better grasp who they are in Christ, and thus better grasp all the success that is just waiting out there with their name on it. Imagine an entire generation of people *of* authority and *under* it. Imagine homes where love rules and children never learn how to spell the word "divorce". Imagine the marketplace with such loyal laborers that every man's business thrives and the national economy skyrockets! Envision nations moving beyond tolerance and onto unity! The possibilities are endless!

Under cover, overjoyed
every ounce of trust employed
hearts defended not destroyed
and each one moving forward

Kings as servants, slaves as lords
every soul in one accord
all at rest and all restored
under, over, and in between

Section Two ~

SUBMISSION: THE CRITERIA

THE SIX MAIN RELATIONSHIPS OF LIFE

"I have become all things to all men..." 1 Corinthians 9:22

In section one we touched on submitting to God through the scriptural institutions He has ordained for our lives. To say that you must submit to no man because you have chosen to submit to God directly is not only a perversion of submission, but a cop-out. If you are truly submitting to God, then you are submitting to His Word and its undeniable mandates on authority. God would never contradict Himself, and so the "it's just me and Jesus" mentality is a fabricated delusion (not to mention an obsolete one).

So what are the main relationships that God has ordained for our lives? Think of it as the six course meal. The fainthearted will turn up their noses and run, but the brave cry, "super-size it!" And the exact order of the courses doesn't really matter, because "of course" all of us are unique and discover the institutions in different sequence. Some people eat their soup before their salad or even their dessert before their entree'. Sadly though, some eat only their dessert or stop at the appetizer and never move on, thus missing all the satisfaction of the six course spread that God has prepared for them. I hope you have a healthy appetite my friend, because this section of the book, Section 2, is a rather large portion of filling protein. Be brave, set your mind on cleaning your plate, and then dive right in. We'll keep you posted along the way on how deep we're diving just in case you need to come up for air!

THE INSTITUTIONS

Romans 13:1-5 "Everyone must submit himself to the governing authorities, for there is no authority except that which God has established. The authorities that exist have been established by God. Consequently, he who rebels against the authority is rebelling against what God has instituted, and those who do so will bring judgment on themselves. For rulers hold no terror for those who do right, but for those who do wrong. Do you want to be free from fear of the one in authority? Then do what is right and he will commend you. For he is God's servant to do you good. But if you do wrong, be afraid, for he does not bear the sword for nothing. He is God's servant, an agent of wrath to bring punishment on the wrongdoer. Therefore, it is necessary to submit to the authorities, not only because of possible punishment but also because of conscience."

Chapter 4

PARENTAL SUBMISSION

A Child's Perspective of Parenthood

My conception took only one second
The womb, 24 million more
20,000 spent sweating in labor
many thousands spent being adored

10,000 per year on my homework
10 million spent watching me flaunt
500 million to call their job done
How much more of my time do they want?

THE KEY INGREDIENT
(DIVE ALERT: BATTEN DOWN THE HATCHES -- HERE WE GO...)

As the mother of six children, three sons and three daughters, I can tell you that submission is the key ingredient that I try to stir up in my children from the time they are born. Gratitude and submission to God, yes, but originally, gratitude and submission to me and their father. If they are submitted, I can teach them anything. If they are rebellious, I am useless in their lives. Their submission allows me the opportunity to pour everything I am into them, and challenges me to grow so that I might serve them better. That "teachable spirit" is easier to deposit into a child who knows he's loved. I remember my father telling me when my first child was just a year old, "Baby, if she knows you love her you can teach her anything." I have found this to be true throughout the years. If I can instill in my children a love affair with obedience and the influence she carries, then I know they will live a long and happy life after I'm gone. After all, that is God's promise: *"Honor your father and mother "--which is the first commandment with a promise--'that it may go well with you and that you may enjoy long life on the earth.'"* Ephesians 6:2-3.

Growing up, I confused submission with "being good". Therefore my flesh discovered that it could be good on the outside, and yet rebel quietly on the inside. Hidden rebellion. Still, "out of the abundance of the heart, the mouth speaks" (Luke 6:45), and so over and over again in my "good" childhood, my mouth would get me in trouble. For years after I was grown with children, my mother and I would be chatting about my teen years and I would come away wondering if we were talking about the same person. What I remembered was how hard I had polished the outside of the cup, and yet what my mother had seen was what needed cleaning on the inside. I think we both would have benefited from seeing the other's point of view, because the outside and the inside are both important parts of a person. Jesus seemed to agree in Matthew 23:26 when he spoke to the Pharisees about cleaning the inside and the outside of the cup, but in my mother's defense, He did say that if we'd start with the inside, the outside would take care of itself.

"Listen to your father, who gave you life, and do not despise your mother when she is old."
Proverbs 23:22

ONLY THE YOUNG DIE GOOD

"Is is good for the young to submit to the yoke of his discipline. Lamentations 3:27 (NTL), or as the NIV puts it, "It is good for a man to bear the yoke while he is young". Probably the flesh's first encounter with death is when a toddler gets his or her hands spanked for the first time during a battle of the wills with mommy. I remember after my sixth child was born and was just a few days old, one of my other daughters asked, "Mama, do you think Jenesis has sinned yet?" "What an interesting question", I thought. I answered no, but then as I chewed on it for a while I realized that flesh is flesh, even if it's only just a few days old, and from the moment it is born it must be trained to surrender itself to the self-control of the Holy Spirit. John 3:6 says, "Flesh gives birth to flesh, but the Spirit gives birth to spirit." John 6:63 adds, "The Spirit gives life; the flesh counts for nothing", and of course you can't argue with Mark 14:38, which says, "The spirit is willing, but the flesh is weak.". Of course, no one in their right mind would spank a newborn for having a flesh fit (which newborns do have from time to time when all is well, they are full and dry, but they just want to cry), but I do believe there is a way to begin training our precious sons and daughters from the moment we bring them into this world.

> *"From birth I have relied on you; you brought me forth from my mother's womb. I will ever praise you"*
> *Psalm 71:6*

We decided with our very first child to put them on a feeding schedule, nothing that couldn't be altered in a pinch, but definite feeding times that came every three-four hours during the day and immediately began "stretching" the child's appetite through the night. I've heard severe stories about hard-line moms who watched the clock, and so I must clarify that while we never served our schedule, it most certainly served us -- so well in fact that we have never had a 2 a.m. nurser in the whole bunch. Did we do that because we were selfish and wanted more sleep? Ok, who wouldn't want more sleep, but no we were not trying to be selfish. We did it because we saw an opportunity to train up our children in the way they should go from the moment they were born, knowing that long before they could reason with their minds they could perceive with their spirits. Somehow, this art form we developed at campsmith resulted in well-trained toddlers who all by-passed the "terrible twos". Those well-trained toddlers then turned into focused students who then blossomed into responsible teenagers. At the time of this writing only 2 of our children are teenagers, but the results have been so rewarding that the younger ones are gladly following in the prosperous footsteps of their older brothers and sisters .

> *"A wise child accepts a parent's discipline; a young mocker refuses to listen." Proverbs. 13:1*

exHONORate ME!

To exonerate a person means to free, excuse or exempt

them. Many sons and daughters, young and old, seek to be exonerated from honoring their mothers and fathers. For years Chris and I have had a special relatability with teenagers. We've had them in our home, we've held them in our arms and met them right where they were, and in that time I have heard just about every argument on the exemptions of submitting to parents. "My mom's a crack addict and I can't be expected to submit to her or honor her!" While my heart would grieve for that youngster, my spirit would traverse back to the ten commandments and wonder why God didn't put any disclaimers on the fifth one. He didn't say, "Honor your mother and father IF they are worthy of honor". Nor, "Honor your mother and father unless you have righteous reason to defy them". It's as if God considers them worthy of honor just for getting you here.

"And you will say, 'how I hated discipline! If only I had not demanded my own way! Oh why didn't I listen to my teachers? Why didn't I pay attention to those who gave me instruction? I have come to the brink of utter ruin, and now I must face public disgrace." Proverbs 5:12-14

The Hebrew word used for "honor" used in the fifth commandment in Exodus 20:12 is "kabed" (Strongs #3513). One of its definitions is to "promote". So in essence, the fifth commandment is really a command for you to promote your parents. Did you know that only you can give your parents a promotion? Isn't it interesting that God didn't order mothers and fathers to promote their children, but the other way around? God has literally put promotion within the hands of children. Therefore, whenever I hear a youth, or for that matter anyone of any age complaining that their mother or father is not responsible enough to receive honor,

I immediately ask them the question. "Well then, when's the last time you gave them a promotion?

"It is better to be a poor but wise youth than to be an old and foolish king who refuses all advice. Such a youth could come from prison and succeed. He might even become king, though he was born in poverty. Everyone is eager to help such a youth, even to help him take the throne. He might become the leader of millions and be very popular."
Ecclesiastes 4:13-16

In Scripture, Rebekah was a woman who made some bad choices as a mother. She was Isaac's wife, and Abraham and Sarah's daughter-n-law (no pressure, of course). When she devised the deceitful plan for her younger son, Jacob, to usurp his twin brother Esau's rightful birthright blessing, Jacob tried to convince her it was wrong but she still demanded his obedience to her plan. I have met many sons and daughters, young and old, who are put in the same precarious places today with the decisions their parents make. Still, studying what happened to Jacob and Rebekah is light at the end of the tunnel. Many have studied Genesis 27 and wondered how Jacob got by with such extravagant deceit, and how the blessing was allowed to remain on him by such a holy God. After all, God honored the blessing and still today He is known as "The God of Abraham, Isaac and Jacob", not "the God of Abraham, Isaac and Esau". Why? The answer is in verse 13. "His mother said to him, "My son, let the curse fall on me. Just do what I say." Rebekah offered to take the punishment for what she was asking Jacob to do, and as a result she did, never seeing Jacob again for the rest of her life. She could have been today's crack addict mom giving bad advice to her son. But somehow and some way, through the concept of honor and obedience, God was able to bless Jacob and make him a mighty nation. Let's not forget that from him sprang forth the twelve tribes of Israel, and from one of those, the tribe of Judah, came Jesus Christ Himself many years later. I am not condoning sin or the breaking of the law, in fact, if you are asked by one authority figure in your life to do something which involves breaking the law in any fashion, you should opt to submit to the higher authority that forbids you from fulfilling their request. Still, when those over us make wrong decisions that put us in difficult places, God keeps good books and will deal with them directly. He will also deal with us directly if we do not honor them in the midst of their infractions. If we will seek the Lord with sincere hearts of submission, He will give us creative ways to honor those parents who do not honor Him.

While dying on a cross, Jesus' last act on earth was to take care of His mother:

"And when Jesus therefore saw His mother, and the disciple whom He loved standing by, He said to His mother, 'Woman, behold your son!' Then He said to the disciple, 'Behold your mother!' and from that hour that disciple took her to his own home".
John 19:26-27

I have begun to enjoy seeing the eyes of dissatisfied sons and daughters of all ages light up when explaining to them just how much of their parent's progression is dependent upon their revelation of honoring them. Even though the parent is the adult and should have been the strong one, God has somehow put an even stronger force within the hands of children in case they were not. He gives them the choice to forgive and to learn. He gives them the choice to be on the honor roll and add years to their own lives. "Honor your father and your mother, so that you may live long in the land the LORD your God is giving you". Exodus 20:12. I have received many reports from families now on how God is tenderizing the generations in their families, all thanks to the simple concept of giving honor where it's due. And I'll never be convinced that even the worst, most abusive, most selfish parent in the world isn't due some sort of honor. They certainly are in greater need of a promotion, that's for sure. Even if the last good thing they ever did was giving birth to you, that is certainly enough.

"Listen, my child, to what your father teaches you. Don't neglect your mother's teaching. What you learn from them will crown you with grace and clothe you with honor."
Proverbs. 1:8

FIVE BROKEN GLASSES

Once I had a dream that shed new light for me on how serious God is about parental submission. I was already an adult and was married with five children. The dream however was about me and my step-father, whom I had experienced some rocky roads with during the eight years that he raised me. I dreamed that I stood washing dishes at a sink as my step-father entered the room. We made small-talk, saying things like, "How are you?".... "Oh, I'm fine! How are you?". But I knew that everything wasn't fine. I could see just beneath the soapy water that there were five broken glasses in the sink, complete with jagged edges and sharp splinters. Even though I knew at any moment I was going to slip my hand into the sink and bleed that water red,

I continued to pretend everything was fine and made small-talk with David. It sort of summed up my relationship with him and the level of communication we had plateaued at after I'd left home at eighteen. After some other details in the dream, I woke up very disturbed and asked the Lord what it meant, specifically the part about the five broken glasses. Very clearly, I heard Him say, "You have broken the fifth commandment". Horrified, I grabbed my Bible to count through all ten and see which one I'd broken, and then landed upon #5: "Honor your mother and father". I exclaimed, "But Lord! He is NOT my father, he's my step-father!" I was appalled to think the Lord could not understand this and thereby offer to exempt me from honoring him. It was then that Jesus reminded me that He too had had a step-father. Whoa! The Lord showed me my heart! He showed me the unforgiveness in it and I wept like a baby. All these years I had thought God was siding with me about the hurts I had experienced as the teenager of divorced parents, and while He had indeed held me in His arms through it and visited me in my room as I would lay in my bed crying many nights, I began to see another side of things and how I had crossed a line and walked over into the blatant sin of unforgiveness. He showed me how difficult it must have been on David -- raising a child not his own -- and how much David had done and sacrificed for me. He showed me how gifted David was and how much he loved the Lord. He showed me how unforgiveness had caused me to filter all my childhood memories through my woundings, and required it of me to finally clean that filthy filter. Suddenly, the air got clearer.

That very morning, I realized that perhaps I'd had a part to play in our plateaued relationship. I had forgiven David "amen", but not enough to move on beyond small talk. I had longed for it and prayed for it, even fasted for it, but I had never dreamed that I was the one in charge of giving my step-father a promotion. It was then that I saw that honor was not the absence of malice, but the presence of praise. So that day, at 6:30 in the morning, I called my step-dad long distance and begged his forgiveness for breaking the fifth commandment. I relayed the entire dream to him. I told him how I had prayed for years for God to put it on his heart to apologize to me, but had somehow failed to see the crimes in secret that I myself had committed against him. He forgave me, released me, and blessed me. I felt like a load of bricks fell off my chest. I had never in a million years thought that I would be the first to say "I'm sorry", in fact I had imagined for years the day he would get down on his knees and apologize first, but now all of a sudden the air was so clean and sweet that I didn't care! What a petty desire! I loved him so much and our relationship grew and grew.

"...I do exactly what my Father has commanded Me".
John 14:31

FROM HEALING TO WHOLENESS

About a year later, an amazing thing happened. In fact, four in one week. Number one, I received a prophecy from a friend concerning a book I was going to write. He said that this book would include stories about my childhood, and would even deal with the hard times I had gone through with my family, specifically my step-father. I was shocked that God would reveal that to him. Still, I remember hearing it and thinking, "Yeh right! I could never and would never tell stories that would drudge up all these things God has finally healed! It would take a miracle to write a book like that!" One night that week as I was meditating on the prophecy I began to innocently "drudge up" some very old memories. I remembered how I had once turned to someone in my teen years as a confidant concerning family troubles, but had ended up hurting my step-dad deeply when this friend told his parents and they contacted my step-dad about it. I remembered the pain and the shame involved. But to God's glory, (and this was miracle #2) all these years later as an adult, I ran to my closet that night where I wept and the Lord ministered to me with one final blow to the enemy concerning this area of my life. As strange as it may sound, I tell you the truth that as I cried out to God to go beyond healing into wholeness, I felt a hand go down deep into my insides and pull out what felt like a large root. As the hand emerged, which I believe was God's, I heard a huge roar like the roar of a lion, and I heard it with my ears in the spirit as God's hand pulled this root from my soul and delivered me from a spirit of rage. Like the layers of an onion, the Lord had begun a work many years before which were reaching the core of me on this night. What he'd done the year before had healed my relationship with my step-dad, but what he did on that night in my closet finally made me whole as a parent.

Within 24 hours, I had a knock on my door, and this was the third and most significant gift of the week. I answered it and was surprised to see my step-father standing on my front porch. He was hundreds of miles from home, and had stopped through Nashville while traveling on business. It was raining outside, and so I ushered him in quickly but could find no place for him to sit since every chair and sofa were piled high with lounging children stuck inside on a dreary day. He offered to take the floor, and as he did he got right to the point. He said he'd been thinking about the next book that I would write, and how he had some suggestions on who I should let publish it. He had worked in the Christian Booksellers industry for years, and so I knew his advice was solid. I decided to step out on a limb and tell him about my friend's prophecy concerning a book of mine that would include dealing with family issues, and his response shocked me. "You know Laura, you and I went through some pretty difficult days, and I think it would be good for you to write about it and maybe help other people who are still there". As if I wasn't shocked enough at his words, it was then that I noticed his position on the floor. He was on his knees. I felt like laughing and crying out loud, and I think I did both as I thanked David over and over for confirming this obvious word from the Lord. A few days went by and I went to a Christian bookstore to make a small purchase. It was there that miracle #4 occurred. While browsing at a certain book table, I turned to see two faces from my past. It was the couple whom I had just been thinking of just a few nights before, the ones who had been caught in the middle of a family under fire when I had confided in their son years before. I had not seen them in over twenty years, and I was once again, stunned at the depth of the healing work God must be trying to do in my life! We chatted and got caught up, and while neither of us plunged into anything deep, I made sure they knew how well Mom and Dave were doing and what great grandparents I thought they were. They could see all that God had done, and I walked away feeling like God had given me a huge cherry on top of an already perfectly orchestrated week. A work of God that had begun many years before on the knees in prayer, had now culminated all in one week, again on the knees, this time in forgiveness, and God was now able to bring complete closure and usher in complete destiny that he had predestined for me before the foundations of the earth. I believe much of it is being fulfilled in the pages of this book.

God will see your true devotion
Through your heart for pure promotion

Honor those who gave you birth
And you will find your own self-worth

"Children, obey your parents in everything, for this pleases the Lord." Colossians 3:20

"My son, keep your father's commands and do not forsake your mother's teaching. Bind them upon your heart forever; fasten them around your neck. When you walk, they will guide you; when you sleep, they will watch over you; when you awake, they will speak to you."
Proverbs 6:20-22

Chapter 5

MARITAL SUBMISSION

The Terms of Endearment...

"Dearly beloved we're gathered here
To do away with views severe
Of matrimony's kings and slaves
that take strong wedlocks to their graves

If both can say, 'I'll serve you well'
'Come rain or shine, come heav'n or hell'
And fathom making one from two
You'll be allowed to say, 'I do'"

LEARNING & UN-LEARNING
(DIVE ALERT: FLOOD BALLAST TANKS AND DESCEND)

Welcome to the chapter on marital submission, the chapter that most outsiders think the whole book is about! Please make note that there are nineteen other chapters in this publication, that hopefully, if all explored with the time they deserve, will help you grasp the idea that submission is not just an issue limited to domestic concerns. I am also enthusiastic about the following chapter, "Mutual Submission", which will deal with many areas where men submit to women, and vice versa. I suppose you could say that out of all that can be learned in the twenty chapters in this book, chapters 5 and 6 are dedicated to "un-learning" and doing away with many submission myths and rumors. It's been a long-time-coming.

As excited as I am to see light bulbs go off for people concerning this timely topic, I have to admit I was apprehensive about writing this book. *"A book on submission: thanks a lot God. Who's gonna buy it?!"*, I would whine over and over again. Even though I had developed a keen appreciation for the true art of submitting and being submitted to, I still realized the huge mountain that lay ahead of me. Say the word submission and you get the same scowls and grimaces you get when discussing enemas, taxes and patience. People rank the word right up there -- or down there -- with death.

THE WHO'S WHO OF MARRIAGE

So if submission is something required of both men and women, one to another and ultimately to Christ, then who decides within the bounds of marriage who submits to whom and when? Could it be possible that the spheres of authority change from time to time within a healthy marriage? And what about in ministry? Do mantles of authority trade shifts and rest on both sets of shoulders in the arenas of parenting, business, and in day to day matters around the house, or does God intend for the man alone to bring home the bacon and for the woman to greet him at the door with skillet in hand to cook it in? Even if the woman does so, and does so very well on a regular basis, it would appear that she is still exercising a measure of authority over that skillet in her hand (the one she will not hit her husband with as he walks through the door, bacon in tow).

With those questions in mind (and before answering too soon), take a walk back in time with me to this article which appeared in Housekeeping Monthly Magazine on May 13th, 1955, a time when the divorce rate was more than 50% lower than it is today.

"THE GOOD WIFE'S GUIDE: Have dinner ready. Plan ahead, even the night before, to have a delicious meal ready, on time for his return. This is a way of letting him know that you have been thinking about him and are concerned about his needs. Most men are hungry when they come home and the prospect of a good meal (especially his favorite dish) is part of the warm welcome needed. Prepare yourself. Take 15 minutes to rest so you'll be refreshed when he arrives. Touch up your make-up, put a ribbon in your hair and be fresh looking. He has just been with a lot of work-weary people. Be a little gay and a little more interesting for him. His boring day may need a lift and one of your duties is to provide it. Clear away the clutter. Make one last trip though the main part of the house just before your husband arrives. Gather up schoolbooks, toys, paper, etc. and then run a dust cloth over the tables. Over the cooler months of the year you should prepare and light a fire for him to unwind by. Your husband will feel he has reached a haven of rest and order, and it will give you a lift too. After all, catering for his comfort will provide you with

immense personal satisfaction. *Prepare the children.* Take a few minutes to wash the children's hands and faces (if they are small), comb their hair and, if necessary, change their clothes. They are little treasures and he would like to see them playing the part. *Minimize all noise.* At the time of his arrival, eliminate all noise of the washer, dryer or vacuum. Try to encourage the children to be quiet. *Be happy to see him.* Greet him with a warm smile and show sincerity in your desire to please him. *Listen to him.* You may have a dozen important things to tell him, but the moment of his arrival is not the time. Let him talk first remember, his topics of conversation are more important than yours. Make the evening his. *Never complain.* If he comes home late or goes out to dinner, or other places of entertainment without you. Instead, try to understand his world or strain and pressure and his very real need to be at home and relax. *Your goal:* <u>Try to make sure your home is a place of peace, order and tranquility where your husband can renew himself in body and spirit.</u> Don't greet him with complaints and problems. Don't complain if he's late home for dinner or even if he stays out all night. Count this as minor compared to what he might have gone through that day. *Make him comfortable.* Have him lean back in a comfortable chair or leave him be down in the bedroom. Have a cool or warm drink ready for him. Arrange his pillow and offer to take off his shoes. Speak in a low, soothing and pleasant voice. Don't ask him questions about his actions or question his judgment or integrity. Remember, he is the master of the house and as such will always exercise his will with fairness and truthfulness. You have no right to question him. A good wife always knows her place."

THE CHICKEN AND THE EGG

What happened to us between 1955 and now? Did such controversial views of a wife's role in marriage result in high divorce rates and thereby liberate women from such "drudgery", or did high divorce rates evolve these women into working-moms, thus resulting in their transformation in society today? It's the chicken or the egg debate, and rather than argue over which came first, women's roles or women's rights, it is best for us to focus our attention on the generation we have awakened in -- one that demands a cure for dying marriages.

At the time that article was written, 1955, the divorce rate in America was between 23% and 25%. Today, in this new millennium, we are nearing 50%, and talk radio insists we're nearer to 51%. The following chart, provided by the Department of Health and Human Service and the National Center for Health Services, shows that the divorce rate peaked in the early 1990's then began to fall again. Today -- despite what the precise numbers -- we are still fast approaching the uncomfortable truth that for every two marriages there will be one divorce. Considering that in 1900 the divorce rate was just 7.9%, and according to the below chart has increased at times within the range of 40-45% during one century, does that mean that by the end of this current century we will increase another 40-45% and skyrocket to a divorce rate of over 90%? Will anyone want to even get married anymore? These are questions worth answering and problems worth solving, otherwise, marriage will one day have such a bad name that mankind will bypass it altogether and give birth to a generation that blindly reduces covenant to cohabitation.

Marriages and Divorces, 1900–1998

Year	Marriage Number	Divorce Number	Divorce Rate
1900	709,000	55,751	7.9%
1910	948,166	83,045	8.8%
1920	1,274,476	170,505	13.4%
1930	1,126,856	195,961	17.4%
1940	1,595,879	264,000	16.6%
1950	1,667,231	385,144	23.1%
1960	1,523,000	393,000	25.9%
1965	1,800,000	479,000	26.6%
1970	2,158,802	708,000	32.8%
1975	2,152,662	1,036,000	48.1%
1980	2,406,708	1,182,000	48.3%
1981	2,438,000	1,219,000	50%
1982	2,495,000	1,180,000	47.7%
1983	2,444,000	1,179,000	48.3%
1984	2,487,000	1,155,000	46.3%
1985	2,425,000	1,187,000	49%
1986	2,400,000	1,159,000	48.3%
1987	2,421,000	1,157,000	47.8%
1988	2,389,000	1,183,000	49.5%
1989	2,404,000	1,163,000	48.3%
1990	2,448,000	1,175,000	48.1%
1991	2,371,000	1,187,000	50.1%
1992	2,362,000	1,215,000	51.5%
1993	2,334,000	1,187,000	50.8%
1994	2,362,000	1,191,000	50.5%
1995	2,336,000	1,169,000	50.1%
1996	2,344,000	1,150,000	49%
1997	2,384,000	1,163,000	48.8%
1998	2,256,000	955,000	42.4%

All divorce statistics include annulments. Divorce rates for 1941–1946 are based on population including armed forces overseas. Marriage rates are based on population excluding armed forces overseas. NOTE: Marriage and divorce figures for most years include some estimated data. Alaska is included beginning 1959, Hawaii beginning 1960.

GOING, GOING, GONE?

Statistics from this chart of marriages and divorces recorded in the United States in the 20th century is provided by the Department of Health and Human Services and the National Center for Health Statistics (www.dhhs.gov). When you look at the figures for 1998, their most current study, you have to rejoice at the 2,256,000 marriages that took place, but then wonder what caused the 955,000 divorces -- almost one million. Since each divorce represents two people, this means that there are around two million people walking around in our country today who are asking themselves what went wrong. All of us have been touched by divorce in some way, and we all know those who were as relieved by their divorces as they were remorseful. But all of them, saddened or satisfied, wonder at some point what they could have done differently. Consider the following ten statistics:

1. Adults and children are at increased risk for mental and physical problems due to marital distress (e.g., Cherlin & Furstenberg, 1994; Coie et al. 1993; Coyne, Kahn, & Gotlib, 1987; Cowan & Cowan, 1992; Fincham, Grych, & Osborne, 1993).

2. Mismanaged conflict and negative interaction in marriage predicts both marital distress and negative effects for

children (e.g., Gottman, 1994; Markman & Hahlweg, 1993; Clements, Stanley, & Markman, 1997; Cowan & Cowan, 1992; and Grych & Fincham, 1990).

3. Marital problems are associated with decreased work productivity, especially for men (e.g., Forthofer, Markman, Cox, Stanley, & Kessler, 1996).

4. Many more couples live together prior to marriage than in the past--recent estimates are in the range of 60+% (Stanley & Markman, 1997; Bumpass & Sweet, 1991). These couples are less likely to stay married, probably mostly due to the fact that they are less conservative about marriage and divorce in the first place.

5. Money is the one thing that people say they argue about most in marriage, followed by children (Stanley & Markman, 1997). But, there is a lot of reason to believe that what couples argue about is not as important as how they argue (Markman, Stanley, & Blumberg, 1994).

6. Married men and women in all age groups are less likely to be limited in activity due to illness than single, separated, divorced, or widowed individuals (National Center for Health Statistics, 1997).

7. Children living with a single parent or adult report a higher prevalence of activity limitation and higher rates of disability. They are also more likely to be in fair or poor health and more likely to have been hospitalized (National Center for Health Statistics, 1997).

8. "The fastest growing marital status category was divorced persons. The number of currently divorced adults quadrupled from 4.3 million in 1970 to 17.4 million in

1994." (Arlene Saluter, *Marital Status and Living Arrangements: March 1994* , U.S.. Bureau of the Census, March 1996; series P20-484, p, vi.).

9. Younger people in the U.S. who are marrying for the first time face roughly a 40-50% chance of divorcing in their lifetime under current trends (U.S. Bureau of the Census, 1992, p. 5).

10. The "triple threat" of marital conflict, divorce, and out-of-wedlock births has led to a generation of U.S. children at great risk for poverty, health problems, alienation, and antisocial behavior. **(Facts About Marital Distress and Divorce** Scott M. Stanley & Howard J. Markman / University of Denver.

THE WONDER DRUG

Before we could discuss the issue of this chapter, Marital Submission, we first had to establish that a need for it even existed. If it ain't broke, don't fix it, right? Well, as you can see from the statistic thus far, many marriages today are definitely broken. An invasive poison has infected our pledges. But what if there was an immunization against it? Ultimately God is the Great Physician, but what antidote would He offer us? What serum can we drink and what pill can we swallow that will be the ounce of prevention that annuls our need for a pound of cure later on? I submit to you that the remedy is submission! One to another, husband to wife and wife to husband, resulting in an impenetrable unity in times of conflict, not to mention the sweet miracle of watching two become one.

As I stated in chapter two, many years ago when

submission was still a scary word to me there came a time when I heard the Lord saying that He was "taking me under" before He would elevate me into any place of substantial leadership. A time of testing, to see if He could entrust others to my care. He loves mankind so much! It was basic sowing and reaping, and He was requiring me to submit before I could be submitted to. I had this knowing that the intensity in which I ran after this humility would be the intensity by which God would measure my authority back to me. Having always been a formulated 1-2-3 kind of person, I decided that I would get this "training" over with very quickly and submit to my husband whenever necessary as a means by which to expedite God's promotion. If I had heard God as well as I thought I did that day, I would have heard Him laughing. You see, because I thought submission was solely a women's issue, I saw marital submission as the home-run of character training. I didn't know it was just first base. I had no idea what God would require of me in the months and years to come in submitting to pastoral leadership, governmental leadership, and even my parents once again. I had no idea that it was protection and not restriction. I saw it as a season of life that I would prove myself in quickly -- sort of like going on a fast with an ending date in mind -- and that it would all be over with and I'd move on to the real stuff of life. I had no perception of the capacity and power involved in a lifestyle of trust and submission. I also had no idea that my decision to trust Chris more was affecting anyone else but me. In other words, the thought never crossed my mind that my private decision to submit myself to Chris' wisdom during conflict catapulted my husband into a whole new level of training too! It also never occurred to me that when I let go of certain reins, Chris actually had a choice on if he would even pick them up or not. I assumed we had a deal! But my true heart was revealed in those moments when the reins lay on the ground with no one leading the cart, and in fear, I would run and grab them once again, feeling justified in having done so.

> *"Better to live on a corner of the roof than share a house with a quarrelsome wife."*
> Proverbs 21:9

FADING LINES

So how does submission come in handy during moments of conflict? Well, consider traffic when it merges. I was recently stuck in interstate construction in which I sat at a dead stand still in the same lane for more than thirty minutes. When we did move it was at a crawling 5 mph, and I was very frustrated that day with the fact that they'd chosen to merge three lanes of traffic into one in order to repaint the highway's fading lines (the same fading lines I'd been complaining about for months). With all that time to sit and think, I wondered why it bothered me so much to yield to drivers and let them merge into my lane in front of me. It's difficult to want to let someone cut line when you've worked so hard for your inches of progression! But I also saw very clearly that if I didn't yield I was going to cause a wreck, especially with one woman who literally forced her way into my lane without receiving the friendly head-nod invitation from me first! What's funny is that just a few minutes later once we'd regained normal speed, I looked in my rear-view mirror and she was once again behind me.

There are many times on the road of marriage when two lanes must merge into one. One opinion must be made out of two. Merging traffic is not a bad thing, nor is it permanent, but many of us refuse to yield in fear that we will never again have our own lane. We view it as impeding our progress instead of seeing the highway we are building. Even when we have complained about the fading lines of authority in our own household, we do not want to make the sacrifices once under construction that may require us to yield to our partner. I have known many strong women, myself included, who would complain about their husband's lack of ability to be firm in specific areas such as disciplining the children or governing finances, and yet when an opportunity arose for him to spread his wings and learn, their criticism and fear of his failure caused them to intervene too soon and prevented him from making any headway. In the end, that woman is left even more frustrated, more exasperated, and less able to trust her husband the next time. What's worse is how incompetent the husband is made to feel, and it is an incompetency that could very well prevent there from ever being a next time.

In those moments, when a man and a woman are at an impasse and the immovable object meets the unstoppable force, God has a design to produce the perfect merger. It is submission. So now the question is, who merges and who yields? Who submits to whom? Is it always expected of the wife or do we indeed each have different spheres of authority within our marriages? Let's take a minute and look at what God has to say about it and I think you will find it quite liberating.

TWO HEADS & YOU'VE GOT A MONSTER

> Mark 10:8: *"...and the two will become one flesh. So they are no longer two, but one."*

Although there are checks and balances in the governmental structure of our nation, ultimately the President is the head hauncho. He's the point guy. The one who gets to bear the title and receive all the kudos when the nation prospers, and the one who catches all the flack whenever it doesn't. It is the same in any corporation, club or household. There must be a point person. Although the husband and wife will each be point people over various responsibilities within their home, there has to be the one person whose wisdom will be defaulted to when no wisdom can be agreed upon. We see this in times of national crisis, when the President receives counsel from many advisors who know much more about their particular spheres of authority than he does, and yet they all submit their info to him, he reviews it as a whole, and then brings a unified decision to us, the general public. It is his face on t.v. that calms us down when he tells us everything is ok. Even if you don't like him, you know he has the power to do something about the situation. Can you imagine, in war-time for instance, how alarming and even damaging it would be to see on t.v. all the flying political opinions of various cabinet members prior to their submission to the President? Even if you think it would improve America's democracy, just imagine the divided front it would present to the opposing nation!

The same is true in any home, and God's desire is for every home to have a godly man to whom it can be entrusted. "For man did not come from woman, but woman from man." 1 Corinthians 11:8 This passage shows the order in which God created us in the Garden of Eden, the first household and the first union between man and woman. Genesis 2:20-25 says "So the man gave names to all the livestock, the birds of the air and all the beasts of the field. But for Adam no suitable helper was found. So the LORD

God caused the man to fall into a deep sleep; and while he was sleeping, he took one of the man's ribs and closed up the place with flesh. Then the LORD God made a woman from the rib he had taken out of the man, and he brought her to the man. The man said, "This is now bone of my bones and flesh of my flesh; she shall be called 'woman,' for she was taken out of man." For this reason a man will leave his father and mother and be united to his wife, and they will become one flesh. The man and his wife were both naked, and they felt no shame."

We see here in the precious account of creation how man gives life to woman but woman gives life to the world! Each role carries precious privileges and there is no room for the mind set that one sex is superior to the other. The Lord gave woman to man as a gift. Not to compete but to complete. Any woman who does not understand that man is incomplete without her will never feel treasured enough to support him. He may be the stronger vessel by physical standards, but God says, "It is not good for man to be alone". Genesis 2:18 Without both sexes' understanding that they are interdependent on the other, neither will ever experience the true security, conquest or freedom that comes from oneness. I love 1 Corinthians 11:11-12 which explains it so beautifully: "In the Lord, however, woman is not independent of man, nor is man independent of woman. For as woman came from man, so also man is born of woman. But everything comes from God."

THE MARRIAGE WALL

Some friends of ours recently built a house that was quite unique, not to mention mind-boggling. It was a high quality two story brick home that took only six weeks to build.

The reason was because it came preassembled in four pieces that were cut to amazing precision and then lowered onto the foundation on their property with huge cranes. From there it took only another six to eight weeks to complete. Unlike the "prefab" homes that were popular a few decades ago, this is a trend that's currently very popular in Japan -- an American invention -- but one that is being shipped overseas by the boatloads every day. Compared to customary construction it looks like a fine art. We were amazed to hear their daily progress stories of how each section was securely planted and came complete with painted walls, cabinets, appliances and even carpet if you so desired. The interesting thing about the four adjoining pieces -- all the different areas of the home that must come together perfectly without even the slightest gap -- is what they call the support structure that joins them. It is called the marriage wall. Interesting. No part of the house was more important than the other, no part would experience less attention to detail or less traffic once built for that matter, but every segment had to submit itself to detailed specifications in order for the whole house to stand. I remember one day they experienced a sizable set-back when one piece was off by just two inches!

Imagine right now the gaps that are in your home that could be threatening the entire structure. Places where you and your spouse are not coming together, or places where one of you doesn't measure up. Perhaps you're close -- within a couple of inches -- but bringing closure to that tiny gap could be the very key to your long awaited well-built marriage. Submitting to authority helps close those gaps that will harm you in the long run if ignored. It may require temporary sacrifice, but will result in a lasting pay off. Give a little, get a lot.

AROUND THE HOUSE

"A quarrelsome wife is like a constant dripping on a rainy day." Proverbs 27:15

In my home, submission has had an interesting history. I am married to a wise man, but I can honestly say that I see evidence of where my submission has allowed him to acquire that wisdom. Wisdom does not come from a book or a conference, but from trials that occur in the pressure cooker of life. For years during various pressure cooker "discussions", my refusal to yield to Chris' judgment hid behind an interesting mask. My husband was so sympathetic and attentive to my side of things, that by the end of our "discussion" I had always talked him out of what he had felt so firm about just five minutes before. Because we always ended in peace and oneness, I always assumed that it was submission. I cannot remember a single one of those encounters where Chris did not listen, but I also cannot remember many where I did. I don't have any attorneys in my family, but Chris says I should have been the first. My father was a savvy award-winning salesman and so maybe I got that gene. All I know is that God gave me a merciful man by which I could learn to trust in authority, and for many years I abused that grace.

Once my eyes were opened to how difficult I was to deal with in the midst of confrontation, my heart was made sad at how much Chris had endured. Endured and yet loved me with an increasing extravagance! It truly was his kindness that led me to repentance. He was never begrudging about his sacrifices to me and my ideas, but the hard truth was that along the way he had become convinced that I truly had the best ones. Add to that my growing ministry of training others to hear the voice of the Lord and you get an intimidating front that cannot be argued with. In the midst of a very happy life, I woke up one day to the fact that my house was in improper order from top to bottom, and that my husband was submitting to me more often than I was to him. Because of his humility there was a measure of peace in our home, but I suddenly recognized that he was not the king God had created him to be, and was confronted with the thought that if he was not a king, then I was not a queen. I also finally faced the fact that our pattern of reaching peace at the end of an argument was not submission, but mere agreement. <u>Agreement is what happens when two forces eventually come together, but submission occurs when one force swiftly agrees to succumb to another for the good of the whole.</u>

So this is where my desire to quickly learn submission and get on with life had landed me: taking me beyond the conflict resolution mind set of submission into the full blown arena of seeing my husband become a king. It was suddenly love and not duty. I decided to take submission from the defensive to the offensive, and although I finally wasn't thinking about what was in it for me, the rewards I reaped from heaven and home were, and still are to this day, inconceivable.

SAD BUT TRUE

> *"Better to live in a desert than with a quarrelsome and ill-tempered wife." Proverbs 21:19*

It is very disheartening to me how many women today refuse to submit to the authority God has graced their husbands with. <u>Even if he is an unbeliever, God's word</u>

says your husband will be won by your demeanor. "Wives, in the same way be submissive to your husbands so that, if any of them do not believe the word, they may be won over without words by the behavior of their wives, when they see the purity and reverence of your lives." (1 Peter 3:1-2). I have actually had women tell me that not only has God released them from submitting to their husbands, but that He has told them to divorce them too! One woman who'd been married several times informed me that God had given up on her current husband and told her it was ok if she did too! I refuse to see how that lines up with "I hate divorce" (Malachi 2:16), or Luke 18:1 which says, "Then Jesus told his disciples a parable to show them that they should always pray and not give up".

I long for women like that to experience the comfort in trust. I long for them to acknowledge that in Scripture, God often called strong women of faith to submit to their husbands' advice, even if at times it was not wise or godly. Abram (whom God later renamed Abraham) asked Sarah to lie to a Pharaoh and state that she was his sister so that the would not see her beauty and kill Abram to attain it, and Sarah obeyed. More than once in fact! Another time it was to a king! Still, when Pharaoh found out, his anger was not toward Sarah. And while he could have been angry at Abram, Genesis 12:15 says, "He treated Abram well for her sake, and Abram acquired sheep and cattle, male and female donkeys, menservants and maidservants, and camels. But the LORD inflicted serious diseases on Pharaoh and his household because of Abram's wife Sarai." From this story it appears that God honored Abram's request due to Sarah's submission to it, and although it was wrong, they were protected in the midst of it due to their unity. God dealt with them later concerning it, but did not publicly humiliate them. Humility vs. humiliation. Today, <u>many wives whose unbelieving husbands put them in compromising positions might be comforted by that thought as they stand in submissive faith waiting for God to transform their men.</u>

Many women want the "Queen Esther anointing", but fail to remember that Esther was only elevated to the position of queen because the queen before her, Queen Vashti, had rebelled against her husband, the king, and his wishes. He was then advised by his counselors for the sake of the example set before the entire kingdom to find another queen. Vashti's rebellion made way for Esther's submission. "Then Memucan replied in the presence of the king and the nobles, 'Queen Vashti has done wrong, not only against the king but also against all the nobles and the peoples of all the provinces of King Xerxes. For the queen's conduct will become known to all the women, and so they will despise their husbands and say, `King Xerxes commanded Queen Vashti to be brought before him, but she would not come.' This very day the Persian and Median women of the nobility who have heard about the queen's conduct will respond to all the king's nobles in the same way. There will be no end of disrespect and discord. Therefore, if it pleases the king, let him issue a royal decree and let it be written in the laws of Persia and Media, which cannot be repealed, that Vashti is never again to enter the presence of King Xerxes. Also let the king give her royal position to someone else who is better than she. Then when the king's edict is proclaimed throughout all his vast realm, all the women will respect their husbands, from the least to the greatest.'" Esther 1:16-21

Another convincing story in Scripture is in Matthew 2

when baby Jesus was in danger of being killed by Herod. It is interesting to note that God did not warn Mary, the mother of Jesus whom He had revealed Himself to and conceived His only Son in, but instead alerted her husband, Joseph, in a dream in which he told him to take Mary and the child and flee to another country. Mary had heard so clearly and so directly from God up until that point about the destiny of this child, that she really would have had every right to question Joseph's intervention in it. After all, God had come to her first and said she was His chosen one. The angel Gabriel had declared to her in Luke 1:28 "Greetings, you who are highly favored! The Lord is with you." But because Joseph was Mary's husband, she chose to trust him, pack up her things and a baby in the middle of the night and move to another country! Could we do the same? As a result, Jesus' life was spared, as was her own. It revealed Mary's heart and also reveals one of the reasons why God chose her to begin with.

AUTHORITY VS. SUPERIORITY

God is calling for submission from equals. For Galatians 3:28 says, "There is neither Jew nor Greek, slave nor free, male nor female, for you are all one in Christ Jesus.". Well, if that's true, then it makes you wonder why He also said in Ephesians 5:22-25, "Wives, submit to your husbands as to the Lord. For the husband is the head of the wife as Christ is the head of the church, his Body, of which he is the Savior. Now as the church submits to Christ, so also wives should submit to their husbands in everything." Perhaps it's because God understands that true submission is not conceding and complying, but mutual commitment and cooperation. God did not invent submission in order to make man lord over woman at a higher rank, but to give husbands and wives a way to work together without chaos. This is the perfect picture of what Christ, who was equal with God, did as He submitted himself to His Father in order to carry out the plan of salvation. He was obedient even to the point of death (Philippians 2:8). Moreover, although equal to man under God, the wife should submit to her husband for the sake of her household. She should not tear down with her own hands the structure which God has put in place to prosper and protect her. It is by choice, not force, and we are actually able to serve God through this union.

Perhaps people would not feel so threatened by submission if they understood that it draws lines of authority and not lines of superiority. I know for me it meant a life realignment in which I acknowledged Chris as the head of our home but also acknowledged myself as the crucial neck which supported his headship at every turn. It was also quite freeing to me that we each did have varied fields of authority within that home life, meaning that I would oversee various domains and that Chris would submit to the solutions that he'd given me liberty to pursue.

"...a prudent wife is from the LORD." Proverbs 19:14

DESIGNATED DRIVERS

Functionally, Chris and I still sit and discuss everything that concerns our home. We are true co-laborers for the large family we have co-partnered with God to bring into this world. However, I have moved beyond persuasion and into the full trust that sometimes God will give Chris a totally illogical solution that He requires me to submit to for the sole purpose of growing my faith. I no longer take such issues personally or see them as defeat, but view them as God's way of protecting me. He could protect me by my own prayers, most certainly, but when I submit to the covering prayers of another whom He's placed one rung up on the ladder and given a better view, then I have at that point had to exercise faith, and that's where the pleasure of God kicks in. "And without faith it is impossible to please God, because anyone who comes to him must believe that he exists and that he rewards those who earnestly seek him." Hebrews 11:6.

Still, there are many areas where Chris submits to me, in and out of our home. He truly believes not only in "wives submit to your husbands as to the Lord" (Ephesians 5:22) but also in the verse above it which says, "Submit to one another out of reverence for Christ." (Ephesians 5:21). With that in mind he is not offended when he is asked to cook, clean or change diapers. What's more is, he doesn't wait to be asked, but is secure enough in the Lord -- and in love enough with me -- to just do it unannounced. Concluding that he is the better ironer of the two of us, Chris does all the ironing at campsmith, including all of my clothes. Also, he tucks the children in each night and has since they were little, praying the Aaron blessing over them from Numbers 6:24-26: "The LORD bless you and keep you; the LORD make his face shine upon you and be gracious to you; the LORD turn his face toward you and give you peace." Our little Jude can literally not go to sleep until Daddy "blesses" him. I used to feel guilty that I didn't tuck the children in like most mommies do, but now I see the benefit they get from having their daddy do it, the same benefit I get from having my Heavenly Daddy do the same to me each night. I believe that because of Chris' willingness in taking the time to tuck in six children every night, they will grow up and better know the love of the Father, and better rest in it at the close of each day for the rest of their lives.

We will move into more areas of reciprocal submission in the next chapter, "Mutual Submission" but let me just state that the areas of authority that Chris and I walk in not only shift from time to time at home, but also in ministry. He is an ordained Elder at the church we attend, Harvest International Church in Hermitage, TN, and I am often called to submit to his authority in that "house". However, I am an ordained minister -- Rev. Laura Smith -- and am often called to speak at churches and conferences all over the country. Because Chris is my spiritual covering, I enjoy having him at my side whenever I speak, but ultimately that means that he travels with me just to sit in the audience and pray. It means the world to me, and so whenever he can he does it as a pure act of service to me. Another example of Chris' submission to me would be the summer when I accepted the position of Prayer Coordinator for the Promise Keeper's Conference in Nashville. As part of the Executive Staff, it was my job to coordinate and oversee prayer for the entire event, for the 4 months before and of course during, which meant finding men and women who would serve behind the scenes in prayer. Chris came and offered himself to work for me in whatever capacity I would place him in, realizing that this meant him sacrificing his attendance of the popular men's event itself. So, on the weekend of the conference, Chris was the head of our home as we prepared for the day and ate breakfast as a family that morning, but then as soon as we walked out the door and into the 17,000 seat arena in downtown Nashville, Chris submitted to my authority there and carried out whatever job I asked him to do.

Shifting spheres of authority. "Submit ye one to another". It truly is like a well-choreographed dance, and brings to mind Acquilla and Priscilla, a couple whom Paul mentions seven times in his writings -- in Acts, Romans, 1 Corinthians and 2 Timothy. They were his "fellow workers in Christ" (Romans 16:3) and yet they are never mentioned in Scripture apart from each other. They ministered alongside of each other and were a picture of what God intends married couples today to model.

Speaking of Promise Keepers, I have another story about men submitting to women. When Promise Keepers came to Nashville that summer, it was my responsibility to not only find the city's prayer warriors for an on-site prayer room, but to wear a headset during the event and be on call to intervene in any situation in the arena that needed prayer. As soon as I arrived on Saturday morning, I was greeted with the news that there were angry women's lib picketers out on the sidewalk on 5th and Broadway, protesting the event and accusing Promise Keepers of being a male chauvinist organization. I immediately made my way to the prayer room where I informed the group. As we prayed, one brother passionately brought up the fact that men certainly had a lot to repent of to women, and that they had done their share of suppressing women for so long that it was no wonder some had taken their hurts and run ten miles with them. I got an idea. When I asked how many men would be brave enough to go out to that sidewalk and tell those women that, almost every man in the room raised his hand. We made our way out the door and down the sidewalk, and I watched as those courageous men got down on their knees in front of those angry women. They asked for forgiveness for all that men had done to women, and then just as they were praying out loud and repenting before the Lord, two news crews drove up and got the whole thing on film. The women dropped their signs and left. Through the power of love, and through the ability to walk in the opposite spirit, humility overcame pride that day and love conquered all. When the news reporter interviewed True Nguyen, Promise Keeper's Director of U.S. Ministries about the "equality for women" signs that the picketers were sporting, his answer was heaven-inspired. "Do I believe in equality for women? No. Why should women settle for equality when we are teaching men in there to go home, put their wives on pedestals and serve them? I think women deserve much more than equality." I was smiling so wide, the 17,000 seat arena couldn't contain me! What a precious picture of the submission required of men. Only godly men are fearless enough to go there.

> *"Enjoy life with your wife, whom you love."*
> *Ecclesiastes 9:9*

THE LAST WORD

I realize that this chapter has been nearly triple the length of the previous chapters, but I think there is a reason why. Perhaps God is saying something to couples about how key marital submission is to an obedient heart, and perhaps that's because what we do within the walls of our homes determines what we are entrusted with outside of them. It's where the rubber meats the road, and is the perfect place for God to deposit ministry into us, taking us to places of public leadership once we are willing to serve those closest to us in private.

Let's end by capturing the essence of what biblical

marriage is for both women and men.

1 Corinthians 7:3 Both parties in a marriage should fulfill their marital duty to each other.

1 Peter 3:7 A husband's prayers will not "work" if He is not respecting his wife.

Proverbs 12:4 Wives can be a crown on their husband's head or decay in his bones. If she will yield to her husband as her "head", God will actually place her on top as the husband's crown!

1 Corinthians 7:4 Our bodies do not belong to us alone once married.

Hosea 2:2-4 God calls Israel's lack of submission to Him adultery.

Ephesians 5:25-29 Husbands, Jesus loves His Bride with all He is. Do you?

1 Corinthians 11:3 Divine order in marriage.

– Colossians 3:18-19 Wives should submit and husbands should be worthy to be submitted to.

Titus 2:2-5 Young marriages need the help of older, successful ones!

Genesis 16:4-5 Sarah is impatient to the will of the Lord as spoken to her through her husband Abraham, and instead devises a plan for him to birth a son through her servant, Hagar, resulting in devastation and a divided promise.

2 Samuel 6:16:-23 Michal belittles her husband, David, concerning the undignified way in which he extravagantly praised the Lord and was struck with barrenness as a result.

"To the married I give this command (not I, but the Lord): A wife must not separate from her husband. But if she does, she must remain unmarried or else be reconciled to her husband. And a husband must not divorce his wife. To the rest I say this (I, not the Lord): If any brother has a wife who is not a believer and she is willing to live with him, he must not divorce her. And if a woman has a husband who is not a believer and he is willing to live with her, she must not divorce him. For the unbelieving husband has been sanctified through his wife, and the unbelieving wife has been sanctified through her believing husband. Otherwise your children would be unclean, but as it is, they are holy. But if the unbeliever leaves, let him do so. A believing man or woman is not bound in such circumstances; God has called us to live in peace. How do you know, wife, whether you will save your husband? Or, how do you know, husband, whether you will save your wife? Nevertheless, each one should retain the place in life that the Lord assigned to him and to which God has called him. This is the rule I lay down in all the churches."
1 Corinthians 7:10-17

"Many waters cannot quench love; rivers cannot wash it away. If one were to give all the wealth of his house for love, it would be utterly scorned." Song of Songs 8:7

Change my heart God, change my name
Leave me different, not the same
Teach me Lord to trust in you
Through this bond of one by two

Chapter 6

MUTUAL SUBMISSION

"Submit ye one to another..."
Ephesians 5:21

I see you; you see me
You have needs I can meet
But cliches are not complete
Lest I act and give them feet

I could choose to just compete
See your gain as my defeat
Fill my heart with curt conceit
Let my mind, your need delete

Then my breakthrough, bittersweet
Would seem somehow incomplete
And my winnings, obsolete
Even if I had you beat

Better off to not retreat
Find a need that I can meet
Boomerang submission sweet
As the Spirit does entreat

FAMOUS AMOS
(DIVE ALERT: DECREASE POSITIVE BUOYANCY AND SINK DEEPER)

Amos 3:3 says, "Can two people walk together without agreeing on the direction?" Unfortunately, many people do it every day. Parents and children, co-workers, church leaders, and even our nation's own fiercely divided Congress (which does seem to unite in times of crisis). Progress is impossible because every person sees their view as superior and submission as a by-word. To yield is weak, and to concede labels you spineless. After listening to the discord of our nation's leaders on the evening news many times, I can't help but wonder if the janitors make more progress than the senators in Washington on some days.

What would happen, from boardrooms to bedrooms around the world, if just one of the parties involved would consider the other person's point of view and sincerely attempt to accommodate it? It might mean an initial investment of surrendering the will, but the mutual respect and submission that would be birthed in that relationship would be well worth the sacrifice. It would get more accomplished on down the road. Why? Because those involved would finally be walking down that road in the same direction.

"But a Samaritan, as he traveled, came where the man was; and when he saw him, he took pity on him. He went to him and bandaged his wounds, pouring on oil and wine. Then he put the man on his own donkey, took him to an inn and took care of him. The next day he took out two silver coins and gave them to the innkeeper. 'Look after him,' he said, 'and when I return, I will reimburse you for any extra expense you may have.' "Which of these three do you think was a neighbor to the man who fell into the hands of robbers?"" Luke 10:33-36

Ephesians 5:21 says, "Submit to one another out of reverence for Christ." This means women to men, men to women, children to adults and vice versa. In case you are a man who thinks he should never have to submit to a woman, I would ask you what you would do if a woman police officer pulled you over for speeding. I also "submit" to you 1 Corinthians 13:4: "Love does not demand its own way". If you are a woman who thinks she must never come under a man, then I say to you that while it's true Scripture in no way indicates that you are required to submit to every man, God does expect you to "submit to your husbands as to the Lord." (Ephesians 5:22). If you are a single woman without a father in your life, consider submitting yourself to your pastor, not just in church membership but in full accountability to his, or some other male church figure's wisdom. If you are a child or teenager who thinks you are for some reason exempt from submitting to your parents, I give you Colossians 3:20, which says, "Children, obey your parents in everything, for this pleases the Lord." And finally, if you're an adult who thinks children should be seen and not heard because there is nothing you could possibly learn from them, then I offer you not only the words of the prophet Isaiah, "...and a little child will lead them" (11:6), but also the heart-warming story in the gospel of Mark, chapter 10, verse 13-16: "People were bringing little children to Jesus to have him touch them, but the disciples rebuked them. When Jesus saw this, he was indignant. He said to them, "Let the little children come to me, and do not hinder them, for the kingdom of God belongs to such as these. I tell you the truth, anyone who will not receive the kingdom of God like a little child will never enter it." And he took the children in his arms, put his hands on them and blessed them."

SOMETHING IN COMMON

In the early church, in the days just following Jesus' crucifixion, resurrection and return to Heaven, it is interesting to note how interdependent the believers were on each other. For survival sake, they learned to consider others' needs before their own. We read in the book of Acts (2:44-47) that "All the believers were together and had everything in common. Selling their possessions and goods, they gave to anyone as he had need. Every day they continued to meet together in the temple courts. They broke bread in their homes and ate together with glad and sincere hearts, praising God and enjoying the favor of all the people. And the Lord added to their number daily those who were being saved." Acts 11:29-30 again records how some Christians in Judea were in need and so the disciples in another location chose to pitch in and help. "The disciples, each according to his ability, decided to provide help for the brothers living in Judea. This they did, sending their gift to the elders by Barnabas and Saul." Finally, we see in chapter 4, verses 34-35 the result of this mind set in the early church: "There were no needy persons among them. For from time to time those who owned lands or houses sold them, brought the money from the sales and put it at the apostles' feet, and it was distributed to anyone as he had need."

Can you imagine submitting your personal possessions to others like that? Can you imagine being so committed to the cause at hand that you couldn't even see your own agenda? That is mutual submission. Relational ecstasy. Preferring another above yourself. I know from personal experience what it feels like to be given a car for free. A few years ago we gave away a mini-van to a family who was in need of one, and then a few years later when we were the ones in need of a car the Lord brought one right back to us just in time. We even had a woman at our church once offer to give us her house! A pricey new two-story brick home in a nice subdivision, but believe it or not, we felt God's leading that the work in our own neighborhood was not complete, and so we decided to forego the blessing and allow another family to move in. That sweet, generous sister preferred our needs to her own, and hopefully, we did the same for that other family who moved in and are still there to this day. We will both be blessed beyond our wildest imaginations.... just in time!

"You will be made rich in every way so that you can be generous on every occasion, and through us your generosity will result in thanksgiving to God. This service that you perform is not only supplying the needs of God's people but is also overflowing in many expressions of thanks to God. Because of the service by which you have proved yourselves, men will praise God for the obedience that accompanies your confession of the gospel of Christ, and for your generosity in sharing with them and with everyone else. And in their prayers for you their hearts will go out to you, because of the surpassing grace God has given you. Thanks be to God for his indescribable gift!"
2 Corinthians 9:11-15

MUTUAL SUBMISSION AT HOME

"When he had finished washing their feet, he put on his clothes and returned to his place. 'Do you understand what I have done for you?' he asked them. 'You call me `Teacher' and `Lord,' and rightly so, for that is what I am. Now that I, your Lord and Teacher, have washed your feet, you also should wash one another's feet.'" John 13:12-14

As I mentioned in the previous chapter, there are various fields of authority within the scope of any marriage, and it would be wise for both partners to learn to move with grace in and out of those spheres with ease. I have already stated what a servant my husband is to me and to our children in our home which we call, "campsmith". Everyone has daily chores and weekly chores, and Dad jumps right in there and helps out with whatever I allot to him on the chore chart, which I update about every six months. Of course, I'll never forget the time when I issued the new chore chart and assigned Dad the weekly chore of taking me out on a date! He submitted with a smile. But within our busy home, there is much need for delegation and cooperation. We've learned to submit to one another and work as a team to get even the smallest tasks done, like meals, which for a family of eight require preparing twenty-four plates a day. I have not folded laundry in almost ten years due to our foolproof delegation plan. When you are five years old you are taught to fold washcloths, and when you're seven you graduate to towels. On up the line everyone has an assigned field of apparel authority, and they are expected to use that authority with excellence as they serve their family with it.

I also enjoy hearing how various couples handle the finances in their marriage, or I should say, *who* handles them. In our home, I used to pay all the bills and balance the checkbook until about seven years into our marriage when the Lord flat-out told both of us that Chris was to take it over. By that I mean it was a strong prompting we were both feeling, even though I was content and more secure in having full control over it myself. And that was what God was addressing. True, at the time I had more time and more ability to keep our account "in check", but by taking the financial authority out of my hands and putting it into Chris', it not only forced me to trust him at a higher level that I frankly did not want to go to due to fear, but it also catapulted Chris into a higher realm of responsibility and accountability. The first few months were a four letter word that starts with "h". Hard (gotcha). And for several years I was still secretly thinking I could handle things better. But as God began to chip away at my control issues and Chris' discipline issues, we both emerged new creatures. To this day he still handles our complete family finances including those of our businesses and ministries that God has since entrusted to us.

But God did not stop there. Just when we thought we had everything figured out and were finally smug in our doctrine about who should handle the finances in every home -- the husband -- our pastors, Brad and Sheila Watson rocked our boat. When I first found out that Sheila handled all their family finances, I had the passing thought, "Well I'll just have to pray for more submission for Sheila that she will entrust their finances to Brad's care!". For years after God did this work in my home, I assumed He would require the same format from everyone. One size fits all. I still had so much to learn about how God is after the heart and will sometimes appear to contradict Himself in an attempt to teach the right lesson to the right person. He knows what it takes with each of us. As Brad and Sheila became our close friends, I saw how well their system of financial operation worked for their household. I saw that even though Sheila writes the checks and pays the bills, she submits all purchases to Brad and they come to a place of agreement with him overseeing the process alongside of her. On the other hand, Brad submits all his receipts to her and gains her consent on what he can purchase when, but because he has given her full authority in that area of their household, he trusts her to run with it and do the job well, and she does.

If you are a woman and your marriage is stifled by a heavy-handed dictatorship in which your husband is attempting to patrol every area of your home, you may want to suggest to him that he could save himself much stress and many ulcers if he would be willing to take a chance with mutual submission. It will be a free trial in every sense of the word. Just remember that God said the husband was the head of the wife, not the household. If you are that man and are struggling with issues concerning women and authority, think back to the tomb where Jesus was resurrected on that first Easter Morning. It was a woman, Mary Magdalene -- an ex-prostitute at that, whom He chose to reveal Himself to first, authorizing her to spread the word which we are still spreading today! And if you are having difficulty believing that God would ever allow your wife, a woman, to advise you in any field, you may want to consider the words of the Lord to Abraham when he was perplexed about what to do with his servant wife, Hagar and their son, Ishmael:

"But God told Abraham, "Do not be upset over the boy and servant wife. *Do just as Sarah says...*" Genesis 21:12

THE BEST OF BOTH WHIRLWINDS

In the pre-publication editing of this book, Chris and I would sit and muse tediously over each chapter several times after I was finished writing. We also got some voice software that enabled our computer to actually read the book back to us while we just sat, sipped our coffee and listened. Like any writer, I tend to write things and get married to them, and so Chris' objective opinion was useful to me after the creation of this manuscript. During one session, Chris announces to me that he thinks chapter one should be chapter two and that chapter two is much better suited to be the first chapter that draws the reader in. I was stymied. I had poured so much concrete into the foundation of chapter one that I couldn't easily take a chisel and just start sculpting. Still, he said chapter two was more humorous and would put the reader at ease, and so since this was a book on submission after all, I decided to practice what I preach and listen to my husband's sound advice (he's a wonderful writer, by the way). I swapped the chapters, turned off my brain, and left it to God. Well, the elementary editing was finished and now I wanted the book to make one more stop before hitting a publisher's desk. I desired to give it to my three assistants to read (they'd been chomping at the bits to see it), but once again, Chris intervened with an incongruous opinion. He said, "the counsel of a professional editor is more useful to you at this stage than that of three friends who love everything you do -- send it to Sandy Smith." Sandy was a friend of ours who is also the Assistant Features Editor at the Tennessean (TN's statewide newspaper), and so I took Chris' advice, held my breath and submitted to Chris by submitting the manuscript to Sandy. I didn't have to, nor did I want to, but something told me to shut up and do it. An interesting thing then happened. A beautiful thing. Sandy got back with me and her very first note was: "Change chapter one to chapter two and let chapter two be your opening chapter." I laughed out loud! When I told Chris, he laughed too (while eating his crow). I had taken my husband's advise about swapping the chapters (test #1) and then heeded his suggestion about sending it to a newspaper editor (which scared me because news editors are known for their brevity and I am not), but by passing that second test of submission I was actually securing my redemption! Not only did I come out of this squeaky clean -- looking like a really submissive wife *and* a great writer -- but I also now had a professional opinion that said I could have my own way! Ha! God is so hilarious, and He will go out of His way to bless you if you're at least trying to stay teachable. He is always your appeals court. I tell that story to prove that God cares about the places you die to and the strong will you surrender each time you submit to someone in His name. Because it requires faith from you -- faith in the fact that He is bigger than whatever you're relinquishing -- He will give back to you all you gave, and more. "Give, and it will be given to you. A good measure, pressed down, shaken together and running over, will be poured into your lap. For with the measure you use, it will be measured to you." Luke 6:38

FRIEND*SHIPS*

"If someone forces you to go one mile, go with him two miles." Matthew 5:41

Consider again the submarines we discussed in chapter two. Like those subs, friends must be willing to surrender and conceal their own wishes during seasons when they know they need to make time in their schedule to serve a friend in need. In healthy unions, friend*ships* are two-way blessings, and no one party should be taking more than they are giving back to the relationship. Of course, there are seasons when one friend will require much nurturing and aid, and hopefully, they will reap it from the friends they have sown into prior to their time of need.

"A friend loves at all times, and a brother is born for adversity." Proverbs 17:17

> *"Do not forsake your friend and the friend of your father, and do not go to your brother's house when disaster strikes you-- better a neighbor nearby than a brother far away."*
> Proverbs 27:10

> *"If one falls down, his friend can help him up. But pity the man who falls and has no one to help him up!"*
> Ecclesiastes 4:10

> *"My intercessor is my friend as my eyes pour out tears to God; on behalf of a man he pleads with God as a man pleads for his friend. Job 16:20-21*

Job was a man who knew what it was like to have friends in time of need. Unfortunately, they weren't the friends he needed! As Job lost all, children, lands and even his own health, he sat and listened to his three friends reason out his dilemma, but in the end was no more edified than when they'd begun their speeches. Finally, a young man named Elihu stepped in. Humbly, he reprimanded the three so-called "friends" of Job, and even had a few words of correction for Job, but his main goal was not to necessarily remedy Job's situation, but to comfort Job's heart with the faithfulness of God, and that's where his true wisdom was revealed. Job, an older man of great stature, humbled himself and submitted to a younger man's advice and the Lord blessed Job with double portions as a result. We also know that God required Job to forgive his other friends first before being restored, because Job 42:10 says, "After Job had prayed for his friends, the LORD made him prosperous again and gave him twice as much as he had before." Here we see a great man of enduring faith who was not too proud to consider himself above a tri-fold test of submission:

#1) He submitted to God's will during trial even when he didn't understand His ways (although he gave great monologues to God asking why). #2) He submitted to a younger man's wisdom when he recognized God's wisdom upon him. And #3) and most significantly, he submitted to God's command to pray for the very friends who'd condemned him. Three hard tests, but Job passed with flying colors. I know many of us wouldn't survive test #1, would be knocked out of the ring by test #2, and would absolutely refuse to even get back up for test #3. But see the brilliance of God at work! Had Job decided to feel sorry for himself and refuse either of the last two tests, his lack of humble submission would have cost him his future restoration, which he didn't even know was on the way. Trust, which is the core of submission, conceived obedience and gave birth to the celebration of healing, resurrection and divine replenishment.

TONGUE TIED

In true submission, one to another, there is no place for accusation, slander, or gossip. It is impossible to truly love someone with the love of Christ and speak against them. As James 3:6-13 says, "The tongue also is a fire, a world of evil among the parts of the body. It corrupts the whole person, sets the whole course of his life on fire, and is itself set on fire by hell. All kinds of animals, birds, reptiles and creatures of the sea are being tamed and have been tamed by man, but no man can tame the tongue. It is a restless evil, full of deadly poison. With the tongue we praise our Lord and Father, and with it we curse men, who have been made in God's likeness. Out of the same mouth come praise and cursing. My brothers, this should not be. Can both fresh water and salt water flow from the same spring? My brothers, can a fig tree bear olives, or a grapevine bear figs? Neither can a salt spring produce fresh water. Who is wise and understanding among you? Let him show it by his good life, by deeds done in the humility that comes from wisdom." So according to this passage, it is not right for us to bless God and curse others who are made in his image with the same tongue. So then why are so many of us doing it?

> *"So in everything, do to others what you would have them do to you." Matthew 7:12*

I'll never forget the season of my life when God began convicting me about this very thing. He set a standard before me to not say anything about someone in private that I could not say to them in public. This was actually years after He had convinced me to not gossip or slander, which was a tough enough lesson on its own. But this was something different. Something higher. When He put this new challenge before me I was shocked at how it forced my conversations with others to a whole new level. I began noticing how few people knew how to have uplifting conversations about others without including some sort of sarcasm. Instead of "have you noticed how wonderfully gifted so-and-so is?", it came out "she is so talented it makes me SICK!". God began showing me the insecurities involved in comments like this, and so I began to make a gallant effort to speak of others as if they were sitting in the same room with me. Depending on the crowd I was in, I sometimes found it hard if they were engaging in sarcasm or even blatant slander, but I noticed that even one word of true blessing spoken about someone in their absence, especially if the rest of the crowd was sitting there defaming them, set a tone for the rest of the conversation that could not be ignored. Blessing will always win out over cursing, for the power of life and death is in our tongues (Proverbs 18:21).

> *"When words are many, sin is not absent, but he who holds his tongue is wise."*
> Proverbs 10:19

> *"The tongue that brings healing is a tree of life, but a deceitful tongue crushes the spirit."* Proverbs 15:4

> *"Even a fool is thought wise if he keeps silent, and discerning if he holds his tongue."*
> Proverbs 17:28

> *"Through patience a ruler can be persuaded, and a gentle tongue can break a bone."*
> Proverbs 25:15

THE SUBMISSION DUE A FRIEND

So what does this have to do with submission? If I submit to someone, I honor them, and as we established in chapter 4, the Hebrew word for honor is the word "kabed", of which one of the meanings is to "promote". Therefore, if I am an honorable friend who honors her friends in the true sense of the word, then I will never let my words ever do anything but promote them. If I can't give them a promotion, then I don't open my mouth. Even if they are someone that I do not consider a friend, or who does not consider me one, I figure they are still made in the image of God and deserve for me to at least keep my mouth shut. If you'll keep your ears open, you'll be surprised at how many people complain about their elected public officials, but if you were to ask for a show of hands of how many actually pray for them, the results would shock you.

"There are six things the LORD hates, seven that are detestable to him: haughty eyes, a lying tongue, hands that shed innocent blood, a heart that devises wicked schemes, feet that are quick to rush into evil, a false witness who pours out lies and a man who stirs up dissension among brothers." Proverbs 6:16-19

Psalm 7:14   Are you pregnant with trouble?
James 4:11   So, who made you judge?
Leviticus 19:16   Are you a good neighbor or a bad one?
Psalm 101:5   What do you say about your neighbors?
Proverbs 19:11   When's the last time you overlooked an offense?
Ephesians 4:2   Make allowances for each others faults.

"Therefore, if you are offering your gift at the altar and there remember that your brother has something against you, leave your gift there in front of the altar. First go and be reconciled to your brother; then come and offer your gift." Matthew 5:23-24

SUBSERVIENCE

God's Word says that if any of us desire to be great we must first be a servant (Matthew 20:26). If we will be daring enough to believe that our promotion is based on our submission to servant-hood, our destinies will begin chasing us down and running us over long before we could ever get to them ourselves. If every man, woman and child would not think it beneath themselves to submit to other men, women and children, then peace and mutual respect would become the world standard, thereby making war an obsolete, passing trend.

"Therefore, as God's chosen people, holy and dearly loved, clothe yourselves with compassion, kindness, humility, gentleness and patience. Bear with each other and forgive whatever grievances you may have against one another. Forgive as the Lord forgave you. And over all these virtues put on love, which binds them all together in perfect unity. Let the peace of Christ rule in your hearts, since as members of one body you were called to peace. And be thankful." Colossians 3:12

Harmony
You and me
and God makes three
His recipe

Let's agree
and guarantee
no third degree
catastrophes

Thereby decree
God's irony
A symphony
You, Him and me

"Two are better than one, because they have a good reward for their labor. Though one may be overpowered by another, two can withstand him. And a threefold cord is not quickly broken."
Ecclesiastes 4:9 & 12

Chapter 7

OCCUPATIONAL SUBMISSION

> Your boss may be an angel
> Your boss may be a jerk
> But unto God you labor
> So whistle while you work

ON THE JOB TRAINING
(DIVE ALERT: NUCLEAR REACTOR HAS HEATED WATER TO 600°F BUT CANNOT BOIL! RETURN TO GENERATOR AND LET OFF STEAM!!)

A thought for you to ponder: Have you ever considered that God may be using your current job to work His character into you? On the job training! I have had many employers over the years, even in my years at home as a freelance writer. Some good, some bad, some wise, some (I'll be discreet)... not so wise, some godly, some ungodly, but they all had one thing in common. Me. I was not only put in a position to touch all of their lives, but they were put in mine to do the same.

I remember back in the early 1980's when Chris and I had not been married that long and I was having to work at a job that I didn't necessarily like but that provided the extra income we needed for us and for our first baby that was already on the way. It was a hard time for me and I hated getting up every morning and going in, but I had no choice. First of all, I am not an office/type/desk person, but because my mother talked me into taking typing in high school, I somehow learned to type ninety-two words a minute and was therefore always able to draw from that later in life as a money making skill. Of course, I had no idea that our world would one day be computer driven with web sites and emails, much less that I would "grow up" to be a professional writer, poet and playwright who would starve without those skills. But this was long before my literary debut and all I knew was that I was stuck behind a desk making calls to people about their overdue payments and documenting those conversations. What I learned about credit and the importance of financial integrity from that job would stick with me for the rest of my life, but I had no idea that God was using the people in that office to work relational integrity into me, as well as submission to authority.

First of all, everyone in that office were heathens. I'm sorry, but they were. If I wasn't listening to one gossip about her boss as soon as he walked out of the room, I was intercepting calls for another one's lover while she was busy lying to her husband on the other line. The men that I worked for were old, fat, out of shape, out of breath and out of their minds most of the time. They were also in the health care industry! One of my jobs was to actually remind them of things they had said to clients the day before through written documentation. And as if that wasn't bad enough, there was my direct manager who drove me bonkers. Raspy and deep, her two-pack-a-day voice would always jolt me like fingernails on a chalkboard when yelling orders to me from across the hallway. I will say in her credit that she had beautiful nails. However, the only reason that I knew this is because when she would race across the hall to scold me for the third time about the second-rate job I had done four days before, I would sometimes not even look up but would instead just bow my head and watch her hand pounding on my desk. I'll never forget though the humiliating time that she pounded and screamed, "Look at me when I'm talking to you!". I felt so belittled that I wanted to burst into tears. There I was, pregnant and hormonal anyway, knowing that God had opened the door for me to be here and receive His extra provision for our baby, and yet I came face to face that day with the fact that He had something else up his sleeve. As much as I hated to admit it, that woman did deserve my respect. Not my admiration and not my esteem, but my respect. She was, after all, my employer, and the day I took that job from her I had placed myself under her authority. Had there been no baby, I'm sure I would have booked and run, and while some would argue that it's not worth it to work in an atmosphere like that, I somehow recognized in the middle of it the higher purpose of why God had me there. My submission to them would gain me God's favor ("...for God has set himself against the proud, but he shows favor to the humble." 1 Peter 5:5) which would then gain me their friendships, ("By this all men will know that you are my disciples, if you love one another." John 13:35) which would then someday gain God their hearts. I must say that after the baby was born, these people were very kind to me. When the door opened for a better higher-paying job, I took it and left the company, but

I could tell that my time there had accomplished what God wanted. I was able to see traces of God's thumb prints around the place as I left. He still had so far to go with my heart that only wanted to submit to deserving perfect leadership, but at least he had messed me up enough with that bunch to wonder if there was any such thing. After all, If God had said to submit only to perfection, we'd all still be waiting around for Moses to come down off the mountain.

"SLAVES, OBEY YOUR MASTERS..."

More than a half-dozen times in Scripture God has Paul deal with the topic of slavery, and the things he wrote would have been considered politically incorrect in our day and age. But if we can look past the words and into the heart and spirit in which these commands were given, we will find a tiny key that unlocks a very big door concerning the benefits of occupational submission.

> *"Slaves, obey your earthly masters with respect and fear, and with sincerity of heart, just as you would obey Christ. Obey them not only to win their favor when their eye is on you, but like slaves of Christ, doing the will of God from your heart. Serve wholeheartedly, as if you were serving the Lord, not men, because you know that the Lord will reward everyone for whatever good he does, whether he is slave or free."* Ephesians 6:5-8

And consider these words next time you feel dissatisfied at your job. If God is not releasing you to leave and has some reason for you to stay, be encouraged and do your job unto the Lord.

"Slaves, obey your earthly masters in everything; and do it, not only when their eye is on you and to win their favor, but with sincerity of heart and reverence for the Lord. Whatever you do, work at it with all your heart, as working for the Lord, not for men, since you know that you will receive an inheritance from the Lord as a reward. It is the Lord Christ you are serving. Anyone who does wrong will be repaid for his wrong, and there is no favoritism."
Colossians 3:22-25

And if you find yourself having to submit to the authority of an employer who is harsh or unreasonable, look for ways to win them through your loyalty, diligence and undeserved respect. Through honor (Hebrew *kabed*- "to promote") then you can actually give your boss a promotion.

"Slaves, submit yourselves to your masters with all respect, not only to those who are good and considerate, but also to those who are harsh." 1 Peter 2:18

"For it is commendable if a man bears up under the pain of unjust suffering because he is conscious of God. But how is it to your credit if you receive a beating for doing wrong and endure it? But if you suffer for doing good and you endure it, this is commendable before God.
1 Peter 2:19-20

"Teach slaves to be subject to their masters in everything, to try to please them, not to talk back to them, and not to steal from them, but to show that they can be fully trusted, so that in every way they will make the teaching about God our Savior attractive." Titus 2:9-10

And finally, if your boss is a close friend or even a relative, you should make a point to wholeheartedly come under their authority while at work, trusting that they have the ultimate say-so concerning business matter, despite your valuable input.

"All who are under the yoke of slavery should consider their masters worthy of full respect, so that God's name and our teaching may not be slandered. Those who have believing masters are not to show less respect for them because they are brothers. Instead, they are to serve them even better, because those who benefit from their service are believers, and dear to them. These are the things you are to teach and urge on them. " 1 Timothy 6:1-2

"Obey them not only to win their favor when their eye is on you, but like slaves of Christ, doing the will of God from your heart." Ephesians 6:6

CHECKS AND BALANCE

Of course, God has a lot to say to bosses too. If you are in management of any kind and are the supervisor of an operation, large or small, remember that you ultimately serve someone too-- whether it be the Lord, the home office, or the customer. You should be kind and lead by example at all times. Ephesians 6:9 says, "And masters, treat your slaves in the same way. Do not threaten them, since you know that he who is both their Master and yours is in heaven, and there is no favoritism with him." Colossians 4:1 also states, "Masters, provide your slaves with what is right and fair, because you know that you also have a Master in heaven."

Recorded in the book of Philemon is an amazing story. One of only three personal letters in the Bible, Paul's letter to

Philemon, written about 60 A.D., is a personal plea concerning a slave named Onesimus. Philemon, a Greek landowner and a friend of Paul's who housed the Church of Colosse in his home, "owned" Onesimus as a domestic slave. But Onesimus had stolen from Philemon and run away -- a crime legally punishable by death -- and had run all the way to Rome where he "accidentally" met the Apostle Paul. It was there, in the very jail cell where Paul was himself imprisoned, that Onesimus heard the Good News and responded by giving his life to Christ. Slavery was prevalent in the Roman Empire during this time, and while Christians did not have the political power to change the nation's laws, Paul's higher hope was to transform relationships. With that aim in mind, Paul persuaded Onesimus that the right thing to do was to return home to his master, and then went a step further and wrote to Philemon with a direct challenge. After personally guaranteeing payment for any item stolen or any injustice committed against Philemon, Paul then proceeded to tell him what God had done in Onesimus, thereby requesting that Philemon receive him back home -- not just as a servant but now as a brother in the Lord. At the close of the letter he actually urges him to receive Onesimus and give him the same welcome as if he himself were coming. He tells him that he thinks of Onesimus as his own son and that he actually wanted to keep him in Rome as a helper to him with the gospel there, but acknowledges that the right thing to do is to see the two of them reconciled, this time as family. Bravely, Onesimus submitted to Paul and ultimately, to Philemon, and according to history, Paul was released from prison soon after writing the letter.

In verse 11-12 we see the whole moral of the story, "Onesimus hasn't been of much use to you in the past, but now he is very useful to both of us. I am sending him back to you, and with him comes my own heart." Whether Paul knew it or not, Onesimus means "useful". Today, despite our job histories or work reputations in the past, may we each strive in the end to be like Onesimus and choose to be useful to those whom we serve.

A SPIRIT OF EXCELLENCE

Practically speaking, what is the left-foot right-foot of occupational submission? What are the simple things that all workplaces have in common and can expect from their employees? In no certain order, here are a few:

1) Be on time. Fulfill the hours you have agreed to put in, and don't falsify work time.
2) Go the extra mile. Matthew 5:41 says that if you are asked to go one mile, go two, and so apply this principal whenever possible in all that is requested of you at work. Give it your all!
3) Labor cheerfully. If it is not a task that you should undertake, then say so, but if you accept an assignment, do it with a smile and not begrudgingly.
4) Speak life, be positive and build relationships. Ephesians 4:29 "Do not let any unwholesome talk come out of your mouths, but only what is helpful for building others up according to their needs, that it may benefit those who listen."
5) Honor management however you can. Avoid slander and anyone who partakes in it.

> *"If your boss is angry with you, don't quit! A quiet spirit can overcome even great mistakes." Ecclesiastes 10:4*

When the godly are diligent, those they serve will prosper

alongside of them. We see this in the story of Joseph, who had been taken as a slave to Potipher's house in Egypt and yet was so faithful that God's favor promoted him very quickly. "When his master saw that the LORD was with him and that the LORD gave him success in everything he did,   Joseph found favor in his eyes and became his attendant. Potiphar put him in charge of his household, and he entrusted to his care everything he owned. From the time he put him in charge of his household and of all that he owned, the LORD blessed the household of the Egyptian because of Joseph. The blessing of the LORD was on everything Potiphar had, both in the house and in the field." Genesis 39:3-5

Daniel was another who was promoted due to his spirit of non-compromising excellence. Taken captive as a young boy and deported to Babylon by Nebuchadnezzar in 605 B.C., he served in the government for about seventy years during the reigns of Nebuchadnezzar, Belshazzar, Darius, and Cyrus. Daniel 5:12 says, "This man Daniel, whom the king called Belteshazzar, was found to have a keen mind and knowledge and understanding, and also the ability to interpret dreams, explain riddles and solve difficult problems. Call for Daniel, and he will tell you what the writing means." Throughout his service to various kings, his fellow advisors would envy his favor and plot against him. But each time, God proved himself faithful to Daniel and rescued him dramatically, including closing the mouths of lions when Daniel was thrown into their den and locked up for a night after refusing to pray to anyone other than his God. Although Daniel was a captive, he prospered due to the excellence and humility in which he served those over him, and as a result the name of his God was glorified throughout the *whole world.* Daniel 6:25-26 proves this and shows King Darius issuing a decree to every nation in the world that Daniel's God was to be praised. We will cover this story in more detail in another chapter, "Governmental Submission", but for now just remember that you too can glorify God right where you are at the job you are in, with far-reaching effects for the kingdom.

> *"Do you see a man skilled in his work? He will serve before kings; he will not serve before obscure men."*
> *Proverbs 22:29*

THE PRICE OF FAVOR

Over the years, I have seen my husband work a myriad of jobs -- all with excellence. Although he's been in the music business industry for over twenty years, there have been many times when our budget required a boost and he would never fail to do his part in keeping our huge family afloat. I've seen him be a dapper record business executive by day, with many men and women and artists under his management, and then come home, jump into his jeans and go deliver pizzas. During one long season in particular, I saw him get up at 4 a.m. everyday of the week to roll and throw papers, only to come home and have to scrub the newsprint off of his hands before going to work to shake hands and make record deals all day long. He has landscaped, built furniture, hung wallpaper, delivered periodicals, and even walked neighborhoods to count heads for the U.S. Census Bureau. Many of those jobs he took on during a four year tenure, after obediently following the Lord's instruction to give up the president's seat he was holding at Reunion Records, a Christian record label with artists such as Michael W. Smith, Third Day, etc... . The very day he resigned he was offered another lucrative contract by another international record label, but because he was secure enough in his relationship with his Provider, he was able to follow God's prompting to walk away and begin putting feet to his life-long dream of building a design God had given him for taking ministry to a higher level in the music industry. I have seen my husband earn everything from six-digits to sub-digits but he has never failed to work hard wherever he was and submit fully to whomever he was serving. He is indeed a man of authority, but because he was never afraid to also be a man under it, God has rewarded his humility with more favor that I've ever seen on a man in my whole life. I've never met a person who didn't like Chris Smith. Myself included!

A CONFLICT OF INTEREST

Let me take a moment and speak briefly about what to do if you are asked to do something compromising at work. Does occupational submission mean that you must submit at all times in all circumstances? I get asked this all the time. I also hear that question applied to parental submission, governmental submission and marital submission. "Should I break the law if my husband tells me to?". Knowing that nothing is one size fits all, I am going to give you my best answer.

In each of those situations, stop and ask yourself if there is a higher authority. If your boss asks you to go against your values in some way, let's say to underhandedly conceal information involving deceit and you know you shouldn't do it, you have two choices. One is to quit that job and walk away. But wait a minute. Has God placed you there for a reason? Then, choice number two would be to calmly confront the boss and offer the right thing to do. If that does not work, you have two more choices. Number one would be to go to his or her boss and disclose the situation. If that still does not work, then you are forced to go back to number one in the first set of options: leave that job.

You are never expected, in the name of submission, to break the law, or God's heart. That applies to your marriage, job, parents or governmental laws. When King Saul asked his armor bearer in 1 Samuel 31 to draw his sword and kill him because the Philistines had wounded him and he didn't want it said they'd killed him, the armor bearer could not. He chose to obey the sixth commandment instead. If you are asked to do anything which conflicts with the ten commandments or with your personal set of values God has set for your life, you are allowed to claim amnesty under a higher law. It may cost you your job, but it just might gain you great respect. Even promotion.

Last week I heard a story about a young man, a boy I'd seen grow up at my church, who entered the military. Fresh out of boot camp and with eager expectation, he abided by every law, synchronized every step, and obeyed every Officer's command. Praying for God to use him on his new assignment, it happened in a way he wasn't expecting. His Commanding Officer was a man of great caliber, and I'm sure my friend, like any good soldier, asked "how high" whenever he said, "jump". But during drills it seemed that the Commanding Officer had a propensity to use the Lord's name in vain time and time again and it burdened the young soldier greatly, encroaching upon his values. Not only did it break the third commandment, but it was breaking the young soldier's heart and spirit, which defeated the purpose of his training. He decided the best thing was to talk to the Officer. Trusting in a higher authority, he went to his office one day and asked for entry.

"May I speak freely, sir?". He was granted permission. He went on to explain how despite his respect for the Officer, that respect could not compensate for the offense he felt every time he heard His God's name used in vain. He explained and waited for a response. "All right soldier... I'll try to watch my mouth", the Officer said. Wow! We see here how in an instant one man's courage changed another man's values, shedding light in a heart and maybe even on an entire platoon. Perhaps even a country!

Bob Dylan, in my opinion, is one of the greatest, not to mention one of the most unusual Musical Prophets of our time. He wrote a song which I believe relates to this chapter on occupational submission substantially. It was released in 1979 on the *Slow Train Comin'* album and won Dylan his only Grammy (Best Gospel Performance) until the *Time Out Of Mind* album in the late 90's. It was written during his conversion, and was his last top-forty single (#26 in Billboard). It's called "Gotta Serve Somebody", and tells many stories. It's repetitive and simple, with seven verses and the same elementary chorus in between them. He says that whether you are an ambassador, a socialite, a rock-n-roll addict or a business man, you are going to have to serve somebody. Whether you like to dance, gamble, drink milk or whisky, you are going to have to serve somebody. He suggests that whether you are poor, blind lame or rich, you are going to have to serve somebody. You may own tanks or banks, cut hair or be an heir, but in the end, you are going to have to serve somebody.

> "...Well it may be the devil or it may be the Lord
> But you're gonna have to serve somebody."

~Slow Train Coming / © 1979 Special Rider Music

Chapter 8

GOVERNMENTAL SUBMISSION

The national anthem do I sing
But I won't vow to anything
Cause it's my right to fail to cling
And disregard 'long live the king'

A Constitution dingaling
I weasel out of everything
Yet claim my rights to porch and swing
With tribe of one where I am king

Praise God for rights to have a fling
And disregard my wedding-ring
To hit your car and cause a ding
Then sue you for the suffering

I flat refuse my pledge to bring
Like Uncle Sam's frail underlings
For if I choose to build a sling
It's my own neck I've right to wring

"Submit yourselves for the Lord's sake to every authority instituted among men: whether to the king, as the supreme authority, or to governors, who are sent by him to punish those who do wrong and to commend those who do right. For it is God's will that by doing good you should silence the ignorant talk of foolish men. Live as free men, but do not use your freedom as a cover-up for evil; live as servants of God. Show proper respect to everyone: Love the brotherhood of believers, fear God, honor the king."
1 Peter 2:13-17

THE PLEDGE OF ALLEGIANCE
(DIVE ALERT: FULL STEAM AHEAD!)

Have you ever said the pledge of allegiance? Well then you're hooked. It's not just some sweet poem we quote on July 4th, it is a *pledge* of *allegiance*. Webstser's defines allegiance as "the duty of a subject to his government or superior; loyalty; an oath of homage." My thesaurus says it is a tie or obligation. So with hand on heart, every time we stand and recite this pledge we are submitting ourselves to the laws of the land -- "the republic for which it stands".

"I pledge allegiance to the flag
Of the United States of America
And to the republic for which it stands
One nation, under God
Indivisible, with liberty and justice for all"

Please note that not only have you pledged alliance with your nation, but you've acknowledged it as being a nation under God's leadership. Revelation of those two details could save our nation.

AGAINST THE LAW

Some people spend their whole lives resisting the governing authorities in our land. It's like they get a great high out of outsmarting Uncle Sam in some way, especially financially. They don't realize they're taking money out of their own pockets. Steal a little, lose a lot more.

Of course, I'm one to talk. Every time I get in my car I am tempted to break the law by speeding. Think of it: No bells and buzzers go off each time we pass a speed limit sign and decide to disregard it, but if we don't obey it we have broken the law. A law set in place by leaders who aim to do us good and keep us safe. They don't slow us down on the roads to make us late to work, but to ensure we get there safely.

One morning, I was driving to a leadership meeting at church and as I looked at the clock I noticed I was about to be late. If I picked up speed and caught every green light I could make it on time. Pastor had asked that we be there on time and so with his face in mind I picked up speed. When I looked at my speedometer and noticed I was doing twenty miles over the speed limit, I was faced with a decision: Should I slow down and disobey my pastor, or speed up and disobey my state government? The pastor or the governor? What to do? The Holy Spirit whispered loud inside of me and said, "Aha! Now I've got you thinking!"

He went on to give me the bigger picture. He said, "You are stuck this time and will disobey one or the other of your leaders today, but the real issue isn't about submission to them but about your submission to Me with your schedule". My mind was racing but he continued in a very linearly fashion. "You speed because you are late. You're late because you're too busy. You're too busy because you crave accomplishment. You crave accomplishment because you don't know how much I love you.".

Shrinking I asked, "So.... I speed because I don't know You love me?" I felt a hallowed nod, "yes". Wow. By the time I got to church I'd already had church in the car.

"How much more should we submit to the Father of our spirits and live!" Hebrews 12:9

THE LETTER OF THE LAW

Society is governed by a set of established rules. One of the most elementary social institutions is that of Law, and perhaps it is one of the most vital. If all persons did as they pleased with no consideration for the rights given to others, the entire community would eventually fall. If individual members of that community fail to acknowledge that they each have certain commitments and duties to that population, the people will not prosper. What the law helps accomplish is a regard and an enforcement of those commitments and duties. Therefore, the law institutes the rules that shape the rights and obligations for a person and his or her community.

The law also specifies punishments for people who disregard the rules, and details how a society's laws and punishments should be carried out. Still, there are ways that a land's laws can be changed. It happens more often than one might think, and thanks to active citizens, laws often see changes whenever there are new needs or attitudes within a society that warrant consideration. First let's consider what the laws of the land are in the United States.

Think of America's laws like a big tree. On that strong tree are two distinct branches, one of which is Public Law and the other, Private Law (also called Civil Law). Public law outlines citizens' rights and duties as functioning members of a society, and Private Law lends itself to establishing the rights and duties that individuals have in their relationships with each other. On those two branches are other specific branches. Public Law has four.

PUBLIC LAW includes:

1. Criminal Law, which deals with arson, bribery, burglary, extortion, forgery, kidnapping, larceny, manslaughter, murder, perjury, rape, and robbery.

2. Constitutional Law, which maintains civil rights, federal and state powers, relations between the states, separation of executive, judicial and legislative powers, civil rights and liberties.

3. Administrative Law, which encompasses consumer protection, currency, environmental protection, interstate commerce, public safety, social welfare, taxation, worker's wages and hours, includes communications and telecommunications.

4. International Law, which oversees arms control, extradition, hijacking and piracy, human rights, territorial waters, uses of outer space, uses of the ocean, and war crimes.

PRIVATE LAW has six branches. They are:

1. Contract and Commercial Law, which includes credit purchases, employment contracts, guarantees, insurance policies, patents, promissory notes, sales contracts, and subscriptions.

2. Tort Law, which contains invasions of privacy, personal injury, product liability, professional malpractice, slander and libel, traffic accidents, trespass, and unfair competition.

3. Property Law, which regulates landlord and tenant relations, mortgages, transfers of ownership, unclaimed property and intellectual property.

4. Inheritance Law, which governs estates, probate, trusts, and wills.

5. Family Law, which involves adoptions, annulment, divorce, marriage and child support.

6. Corporation Law, which patrols matter of corporate finance, documents of incorporation, and mergers and acquisitions.

"Everyone must submit himself to the governing authorities, for there is no authority except that which God has established. The authorities that exist have been established by God. Consequently, he who rebels against the authority is rebelling against what God has instituted, and those who do so will bring judgment on themselves. For rulers hold no terror for those who do right, but for those who do wrong. Do you want to be free from fear of the one in authority? Then do what is right and he will commend you. For he is God's servant to do you good. But if you do wrong, be afraid, for he does not bear

the sword for nothing. He is God's servant, an agent of wrath to bring punishment on the wrongdoer. Therefore, it is necessary to submit to the authorities, not only because of possible punishment but also because of conscience. This is also why you pay taxes, for the authorities are God's servants, who give their full time to governing. Give everyone what you owe him: If you owe taxes, pay taxes; if revenue, then revenue; if respect, then respect; if honor, then honor." Romans 13:1-7

CIVIL DISOBEDIENCE

Civil disobedience is not a new term. So what is it? Where did it come from? Who thought of it? Well, simply put, civil disobedience is the intentional public defiance of a law. Many have used civil disobedience as a means of protest to draw attention to what they believe to be unconstitutional guidelines. Through their protest, they hope they will move others to change unfair policies. Other people view civil disobedience as a tool to help bring public awareness to their religious convictions. They refuse to obey laws that they believe encroach upon their personal principles. It is said that the common lawbreaker tries to elude punishment. However, the reputation of an individual who practices civil disobedience is much different. They quickly accept all responsibility for breaking a law. By doing so, they dramatically demonstrate their convictions and opinions about the law they are protesting. They are usually nonviolent, which is another trait that separates them from typical lawbreakers.

In an average society, civil disobedience has its supporters and its critics, and it has been this way throughout history. Claiming that it is justified to disobey a law that is considered inequitable or immoral -- such as laws supporting racial segregation -- they say that the public refusal to obey that law may be the best way to test its constitutionality. For instance, when Nazi Germany called for the annihilation of Jews, many Germans broke the law and hid Jewish families to protect them from death. Others protested publicly. Both were civil disobedience.

There are those, however, who argue that the denial of one law leads to the denial of all law. They believe it is never right, under any circumstance, to intentionally break a law. Others approve only in desperate circumstances, and even then, it must be passive and peaceful. They believe that the democratic process should be the trusted means to change laws without ever having to break them.

HISTORY REPEATS ITSELF

So is civil disobedience rebellion? Isn't breaking a law always a lack of submission? I have grappled with this topic before sitting down to pen the pages of this chapter. Still, there are school children all over the nation refusing to discontinue public prayer in schools. By all definitions they are inciting a rebellion. But by God's law, they are obeying His rules. Therefore, sometimes civil disobedience is actually biblical obedience.

My daughter, Jessica says, "the day we took prayer out of schools we orphaned ourselves. We have now given birth to a generation who doesn't know who they are or that they are God's. There is higher crime and lower self-worth. We must reinstate prayer in schools somehow, some way." Jessica is the TN State Coordinator for Generals of Intercession's multi-generational youth prayer movement,

"The Cause", which is spear-headed by Mike and Cindy Jacobs and many other devoted and impassioned leaders. Believing that God is the God of Abraham, Isaac and Jacob, they are envisioning and building a state-by-state prayer network fueled by the blood, sweat and tears of three generations working together. The teens receive wisdom from the adults and the adults receive passion from the youth. I have been a part of these meetings as we gather around the country in prayer, and the sense of unity amongst the generations is phenomenal. Together we will take back the land and see the curse lifted. "He will turn the hearts of the fathers to their children, and the hearts of the children to their fathers; or else I will come and strike the land with a curse." Malachi 4:6. It is a privilege to work with these young men and women of God, who are literally willing to live or die for the gospel of Jesus Christ.

The truth is, civil disobedience has been around for hundreds of years. Jesus' disciples were ordered by the state to quit preaching, but of course, they opted to obey God rather than mortals. Around 1200 A.D., the Christian theologian Saint Thomas Aquinas argued that whenever the laws of the state contradicted the laws of God, the laws of God must be obeyed without exception. There were actually different religious groups during the 1600's and 1700's that became famous for their civil disobedience. Colonial American Quakers disagreed with war, and therefore refused to pay their taxes which supported it. In the 1850's, American abolitionists disobeyed the Fugitive Slave Law, which tried to find and return runaway slaves to their "owners". In 1872, Susan B. Anthony was arrested for voting. The problem? Women were not yet allowed to vote! Her trial caught the eye of a nation. It is said that American writer Henry David Thoreau was one of the most government that captured runaway slaves and waged war on Mexico to expand its area of slavery. In his essay "on the Duty of Civil Disobedience" (1849), Thoreau declared that people should refuse to obey any law they believe is unjust."

"In the United States, during the 1950's and 1960's, Martin Luther King, Jr., and other civil rights workers deliberately violated Southern segregation laws as a means of fighting racial injustice."

"Peter and the other apostles replied: 'We must obey God rather than men!'" Acts 5:29

DANIEL

There are specific accounts of civil disobedience in the Bible. However, in all of them were law-abiding citizens who subjected themselves to king and country at every turn, acknowledging the authority of the nation they were in, even if there by force. We studied Daniel in chapter seven, "Occupational Submission", but let's look again at his example. He had been taken captive as a young boy where he was deported to Babylon to serve the king. He grew in stature and wisdom and became one of his most trusted advisors. Even with the favor of the Lord upon him, he never demanded his freedom or incited a rebellion to overthrow a king, and he served during the reigns of four of them. When the king's other advisors grew jealous and tried to find something to accuse Daniel of, there was nothing. "At this, the administrators and the satraps tried to find grounds for charges against Daniel in his conduct of government affairs, but they were unable to do so. They could find no corruption in him, because he was trustworthy and neither corrupt nor negligent. Finally these men said, "We will never find any basis for charges against this man Daniel unless it has something to do with the law of his God." Daniel 6:4-5. So they tricked the king into signing a document that banned prayer to anyone else besides himself, and blindly, the king approved it. Here's where civil disobedience kicked in:

"Now when Daniel learned that the decree had been published, he went home to his upstairs room where the windows opened toward Jerusalem. Three times a day he got down on his knees and prayed, giving thanks to his God, just as he had done before. Then these men went as a group and found Daniel praying and asking God for help. So they went to the king and spoke to him about his royal decree: "Did you not publish a decree that during the next thirty days anyone who prays to any god or man except to you, O king, would be thrown into the lions' den?" The king answered, "The decree stands --in accordance with the laws of the Medes and Persians, which cannot be repealed." Then they said to the king, "Daniel, who is one of the exiles from Judah, pays no attention to you, O king, or to the decree you put in writing. He still prays three times a day." When the king heard this, he was greatly distressed; he was determined to rescue Daniel and made every effort until sundown to save him. Then the men went as a group to the king and said to him, "Remember, O king, that according to the law of the Medes and Persians no decree or edict that the king issues can be changed." So the king gave the order, and they brought Daniel and threw him into the lions' den. The king said to Daniel, "May your God, whom you serve continually, rescue you!" Daniel 6:10-16.

Well rescue He did, and the king was so impressed with

Daniel's dramatic salvation that he threw all those who'd tricked him, and their families, into the den of lions and watched them be devoured. Daniel's civil disobedience, or biblical obedience, ended up affecting all the nations of the world: Daniel 6:25-26 says, "Then King Darius wrote to all the peoples, nations and men of every language throughout the land: "May you prosper greatly! I issue a decree that in every part of my kingdom people must fear and reverence the God of Daniel. For he is the living God and he endures forever; his kingdom will not be destroyed, his dominion will never end."

W.W.J.D.?

Jesus did the same. He Himself was a king, but for his entire life had submitted to the governing laws of his land. He constantly came against culture, like speaking in public with women and dining with tax collectors and sinners, but he constantly submitted to his nation's laws. Once he was quizzed about this very topic: We read in Luke 20:20-26, "Keeping a close watch on him, they sent spies, who pretended to be honest. They hoped to catch Jesus in something he said so that they might hand him over to the power and authority of the governor. So the spies questioned him: "Teacher, we know that you speak and teach what is right, and that you do not show partiality but teach the way of God in accordance with the truth. Is it right for us to pay taxes to Caesar or not?" He saw through their duplicity and said to them, "Show me a denarius. Whose portrait and inscription are on it?" "Caesar's," they replied. He said to them, "Then give to Caesar what is Caesar's, and to God what is God's." They were unable to trap him in what he had said there in public. And astonished by his answer, they became silent."

ESTHER

Esther was another beautiful case of submission. She submitted to her husband, the king of Persia, and in fact was only chosen by him because his first wife, Vashti, had refused him in an overt act of rebellion and he feared all the wives in the land would hear of it and do the same with their husbands. Esther was humble, but she was also tenacious and decided to go before the king unannounced, which was a crime punishable by death. Still, she went because the lives of her people, the Jewish people, were at stake. "When he saw Queen Esther standing in the court, he was pleased with her and held out to her the gold scepter that was in his hand. So Esther approached and touched the tip of the scepter." (Esther 5:2) It is worth it to take time and read about Esther's humility, and how even after being made Queen she still obeyed the king and honored him at all costs. Even when she gained favor with the king and he offered her up to half of his kingdom, she chose not to succumb to greed, but to merely ask for the lives of her people, the Jews, which was at stake. Her obedience saved an entire nation, that is, God's chosen people.

"Then Queen Esther answered, 'If I have found favor with you, O king, and if it pleases your majesty, grant me my life --this is my petition. And spare my people --this is my request.'" Esther 7:3

Esther could have lost her life for coming before the king unannounced. By doing so anyway she technically could be viewed as unsubmissive. However, notice how her civil disobedience was not violent or aggressive. Neither was Daniel's or Jesus'. She was patient for the favor of the Lord to kick in, and when it did, she seized the day.

"Obey the king's command, I say, because you took an oath before God. Do not be in a hurry to leave the king's presence. Do not stand up for a bad cause, for he will do whatever he pleases. Since a king's word is supreme, who can say to him, "What are you doing?" Whoever obeys his command will come to no harm, and the wise heart will know the proper time and procedure." Ecclesiastes 8:2

PUT OUT YOUR RE-SCEPTORS

There is a day coming soon when Christians will have to choose whom they will serve on certain issues. God or man. In doing so, my personal view is that we should fight each battle with a sword in the heavenlies and a towel on the earth, meaning that we wage war in prayer about whatever the governmental infraction is against our beliefs in Christ, and yet we serve those enforcing the laws with as much respect and obedience as we can give. Christ put a towel around his waist and washed the dirty feet of men. Notice I didn't say he washed the feet of dirty men. The men weren't dirty, but their feet were. Everywhere they walked their sandals picked up sand and grit. But Jesus' demonstration wasn't His way of subliminally addressing a dirtiness that needed to be cleansed, but instead an act of humility and service which helped wipe it all away.

If we could serve our elected officials in this same way, wiping away all the dirt and mud they trudge through every day by washing their feet in prayer and determining it within ourselves not to judge their hearts just because of the dirt on their feet, then we would find ourselves at the tips of many lowered scepters. It would stay the hand of much civil disobedience. I still sense there are times coming when the voice of reason will not be heard and we as Christians will have to take a stand for our faith and the justifiable demonstrations of it. We will have sit-ins of prayer and show-downs of conviction. Like Daniel, we pray, like Esther we will speak up, but like Jesus we will serve, serve, serve. We will even lay down our lives.

As we seek the Lord in the days to come concerning how He would have us act and react to any governmental interference with our faith, may we pray and obey these 20 scriptures, which are attached to Heaven and all its favor.

"Do not revile the king even in your thoughts."
Ecclesiastes 10:20

1 Samuel 26:9   Saul was an ungodly king, and yet David, already anointed by the Prophet Samuel as the next king of Israel, submitted to his authority at all costs.

Ezra 6:6-10   Imagine such favor with our government that they offer to build our churches and fund God's work!

"I urge, then, first of all, that requests, prayers, intercession and thanksgiving be made for everyone-- for kings and all those in authority, that we may live peaceful and quiet lives in all godliness and holiness. This is good, and pleases God our Savior." 1 Timothy 2:1-3

Psalm 2:2-4   God laughs out loud at kings and rulers who think they are running this world without Him.

Psalm 61:6-7 May every nation's leader dwell in God's presence and have his days increased.

"The king's heart is in the hand of the LORD; he directs it like a watercourse wherever he pleases". Proverbs 21:1

Psalm 72 is definitely the "Long Live the King" psalm.

Proverbs 8:15 God helps rulers write the laws of their land.

Proverbs 25:3 God has given national leaders big hearts.

"Then the kings of the earth, the princes, the generals, the rich, the mighty, and every slave and every free man hid in caves and among the rocks of the mountains."
Revelation 6:15

Proverbs 24:21 Do our children see us honoring our public officials?

Ecclesiastes 8:2 We should obey our public officials and look for the proper time and procedure to speak up about necessary issues.

"Remind the people to be subject to rulers and authorities, to be obedient, to be ready to do whatever is good, to slander no one, to be peaceable and considerate, and to show true humility toward all men." Titus 3:1-2

Luke 2:3 Even Jesus's family submitted to the government.

Acts 26:19 Paul was defending his faith before the king and explaining that although he did not wish to disobey him, he could not be disobedient to the vision from heaven. This is civil disobedience in action.

"Do you refuse to speak to me?" Pilate said. "Don't you realize I have power either to free you or to crucify you?" Jesus answered, "You would have no power over me if it were not given to you from above." John 19:10-11

Acts 13:12 The church can affect the state and its leaders.

Proverbs 16:10 God uses the mouths of national leaders.
"The nations will walk by its light, and the kings of the earth will bring their splendor into it."
Revelation 21:24

QUOTES

"I don't mind how much my ministers talk – as long as they do what I say." ~ Margaret Thatcher

"The stakes...are too high for government to be a spectator sport." ~ Barbara Jordan

"A government which robs Peter to pay Paul can always depend on the support of Paul." ~ George Bernard Shaw

". . . it's a blessing to die for a cause, because you can so easily die for nothing." ~ Andrew Young

"Our government sprang from and was made for the people – not the people for the government. To them it owes an allegiance; from them it must derive its courage, strength, and wisdom." ~ Andrew Johnson

"The spirit of resistance to government is so valuable on certain occasions that I wish it to be always kept alive. It will often be exercised when wrong but better so than not to be exercised at all." ~ Thomas Jefferson

Chapter 9

PASTORAL SUBMISSION

Please pray:

"Father God, I earnestly ask, on this day, for You to remove from my heart and especially my mind, any trace of fear, known or unknown, concerning the structure You yourself have put in place to care for Your many children -- the Church. I acknowledge the need for covenant, and lay to rest any suspicion and mistrust that has hindered me thus far in my life from embracing it. Whether I have been pastored heavy-handedly or lethargically, faithfully or falsely, all of my life or never at all, I acknowledge today that Your teachers are human, need my prayers, and deserve all the trust I can muster up and surrender. In the presence of your angels, I forgive, I forget, and hereby forego the search for the perfect church. If I joined it I would ruin it!"

LOW AND BEHOLD
(DIVE ALERT: YOU ARE NOW 20,000 LEAGUES UNDER THE SEA...)

Because I have no idea who will be reading this book, I must say it is difficult to know how to build the framework for this chapter. At least in the last few chapters the institutions discussed were not foreign to the every day joe -- marriage, parents, workplace, friendships -- but now we're venturing out into controversial water. Building a case for submission is hard enough on its own, but ask how many are truly submitted relationally to God's governmental design for the Body of Christ and the crowd gets thin. Ephesians 4:11-13 defines the design of five offices God has created to best steward His Church with, thus explaining why some refer to it as the five-fold ministry. That is not a biblical term, but a good conceptual one (such as how the words "rapture" and "evangelism" are not included in scripture and yet their concepts most certainly are). We'll look more at the five-fold ministry in a moment, but suffice it to say that even if you are a regular church member at some local fellowship, most of us get uneasy at the thought of telling any of its leaders that we will willingly submit ourselves to their leadership and welcome their voices in our lives. We trust our bosses at work -- even though they are human -- but we consider the office of pastor such an ethereal thing that we wind up awaiting a perfection from them that will never be realized. Because it's a God-job he or she must be perfect. At least very close. That's what we tell ourselves.

Consider again the above comparison: We'd rather submit to a boss than submit to a pastor, in fact, most people probably stay at their jobs longer than they stay at the same church. Why is that? Is it because they know that if they submit to the governing authorities at work they will get paid? Probably so, and I guess that's understandable. Still, it's so very sad how few people understand that there is also a promised compensation for all those who trust in the authorities God has put in place in His Church -- put in place fully knowing they were human. If He trusted them knowing all their weaknesses, then why can't we?

The boss-pastor comparison is also good for the guy who may submit to both, but not in the same capacity (I may use "men", "guy" and "he" generically in this). He thinks nothing of checking in with boss every day, but he hasn't spoken to his pastor or designated church leader in over a month (and that's being nice). Aren't they both mere men?

THE CHARLATAN IN THE WHITE SUIT

If we could forever erase from our minds the sour slant we have towards the guy in the white suit on our t.v. asking for money (which is a bogus thing to whine about since ministries need money to function just like businesses), perhaps we could make some progress on this topic. John Travolta wore a white suit and nobody laughed at him -- well, almost nobody. Actually I liked John Travolta AND the preacher in the white suit. They both were distinct parts of my childhood and I am grateful to them both. John Travolta taught me how to dance and the t.v. evangelist taught me how to pray. I use both of those skills in my everyday Christian life now. The evangelist will remain nameless here, but I used to stay up past my bedtime and watch him on my little black and white t.v. I had won at school selling popcorn jars. I was a junkie. My mom had said I couldn't watch anything like the Exorcist but she didn't say I couldn't watch the televangelists. Unfortunately, most people are less afraid of the Exorcist.

The point is, as much as I loved the evangelist, he was not a fair representation of a pastor. Evangelists have a special grace to compel the lost -- on their tippie-toes with finger pointed in the air if necessary -- and their job is literally to put on the cheerleader skirt and convince the dying that they have an antidote. A pastor's job is a different ball game. Oh, he still puts on the cheerleader skirt, but once he does he doesn't take it off and leave town. If he does have to take it off it's to put on the nurse's uniform and comfort the hurting. When the evangelist finishes his job and moves on, the pastor is the one who stays behind to nurture the gifts that were deposited.

If more people would make the distinction between what they see on t.v. and what they could have in real life, they would not be so afraid to submit to the person behind the pulpit. If they would take the time to get to know their church leaders, in prayer and in person, they would build relationships that would last a lifetime.

THE LONE RANGER

First of all, it is solidly possible for you to have a personal relationship with Jesus Christ and not be a part of a local fellowship. However, you will not grow at the same rate (or really at all) as you would if you were connected to "the Body". As beautiful as your eyes are, they would look ridiculous sitting on your desk like trinkets.

> *"The body is a unit, though it is made up of many parts; and though all its parts are many, they form one body. So it is with Christ. For we were all baptized by one Spirit into one body --whether Jews or Greeks, slave or free --and we were all given the one Spirit to drink. Now the body is not made up of one part but of many. If the foot should say, "Because I am not a hand, I do not belong to the body," it would not for that reason cease to be part of the body. And if*

the ear should say, "Because I am not an eye, I do not belong to the body," it would not for that reason cease to be part of the body. If the whole body were an eye, where would the sense of hearing be? If the whole body were an ear, where would the sense of smell be? But in fact God has arranged the parts in the body, every one of them, just as he wanted them to be. If they were all one part, where would the body be? As it is, there are many parts, but one body. The eye cannot say to the hand, "I don't need you!" And the head cannot say to the feet, "I don't need you!" On the contrary, those parts of the body that seem to be weaker are indispensable, and the parts that we think are less honorable we treat with special honor. And the parts that are unpresentable are treated with special modesty, while our presentable parts need no special treatment. But God has combined the members of the body and has given greater honor to the parts that lacked it, so that there should be no division in the body, but that its parts should have equal concern for each other. If one part suffers, every part suffers with it; if one part is honored, every part rejoices with it. Now you are the body of Christ, and each one of you is a part of it." 1 Corinthians 12:12-27

So yes, you can be a Christian and not join and submit yourself to the teachings of a local church and its pastor, but before long you will cease to function at maximum capacity and will find yourself dragging spiritually. Then emotionally and physically. In covenant fellowship, the teachings you get and the people you meet, good and bad, will challenge you and stimulate growth. You can not challenge yourself. You can challenge others -- with your strengths and your weaknesses -- but you cannot challenge yourself with the surprising ambushes of life that only come from one on one relationships with others. Even if you are strong, as strong as iron, you are still in need of others. "As iron sharpens iron, so one man sharpens another." Proverbs 27:12. You cannot sharpen yourself. And just think of all the people in churches out there who aren't being sharpened because they don't know *you*. Connect to the Body of Christ today. For yourself and for those who are missing out not having you as a part of their lives.

"And let us not neglect our meeting together, as some people do...." Hebrews 10:25

GRAB A TOWEL AND FOLD IT 5 TIMES

"After that, he poured water into a basin and began to wash his disciples' feet, drying them with the towel that was wrapped around him." John 13:5. Jesus was a servant, plain and simple. He did everything He could while on earth to take care of His followers. What people fail to see is how He is still trying to take care of them today through the local church. He is doing it -- to protect, not to restrict -- through the five-fold ministry described below by the Apostle Paul.

"It was he who gave some to be apostles, some to be prophets, some to be evangelists, and some to be pastors and teachers, to prepare God's people for works of service, so that the body of Christ may be built up until we all reach unity in the faith and in the knowledge of the Son of God and become mature, attaining to the whole measure of the fullness of Christ. Then we will no longer be infants, tossed back and forth by the waves, and blown here and there by every wind of teaching and by the cunning and craftiness of men in their deceitful scheming. Instead, speaking the truth

> *in love, we will in all things grow up into him who is the Head, that is, Christ. From him the whole body, joined and held together by every supporting ligament, grows and builds itself up in love, as each part does its work."*
> Ephesians 4:11-16

Roughly, here's how it works: Most likely, an apostle planted your church (founded it) If he didn't plant it, he stepped in at some point to cover it governmentally. A prophet, local or visiting, helps build your church up in prayer and in the spoken word of the Lord. An evangelist visits and grows it. The pastor nurtures and leads it. The teachers study and instruct it. Who could refuse such a safety net? No corporate guru could've thought of a better plan. All the members of the Church, young and old, have gifts that are vital to its success, but these 5 offices are set in place to help mature those gifts and release them into the Body. Not all are called to the "offices" of five-fold ministry, but we all have the ability to minister. For instance, not every believer is an Evangelist, but we are all called to evangelize. Using myself as an example, prophetic prayer had been a part of my daily Christian life for as long as I could remember -- in other words, I have always loved searching out the things of the Lord, hearing His voice and praying what was on His heart (which is the way to really get things done!). But then that gifting within me grew -- sort of like a muscle does when you exercise it -- and I found myself the recipient of invitations to come and minister at churches and speak at conferences all over my city and state. I began finding myself in situations where I was praying for people publicly and suddenly I would "know" things about them and their situations that I could not have known other than by revelation of the Holy Spirit. With their hearts pricked in that place of humility before an all-knowing God, they would surrender their lives or their situations to Him with fresh faith, and as a result I began to see miracles taking place in front of my very eyes -- including healed bodies, healed emotions and healed spirits. We are made up of these three in God's image -- Father, Son and Holy Spirit -- and His desire is for us to allow Him to unfold healing in all three areas. I say that in the humility of the Lord as I await His total healing for myself. Anyway, as my pastor recognized what God was doing within me (all I knew was that I was loving seeing people's lives transformed), he asked me to consider an ordination into five-fold ministry as Prophet. After praying about it with my husband it happened just a few months later. So now as one ordained into prophetic ministry, my job is not to grow a gray beard and stand on a mountain with a big stick, but to release prayer and prophecy into the Body locally, nationally and internationally, training believers in hearing the voice of God. The prophet doesn't just prophesy, he or she trains others to prophesy! This is my fervent passion.

ONE FATHER PER HOUSEHOLD

Even though many five-fold ministers will visit churches and pour into them, it is the pastor who is ultimately accountable before God for the congregation. He must give an account for them, and so his role in that house is truly one of a father. Even though an apostle is the father who plants the church (or ministry) or at least helps oversee it governmentally, it is the pastor who leads it day to day, and so in a sense, the apostle releases the continual care of that house to his "son", the pastor. In the apostle's absence, the pastor has a better pulse on what's happening in the church daily, and so even upon the apostle's return we see him respecting the role God has given the pastor as the leader of that house. We see this in the book of Philemon (who led the church of Colosse in his home) when the Apostle Paul wrote to him with a request. He says, (v.8) "... in Christ I could be bold and order you to do what you ought to do", (then in v.14)... "but I did not want to do anything without your consent, so that any favor you do will be spontaneous and not forced." Paul was an apostle, but he was submitting to Philemon's authority when discussing matters concerning the Colossian church which Philemon pastored.

With all that said, I hope you now see the strategic importance of the role of a pastor. He is God's gift to man, in my opinion (warm smile). While I have heard of some churches that prefer a more pluralistic approach to church government -- like the round table leadership structure -- I am a firm believer that there should be only one father in each house. Many brothers, many sisters, but just one father. In my church, the mother in our house is our pastor's wife, who is also an ordained pastor. Apostles then become like grandfathers who visit and affirm the household, encouraging and imparting to the pastor, who is like a son. 1 Peter 1:12 tells about the prophets of old foreseeing the preachers of the gospel today: "It was revealed to them that they were not serving themselves but you, when they spoke of the things that have now been told you by those who have preached the gospel to you by the Holy Spirit sent from heaven. Even angels long to look into these things." Within the structure of a correctly aligned church, lives blossom and God's wisdom is made manifest to the whole world, including to the angels!

"His intent was that now, through the church, the manifold

wisdom of God should be made known to the rulers and authorities in the heavenly realms, according to his eternal purpose which he accomplished in Christ Jesus our Lord."
Ephesians 3:10-11

FOLLOW THE LEADER

Aside from the five-fold ministers, each local church has leaders that help the pastor oversee and care for that local body of believers. Scripture defines these roles and tells us they are due our honor and submission. So then, we see when studying Pastoral Submission that although not everyone is called to be a pastor, there are those who have a pastoral service to the Body of Christ and they too are in authority over us.

We see in Titus 1:6-8 the qualifications for Elders, and are told that they are "entrusted with God's work", and have authority to "encourage others by sound doctrine and refute those who oppose it." In James we see that it is the Elders who should be called upon to pray for the sick. James 5:14-15 "Is any one of you sick? He should call the elders of the church to pray over him and anoint him with oil in the name of the Lord. And the prayer offered in faith will make the sick person well" Of course, some say that because this is a lower-case "e" and not Elders with a capital "E", that this is merely saying to call on those who are mature and older in the faith. In Acts 20:28 and 1 Peter 5:2 Elders are referred to as "Overseers", and are reminded that they are shepherds of the flocks under their care.

In 1 Tim. 3:8-10 are listed the requirements for those serving as Deacons, part of which is to "keep hold of the deep truths of the faith with a clear conscience." We know there were women deacons too, for in Romans 16:1-2 we learn about a woman named Phoebe. Paul tells them, "Our sister Phoebe, a deacon in the church in Cenchrea, will be coming to see you soon. Receive her in the Lord, as one who is worthy of high honor. Help her in every way you can, for she has helped many in their needs, including me."

"Remember your leaders, who spoke the word of God to you. Consider the outcome of their way of life and imitate their faith." Hebrews 13:7

"Obey your leaders and submit to their authority. They keep watch over you as men who must give an account. Obey them so that their work will be a joy, not a burden, for that would be of no advantage to you." Hebrews 13:17

"Now we ask you, brothers, to respect those who work hard among you, who are over you in the Lord and who admonish you. Hold them in the highest regard in love because of their work. Live in peace with each other." 1 Thessalonians. 5:12-13

There are some intriguing stories in the Bible documenting what happened when God's man or messenger was honored and submitted to: 2 Kings 5:10-14: when Elisha's with specific instructions, strange and humbling, commanded Namaan to bathe seven times in the dirty Jordan river in order to healed of leprosy. He did and instantly was. 2 Corinthians 7:13 tells of how Titus, Paul's special representative sent to oversee the island of Crete, was so welcomed and honored by the people that he felt "happy" and "refreshed". 1 Kings 7:13 tells the story of the widow whom Elijah asked to use her last bit of flour and oil to make him a small cake. She submitted to his difficult requests with all she had left, and God multiplied her supplies supernaturally and she and her family had food for the rest of the famine. A simple verse that speaks volumes is Malachi 4:4 in which God instructs the people to "remember to obey the instruction of my servant Moses." This always struck me as interesting that God didn't say, "obey Me", but rather to obey Moses. Though imperfect men, we see in history where God has a pattern of placing ordinary people in places of leadership and doing extraordinary things through them.

WHERE THE RUBBER MEETS THE ROAD

Or course, it is a privilege to honor to serve and submit to those who care for and encourage you. But what about when the Lord uses them to discipline you? Is that still a privilege? Are they still due honor, even when they've stepped on our spiritual toes? I'll never forget when God started dealing with me on this very issue. I was seeking Him in prayer and fasting concerning the next season of my life and all He had in store for me, and when I awakened on the morning of November 14th, 1993 I had a big surprise awaiting me. I awoke and saw "Hebrews 12:10" written on my bedroom wall. Remembering how Daniel had once interpreted a series of words written by God on a wall with His finger, I was very excited to jump out of bed and run to my Bible to see what exciting message God must be trying to send me. Oh boy, here it was:

"Our fathers disciplined us for a little while as they thought best; but God disciplines us for our good, that we may share in his holiness."

Great. I was scared to death at what God must be about to

do. I backed up a few verses and here's what I found: "...because the Lord disciplines those he loves, and he punishes everyone he accepts as a son. Endure hardship as discipline; God is treating you as sons. For what son is not disciplined by his father? If you are not disciplined (and everyone undergoes discipline), then you are illegitimate children and not true sons. Moreover, we have all had human fathers who disciplined us and we respected them for it. How much more should we submit to the Father of our spirits and live!" Well indeed, the next few years of my life required much discipline. Not necessarily chastisement, but true discipline, which is the training of God. I was thankful that the majority of it came directly through situations at church where I was being raised up into higher places of leadership, because when you have loving relationships with the people at your church God will use that in your life as a wonderful breeding ground for maturity.

Well, during those years, the more God would entrust to me the more He would require of me. I had started out at the director of the church's drama ministry, and since that had been my life work I enjoyed the job immensely and considered it fun. And then Chris and I decided to move into the church's home-group leadership (Harvest is a cell-based church -- a church model which has exploded around the world that uses home groups called "cells" to help multiply and grow the Body with lasting health) and so we began holding weekly cell meetings in our home each week. Our maturity levels had to take a step up, as did our accountability to the group members and to the Zone Leader over us who oversaw us and about three other cell groups. Our cell prospered and grew and so pretty soon we were having to "multiply" and form other cells, so then at that time we were raised up into Zone Leadership. Before we knew it, my husband was also being ordained as an Elder of the church as an advisor to the pastor. Alongside that, my prophetic ministry was growing and Pastor was often calling me forward to deliver words of prophecy that I felt were on God's heart. We had suddenly awakened one morning and realized we were living in a glass house in which everyone in the church knew us and could see inside of our very persons. They knew our children, and since I'd read somewhere in 1 Timothy that Overseer's children needed to be obedient with proper respect, that new level of self-discipline instantly expanded to our entire household. It was a wonderful time. Due to the love and honor given us in the church, it was an easy yoke. Still, I remember times when that high visibility set me up for some key threshholds of decision. There would be times when I was growing in the prophetic utterances of the Lord and would approach Pastor during a church service with what I truly felt was a prophetic word for our body, and he would pray and sense that it was not for that gathering. Those times were hard. #1 because you had something burning in your spirit that never got out. #2 because the whole church had seen you step forward with a word and then also saw Pastor decide to not let you release it in that particular setting. Of course it needs to be said that it is a Pastor's job to oversee each service as a whole to the best of his abilities. So in moments like that, you are truly faced with how much submission is, or is not, in your heart. I now think that some of those messages were truly words that I'd heard God speak, but that He sent them and had Pastor withhold them solely to test what I would do: Consider myself greater than the pastor because I had a word from God, or submit to his judgment with a smile and without hesitation. It was the fulfillment of what I'd seen written on the wall that day, and so with each opportunity to be disciplined, I'd call on the grace of God for humility enough to submit, knowing that the promise was that I would get to "share in His holiness." Sometimes I'd fight rejection, and sometimes even embarrassment, but I now see that God blessed my submission to Pastor immensely and began increasing and multiplying the gift within me. Before long, as I said, he was coming to me and suggesting I be ordained as Prophet. Today, there is hardly ever a time when he doesn't turn the microphone over to me instantaneously -- even without first judging the prophecy himself. I do not consider myself to be the greatest prophet in the world, but my aim is to be the most submitted one. "God sets himself against the proud, but he shows favor to the humble" James 4:6

COMMANDS, CORRECTIONS AND REBUKES

As we take a look at what Scripture says about a church leader's authorization to discipline those in their care, ask yourself this question: "What would I do today if I was "commanded, corrected, or rebuked" by a leader in my church?" Think about it. Would you be offended? Would your pride cause you to find an excuse to leave the church? Or could you trust that these men and women, as iron sharpens iron, are lovingly trying to sharpen you into the image of Christ that you've begged God to help you look like? Despite their imperfections and their own needs for sharpening, do we really believe that mere men have the authority to speak into our lives in such ways? To engage in submission to those training us, knowing that they themselves are flesh and blood in training at higher levels and are required to submit to those in authority over them, is the ultimate trust in God, and most certainly very pleasing to Him.

God's leaders are authorized to:

2 Timothy 4:2 "correct, rebuke and encourage"
2 Thessalonians 3:6 "command"
Colossians 1:28 "admonish and teach"
1 Thessalonians 2:7 "make demands"
2 Corinthians 10:13 "boast" in the fields assigned to them
2 Corinthians 10:14 - "claim authority"
2 Peter 3:7 "warn"
1 Corinthians 5:12 "judge"
Philippians 2:12 expect obedience, even in their absence
Philippians 3:17 have others pattern their lives after them
1 Timothy 2:8 instruct men exactly how to pray

> *"For the appeal we make does not spring from error or impure motives, nor are we trying to trick you. On the contrary, we speak as men approved by God to be entrusted with the gospel. We are not trying to please men but God, who tests our hearts." 1 Thessalonians 2:3-4*

NOT A NEW IDEA

In the Old Testament, God's leaders where also authorized to have say-so in the personal lives of the people, as well as expecting some pretty demanding details from them as they served. Take for instance Nehemiah. No one with any submission issues could have served under Nehemiah! What a great work of God he accomplished, but with a zero-tolerance level for sin. Take a look:

1. When the people were wailing and crying he told them to "HUSH!" (8:11)
2. When one of his workers disobeyed him he threw out

his belongings from the Temple (13:8)
3. He demanded purification (13:9)
4. He confronted leaders (13:11)
5. He rebuked those selling goods at the Temple on the Sabbath (13:5)
6. He commanded the people (13:19)
7. He spoke sharply to them concerning their behavior (13:21)
8. He threatened to arrest those who were hard-headed (13:21)
9. He confronted and call down curses on those who'd married wrongly (13:25)
10. He banished a high priest (13:30)
11. He purged every foreign object from the temple (13:30)
12. And finally, *HE BEAT SOME OF HIS WORKERS AND PULLED OUT THEIR HAIR!* (13:25)

What would you do today if a church leader spoke sharply to you concerning your behavior? What if he or she called down a curse upon you for marrying the wrong person? What pastor could stand up under that report?!!! Nehemiah did, and because he was unafraid to take action after 150 years of Babylonian exile of the Jews, he completed the prophesied rebuilding of the wall in just 52 days!

Now look at Moses:

The entire book of Exodus is a detailed account of one man's ability to lead a mob with God's help. God would give Moses instructions, and then punish the people severely if they did not submit to them. Although most people today would feel it an invasion of privacy, Moses was involved in every aspect of their lives, and nothing about them was hidden from him, spiritually or personally.

In Exodus 31:11 God said to Moses,"They must follow exactly all the instructions I have given you."

Exodus 16:1-36 -- The people submit to Moses concerning their daily portions of food (manna). When some took more than their allotted share, their manna became infested with maggots.

Exodus 17:2 -- To argue with Moses was to argue with God. "Moses replied, "Why do you quarrel with me? Why do you put the LORD to the test?"

Numbers 4:5-15 - Moses and Aaron were to tell the people precisely how to move the Ark of the Covenant whenever it must be transported. Later in 1 Chronicles 13:9-13 when David's people were trying to transport it into the City of David, they disobeyed the precise instruction given by Moses and Aaron and as a result one man, Uzzah, was struck dead just for touching it.

Numbers 4:49 - Moses tells the people where they will work and what they'll carry as they journey.

To disobey God's man, Moses, was to disobey God. Moses said, *"Who are we? You are not grumbling against us, but against the LORD." Exodus 16:8*

What would happen if today we were told by a church leader where to work and what to eat and when? Fully realizing that today's church is structured with more checks and balances than with a one-man-show crusade like Moses was running, it is still worth asking ourselves if we are made of the stuff that would allow someone to speak into our lives on that level. Unfortunately, our westernized world is so far removed from all Biblical models of authority to submission, that many today feel controlled and manipulated when asked to submit at even the most primitive levels. There is always another church down the road to join when something doesn't go our way. Still, if we allow employers, policemen, government officials and parents -- all mere men and women -- to have authority over us, determine our boundaries and control our actions, then why should we have such trouble staying put while our pastors and other church leaders do the same?

"Finally, brothers, we instructed you how to live in order to please God, as in fact you are living. Now we ask you and urge you in the Lord Jesus to do this more and more. For you know what instructions we gave you by the authority of the Lord Jesus." 1 Thessalonians. 4:1-2

REBELLION AGAINST AUTHORITY

Please remember the prayer you prayed at the beginning of this chapter before we move now into this next section. If necessary, go back and pray it again! My real request however is that you make yourself a blank page and ask the Lord to write upon your heart His fresh mandates for any area of your life that you are withholding from Him, including submission to the men and women leaders at your local church.

Rebellion is the opposite of submission. It can be blatant or it can be subtle, but since God sees the heart, make no mistake that He sees a lack of submission as overt rebellion. 1 Samuel 15:23 tells us that to God, "rebellion is as the sin of witchcraft". The New Testament is filled with stories of rebellious individuals that the early church leaders had to confront and deal with. The Old Testament is too. I can't imagine the time wasted since the beginning of creation on this sorry excuse for a distraction. Imagine all the hours totaled up and then spent on something worthwhile in the kingdom: helping others, healing the sick, enjoying our families, or just soaking in the Lord's presence. Who was the first individual to ever rebel? Was it Judas against Jesus? Was it Jonah who wound up as whale chow? Was it Adam and Eve in the Garden? No, the first ever rebellion began with Satan. Isaiah 14 describes his attempt to "make himself like the Most High", thereby securing his fall from Heaven as one of its original angels. When he fell, "Lucifer" took one-third of the angels with him. Jude 6 says, "And I remind you of the angels who did not stay within the limits of authority God gave them but left the place where they belonged. God has kept them chained in prisons of darkness, waiting for the day of judgment. 2 Peter 2:4 & 9 says, "For if God did not spare angels when they sinned, but sent them to hell, putting them into gloomy dungeons to be held for judgment, ...then the Lord knows how to rescue godly men from trials and to hold the unrighteous for the day of judgment, while continuing their punishment." And finally, rebellion will be the driving force behind the Anti-Christ when he appears on the scene at the end of all time to deceive many. "Don't let anyone deceive you in any way, for that day will not come until the rebellion occurs and the man of lawlessness is revealed, the man doomed to destruction." 2 Thessalonians 2:3

Rebellion is a powerful demonic force, a very old spirit, and it is still looking for those whom it may fulfill its lusts through today. Let's take a look in Scripture at the devastations of rebellion:

FASTEN YOUR SEAT BELT

On the week of my 36th birthday, after having penned the opening chapters of this book, the Lord dropped a bomb on me. A good bomb. He reminded me how just a few years before He had led me to steal away to my father's prayer cabin on his farm and read through the entire Bible in just five days. He was now telling me I was going to do it again, only this time, reading through every page of the Bible and looking for stories about submission. With a rigorous 15-16 hour a day reading schedule, and with the cooperation of my family since I was unable to leave town this time, I dove in. I bought a blank journal and by the time I was through (on my birthday), about a hundred of its pages were filled with beautiful sagas on submission. Unfortunately, there were just as many escapades on rebellion. In every single book of the Bible -- from Genesis to Revelation -- I found something. Sometimes just a nugget and sometimes a whole novel. In doing so, I uncovered the following thirty stories or verses about rebellion that "woke me up" in the spirit. In the fear of the Lord I submit them to you for sober contemplation. The first twenty are a montage of God's opinions about submission and rebellion, some as told through His servants as they were overseeing particular disturbing uprisings. However, the final ten are the gravest, as they are actual accounts of how God killed or struck those who would not submit to His leaders. Imagine how you would feel if you picked up your newspaper day after day for a week and in that time read 30 accounts of serious uprisings, betrayals and rebellions going on in the world. There were many more than that as I read, but these were the ones that made me lose sleep. As you get your Bible out and study them I pray you'll throw off all biases, shake in your shoes and realize just how serious God is about this submission thing.

"Do not blaspheme God or curse the ruler of your people."
Exodus 22:28

Galatians 1:7-8 Paul defending himself after being accused of preaching heresy.

The book of Zechariah - God is angry at His people for ignoring His man.

Numbers 17:5 God gives Moses a plan to put an end to the grumbling against him by those he was trying to lead.

I Corinthians 4:3-4 Paul explaining that he frankly doesn't care who decides to judge his authority in ministry because God is the only One who can judge us.

"...and you said to my prophets, shut up." Amos 2:12

Titus 1:10-11 When those in our churches rebel against right teaching (as happened in this passage), they must be silenced, otherwise they may turn entire families away from the truth.

Hosea 4:16 Rebellion leaves you disfellowshipped and unprotected.

2 Timothy 4:14-15 The words of Paul describing how Alexander the metalworker greatly harmed his ministry.

Acts 23:1-5 Paul, with every right to judge, still tried to honor the High Priest under accusation. This was a hard submission, but Paul did it.

"Gaal gained the confidence of the people and led a united rebellion against the king, Ambimelech (In this case God allowed it since it was an ungodly king -- but many of Gaal's men were struck down as a result.) "Then Zebul said to him, "Where is your big talk now, you who said, `Who is Abimelech that we should be subject to him?' Aren't these the men you ridiculed? Go out and fight them!" So Gaal led out the citizens of Shechem and fought Abimelech. Abimelech chased him, and many fell wounded in the flight --all the way to the entrance to the gate." Judges 9:26-40

Lamentations 4:16 Rebellion leaves you unprotected.

1 Thessalonians 4:8 Paul explains how when others reject your instruction, they are rejecting God and not you.

Jeremiah 7:25-26, 28-29 God sends His prophets to warn us. Are we listening?

"While I was there I talked privately with the leaders of the church. I wanted to make sure they did not disagree, or my ministry would have been useless." Galatians 2:2

The Psalms: Many, many of them include the phrase, *"Oh that my enemies would be silent and not accuse me falsely!"*. Well remember that many psalms were written by David, God's anointed, and so every tongue that rose up against David in judgment was in essence a direct rebellion against God. Like a pastor who is falsely accused, David suffered countless trials at the hands of rebellious know-it-alls. In the 150 Psalms there are are over 140 times when David or another psalmist spoke of the betrayal of a friend turned enemy or a flat-out rebellious foe. For instance: *Psalm 41:7-11 All my enemies whisper together against me; they imagine the worst for me, saying, "A vile disease has beset him; he will never get up from the place where he lies." Even my close friend, whom I trusted, he who shared my bread, has lifted up his heel against me. But you, O LORD, have mercy on me; raise me up, that I may repay them. I know that you are pleased with me, for my enemy does not triumph over me."*

2 Chronicles 36:15-16   Despise the words of God's Prophets and arouse a wrath with no remedy!

1 Corinthians 4:4-5   Paul, once again, claims a clear conscience against his accusers and declares that they should leave the judging to God.

Numbers 14:2&4   Israel illegally raised up another leader to pacify and justify their rebellion against Moses and Aaron.

"I know that after I leave, savage wolves will come in among you and will not spare the flock. Even from your own number men will arise and distort the truth in order to draw away disciples after them. So be on your guard! Remember that for three years I never stopped warning each of you night and day with tears." Acts 20:29-31

THE TOP TEN

Now study the consequences of rebellion, or speaking against God's anointed, in the these ten:

2 Chronicles 26:16 & 19   King Uzziah becomes prideful after his rise to power, and decides to enter the temple and burn incense on his own at the altar without aid from the priests. While raging at the priests from trying to stop him,

Uzziah broke out in leprosy.

2 Chronicles 35:22 Josiah didn't listen to King Neco to whom God had warned him through to not go into battle, and Josiah was hit and killed by enemy archer when he went anyway.

2 Kings 5:27 Gehazi, an assistant to the Prophet Elisha, had rebelled against Elisha's wishes to not take compensation from Namaan after Namaan was healed by Elisha of leprosy. As a result, Gehazi and his descendants inherited Namaan's leprosy forever.

Numbers 12:8-15 Miriam, Moses' sister and a known prophetess of the Lord, grumbled against Moses and came under the judgment of God because of it. When God struck her with leprosy, Moses still interceded on her behalf with God and begged him to heal her. He did, but note how Miriam's rebellion caused the entire camp to be held back. Corporate progress is impeded by even one person's lack of submission.

Numbers 14:36-37 A group of rebels are struck down with a plague and die after causing the entire community to grumble against Moses and spreading a bad report about the land.

Numbers 16 Korah became insolent with Moses and decided to incite a rebellion amongst 250 Israelite men against him. It so angered God that He gathered them all in one place and caused the ground underneath them to open up and swallow them whole. They went to their graves alive, along with their households and all of their possessions. God will go to great lengths to remove every trace of rebellion!

Numbers 14:10-12 God is angered by Israel's contempt and rebellion. As the whole assembly schemed to stone Joshua and Caleb -- God's chosen leaders -- God showed up and threatened to strike them with a plague and destroy them once and for all. His chosen people!

Numbers 21:4-6 God gets fed up with Israel's murmuring about how Moses brought them out of Egypt just to make them starve in the desert, and He sends venomous snakes to bite and kill them. Many died that die.

3 John 9-10 John describes an individual who loves calling himself a leader at church but will not acknowledge authority or support other Christian ministries.

2 Kings 2:23-24 Some youths walking down a road see Elisha and make fun of his bald head. Elisha calls down a curse upon them and two bears come out of the woods and maul forty-two of the youths.

May the Lord give us each the grace and gumption needed to submit to our leaders!

BETRAYED WITH A KISS

I would like to state some personal observations on the last five passages listed above, because in them exist many issues that the Body of Christ is dealing with today. First of all, notice how in the story of Korah and in the following one about Joshua and Caleb, both involved a very large group of seemingly convincing people who were murmuring. As a leader of many believers, young and old, throughout my years of serving the Lord in different locations I have seen one too many instances when one person's grievance would be adopted by many as soon as that one stepped forward with a "concern". For instance, many may be questioning a decision that their pastor or other church leader has made, but it remains a mere thought in their mind to wrestle and pray through (which is *all* they should be doing -- the Pastor *needs* that prayer). But then suddenly, Satan gains control of one tongue in the bunch and then all hell breaks lose. "Yes, I've noticed the same thing about Pastor!", or "Yes, the Lord had laid the same concerns on my heart about how that spirit is trying to overtake our dear Pastor!"

Always be on the lookout for such syrupy catch phrases, for they are indeed the kiss of Judas.

What makes my antennas go up concerning these two stories is how many people were involved. In Joshua and Caleb's case, Scripture says "the whole assembly" rose up against them. What if today, your whole church rose up against the pastor? Would you be tempted to side with the majority just because they were so large in number? Far too many people have abused and misused the 1 Timothy 5:19 passage, "Do not entertain an accusation against an elder unless it is brought by two or three witnesses", and totally forgotten that even when Korah had 250 "witnesses" God still judged them for judging God's man. The ground literally opened up and swallowed them, along with their families and "all their possessions". Perhaps even their candlesticks were swallowed up with them because God didn't want a single thumb print of rebellion left. But unlike the first time Moses had seen a swallowing up of this sort at the Red Sea, these people were not Egyptian enemies. They were his friends. He had eaten with them, danced with them, and delivered them from slavery. Their death, although necessary punishment by God, had to grieve his heart. I'm sure Jesus felt the same way when the one from His twelve betrayed him.

NEXT: VENOMOUS VIPERS

Now notice the Numbers passage where the people grumbled and God sent poisonous snakes to bite and kill them. I have seen many instances in my years in church leadership where tongues have wagged in the name of discernment. When the Bible speaks of "being delivered from the jaws of death", I firmly now believe it is describing the sins of the tongue and its devastations. In one such instance, I had a dream one night about poisonous snakes that were being hatched in mass quantities and squirming on the floor beneath my feet. They were tiny, but as a whole they were very intimidating. In the dream I leaped upon my bed, which was in an army barrack (interp: rest in the midst of war), and I began jumping from bed to bed and sure enough, they were under every cot of those in my platoon. Pretty soon in all my leaping, I sprouted wings and began to soar above the snakes. From that new perspective, they were like helpless little worms with no place to go. That very week, an outbreak of accusation was birthed in our church, against the pastors and many of those in leadership, including myself. Some joined forces and left the church. It was hard, and only made harder because it was not the first time it had happened, but we held tightly to one another with daily prayers and even fastings, and the Lord indeed helped us to soar above the accusations and prevail. We began seeing salvations every week at our church, in and out of the church meetings. A constant flow came in. Five one week. Ten the next, and a dozen the next. It still has not stopped to this day. Greater miracles. Hearts and emotions made whole. Druggies saved, prostitutes cleansed, and marriages restored. Lasting fruit. What I saw emerge was a whole army of victors. I speak not just of those of us who were accused, but of the whole church. It was as if our Body had fought off a deadly poison and emerged with a stronger immune system as a result. Hallelujah! Romans 3:13 says, "Their throats are open graves; their tongues practice deceit. The poison of vipers is on their lips.", and James 3:8 describes the tongue as "a restless evil, full of deadly poison", but hallelujah to God, Mark 16:18 declares victory to the Body of Christ and says, "they will pick up snakes with their hands; and when they drink deadly poison, it will not hurt them at all."

Frederick Douglass, an American abolitionist (1817-1895) said, "If there is no struggle, there is no progress."

NEXT: THE MATTHEW 18 RULE

The next note I have (in this very long chapter) is on the letter John had to one of his church leaders, Giaus, about a devise man names Diotrephes. Please note the words, "When I come, I will report some of the things he is doing and the wicked things he is saying about us." In the dealings I have had in respect to uprisings within churches, often being called in as a mediator between feuding parties, I have had to call many people on the carpet about their lack of obeying the Matthew 18 rule. In it is the key to proper resolution of any disagreement. "If your brother sins against you, go and show him his fault, just between the two of you. If he listens to you, you have won your brother over. But if he will not listen, take one or two others along, so that every matter may be established by the testimony of two or three witnesses. If he refuses to listen to them, tell it to the church; and if he refuses to listen even to the church, treat him as you would a pagan or a tax collector" (v. 15-17). So the command here whenever you have a grievance against someone is, #1) Go directly to them. Do not pass judgment. Do not pass it on to others. Do not pass "go"! Go directly to them (monopoly has many spiritual truths in it!). #2 is) If they will not "hear" you, bring in a third party. We have seen many times when having a mediator helped immensely and instantly. It's the same theory our nation's legal system is based on when a judge hears both sides of a story. And #3) if still he will not hear you, take it to the church. I have only seen this happen once in my church, and it happened at my advice. Even then, it was not to the entire church, but since we are a cell-based church (made up of small home groups), I advised a leader to bring one person's habitual sin before her entire cell group since it had been committed individually against everyone in the group and no previous private confrontations had done any good. So back to John's letter. In many of the cases when people left our church after they were confronted with the truth that they had not abided by the Matthew 18 rule, they would in turn, leave disgruntled and accuse us of then talking about them. For instance, if we had proof that they had gone to their friends with an offense about someone else instead of going straight to that person to resolve it, they would then accuse us as the mediators of having talked about them behind their backs and gathering grievances against them. It was, I am sure, injurious to the heart of the Lord as He watched His children bickering. But what we need to see about John's letter to Gaius is that he specifically had to "report some things" to him about the divisive individual. When you choose to disobey scripture and it results in injury to the Body, you immediately open yourself up to become an item of church business by your church leaders. They must work to protect the flock, and according to 3 John 10 that is exactly what will happen. If more people would quit calling their friends for prayer support and instead go directly to the person they are at odds with, we would have fewer split churches today, which make a joke of the gospel to those deliberating embracing it. Personally, I think there is an even higher level of maturity than Matthew 18, and that is Proverbs 19:11: "A man's wisdom gives him patience; it is to his glory to overlook an offense."

NEXT: BALD HEADS

Finally, and on a lighter note, is the last story about Elisha and his bald head. I remember once, "Papa" Don Finto came to speak at my church, which had been birthed out of one of his other churches. It was his birthday, and we were all family, and so Pastor Brad asked me to work up a little dramatic presentation to help celebrate. I did, and in doing so worked up a hilarious parody to the Tammy Wynette song, "Stand By Your Man". I had the audience, and Papa Don, in stitches, especially when I got to the part about his bald head. A few months later I was reading through Scripture and stumbled across this passage about Elisha and the young men who had made fun of his bald head and then been mauled by bears! Of course, they were engaging in the course jesting because they truly hated Elisha and my situation was entirely different, but still it got me thinking. It wasn't like they'd tried to bodily harm Elisha, right? They were just making fun of his head! In the careful study of a trying-to-be-pure heart, I realized just how much God wants His anointed to receive honor. Nothing short of it.

Soon after, I found myself in the same room with Papa Don and I approached him and explained my remorseful revelations. With his typical wide-smile and jovial spirit, he laughed and hugged me. Although he felt there was nothing to forgive, he had seen my heart and so he knew it was important for me to be released. My already loving opinion of him sky-rocketed that day, and hopefully that went both ways.

GOD MEANS BUSINESS

A close friend of mine once shared with me about an odd thing that had occurred at her church. Her pastor had been forced to step down due to a debilitating physical illness, but shortly before doing so he had ordained a man in the fellowship as a deacon, a decision that he probably lived to regret. This man was very cordial and very handsome, and in some ways was like an "Associate Pastor" although he had never been ordained as such. He began ruling the deacons' meetings with a heavy hand, screaming at the people and overspending their money. When the pastor resigned, this man elevated himself into the position of Pastor and the abuse of the Body got worse. At one particular church meeting he declared in prayer, "Lord, if there's anybody among us who is not doing what they're told, TAKE THEM OUT!". Shortly after that he died of a massive brain aneurysm.

"Avoid godless chatter, because those who indulge in it will become more and more ungodly. Their teaching will spread like gangrene. Among them are Hymenaeus and Philetus." 2 Timothy 2:16-17. How would you like to go down in history and be listed in the Bible *by name* as being a gossiper who spreads gangrene in the Body? Yikes!

CHURCH HOPPERS

Covenant should not be taken lightly. I personally think that church membership is a covenant due a similar loyalty as the covenant of marriage. In spirit, not in law. Proverbs 15:12 states that mockers don't like rebukes and so they stay away from the wise, which I think is the perfect explanation for all the church hopping going on amidst the Body of Christ today. If one pastor doesn't tickle your ears, you just run down the road to find someone who will. In 1 John 2, John described a group of people who'd left them and says, "these people left our churches because they never really belonged with us." Ezekiel 16:59 issues a wake up call "This is what the Sovereign LORD says: 'I will deal with you as you deserve, because you have despised my oath by breaking the covenant.'" So many people are looking for the perfect church, instead of realizing that if they find it and join it, they will ruin it. No church is perfect, because it is made up of human beings. No pastor is perfect, despite his God-given right to be honored. He is, after all, a man. So what if he really is walking in error? What if my complaint is legitimate? Isn't he worth me sticking around and prayerfully serving him back into the truth along with all those in his care? I remember once I sat across from a man who was telling me he was going to leave our church because "all of the people were so immature!". I answered, "Perhaps you are right bro, but the last thing we need is for all the mature people to leave!" Ecclesiastes 11:4 says, "If you wait for perfect conditions, you will never get anything done."

PUT YOUR MONEY WHERE YOUR MOUTH IS

"Will a man rob God? Yet you rob me. "But you ask, `How

do we rob you?' "In tithes and offerings. You are under a curse --the whole nation of you --because you are robbing me. Bring the whole tithe into the storehouse, that there may be food in my house. Test me in this," says the LORD Almighty, "and see if I will not throw open the floodgates of heaven and pour out so much blessing that you will not have room enough for it." Malachi 3:8-10

Financial submission is another touchy topic in the Church today. I notice that when a man is truly submitted to God, it will affect his wallet. I am so tired of hearing people make fun of the preacher on t.v. asking for money, and yet never acknowledging the fact that ministries take money to run just like businesses. Even Solomon said, "money is the answer to everything" (Ecclesiastes 10:19). We have no trouble putting our money in invisible stocks and bonds, but we have a hard time putting anything in the plate being passed down our row. Must we really throw the baby out with the bath water just because a few have misused our funds? I have more faith than that, and I also know that whatever I give I give unto God and therefore it will come back to me as blessing regardless of what the recipient does with it. Make note of the what God has to say about tithes (10% of your income) and "offerings" (the gifts that you give above that).

"All the believers were together and had everything in common. Selling their possessions and goods, they gave to anyone as he had need." Acts 2:44-45

"Now a man named Ananias, together with his wife Sapphira, also sold a piece of property. With his wife's full knowledge he kept back part of the money for himself, but brought the rest and put it at the apostles' feet. Then Peter

said, "Ananias, how is it that Satan has so filled your heart that you have lied to the Holy Spirit and have kept for yourself some of the money you received for the land? Didn't it belong to you before it was sold? And after it was sold, wasn't the money at your disposal? What made you think of doing such a thing? You have not lied to men but to God." When Ananias heard this, he fell down and died. And great fear seized all who heard what had happened."
Acts 5:1-5

"The disciples, each according to his ability, decided to provide help for the brothers living in Judea. This they did, sending their gift to the elders by Barnabas and Saul."
Acts 11:29-30

"Moreover, as you Philippians know, in the early days of your acquaintance with the gospel, when I set out from Macedonia, not one church shared with me in the matter of giving and receiving, except you only; for even when I was in Thessalonica, you sent me aid again and again when I was in need. Not that I am looking for a gift, but I am looking for what may be credited to your account. I have received full payment and even more; I am amply supplied, now that I have received from Epaphroditus the gifts you sent. They are a fragrant offering, an acceptable sacrifice, pleasing to God. And my God will meet all your needs according to his glorious riches in Christ Jesus."
Philippians 4:15-19

"But just as you excel in everything --in faith, in speech, in knowledge, in complete earnestness and in your love for us --see that you also excel in this grace of giving. I am not commanding you, but I want to test the sincerity of your love by comparing it with the earnestness of others."
2 Corinthians 8:7-8

"So I thought it necessary to urge the brothers to visit you in advance and finish the arrangements for the generous gift you had promised. Then it will be ready as a generous gift, not as one grudgingly given. Remember this: Whoever sows sparingly will also reap sparingly, and whoever sows generously will also reap generously. Each man should give what he has decided in his heart to give, not reluctantly or under compulsion, for God loves a cheerful giver."
2 Corinthians 9:5-7

1 Corinthians 9:3-14 Paul defends his rights, and other preachers' rights, to earn their living from the gospel. Claiming that they have right to food and drink as much as anyone else, he claims that sowing spiritual seed into others' lives gives you the right to reap a material reward from it.

"Now about the collection for God's people: Do what I told the Galatian churches to do. On the first day of every week, each one of you should set aside a sum of money in keeping with his in-come, saving it up, so that when I come no collections will have to be made." 1 Corinthians 16:1

A CHARGE TO PASTORS AND LEADERS

Let's close this very long chapter with a sobering charge to those who are in any form of leadership within the Body of Christ. Paul told the church leaders at Phillipi to not demand their rights as leaders, but to serve. They had every right to demand, but what Paul is saying is that when we serve the people this will not be necessary. We are leaders, but we are servants, just as our elected officials call themselves "public servants", and the way Jesus washed the disciples' feet to display even He was not beneath serving. Paul spoke in Colossians 1:25 about the church and said, "I have become its servant by the commission God gave me", and so that should be our theme as we engage in servant leadership even today. He said to the Corinthian church, "But the only letter of recommendation we need is you yourselves! Your lives are a letter written in our hearts, and everyone can read it and recognize our good work among you." (2 Corinthians 3:2). He often had to take hits and accusations from those who thought he was preaching the gospel for his own gain, but time and time again he would answer, "If we are out of our mind, it is for the sake of God; if we are in our right mind, it is for you. For Christ's love compels us" (2 Corinthians 5:13-14). As leaders, we should consider all that Paul endured for the people he loved: 2 Corinthians 6:3-10 says, "We put no stumbling block in anyone's path, so that our ministry will not be discredited. Rather, as servants of God we commend ourselves in every way: in great endurance; in troubles, hardships and distresses; in beatings, imprisonments and riots; in hard work, sleepless nights and hunger; in purity, understanding, patience and kindness; in the Holy Spirit and in sincere love; in truthful speech and in the power of God; with weapons of righteousness in the right hand and in the left; through glory and dishonor, bad report and good report; genuine, yet regarded as impostors; known, yet regarded as unknown; dying, and yet we live on; beaten, and yet not killed; sorrowful, yet always rejoicing; poor, yet making many rich; having nothing, and yet possessing everything." Another translation says, "In everything we do we try to show that we are true ministers" (2 Corinthians 6:4). Amen and so be it today.

There once was a Church who matured
Past the grapevine brigade they'd endured
All the fist-fighting dukes
Did receive their rebukes
Making splits and rebellions obscure

Gone for good were the roving disasters
Caused by church hopping saints and hurt pastors
As they followed their leader
Their lives were made sweeter
And lo and behold they grew faster

Section Three ~

SUBMISSION: THE COUNTERFEITS

"The LORD does not look at the things man looks at. Man looks at the outward appearance, but the LORD looks at the heart." 1 Samuel 16:7

The naked eye cannot detect intentions of the heart
But phony imitations can be spotted if you're smart

The bogus simulation of a plastic-coated fake
Will promise you the world then dice it up upon your plate

Beware of perjured promises that seemingly bewitch
Then self-destruct in anger if you dare reveal their glitch

Betrothed to pure betrayal, empty words will build their nest
Then be reduced to fading carbon copies at their best

Confront all shams, destroy all clones, disable heavy yokes
Resist all replications, don't be hoodwinked by a hoax

And then one day all artificial sweeteners will resign
Humanity will taste and see submission redefined

Chapter 10

RELUCTANT SUBMISSION

There once was a prophet, they say
Who didn't say yes right away
It's a whale of a story
But to God be the glory
The prophet learned not to delay!

JONAH

"But Jonah got up and went in the opposite direction."
Jonah 1:3

What an entertaining story is found in the tiny, four-chapter book of Jonah. I've read magazine articles that were longer, but few that are more unconventionally educational. It is different from all of the other Old Testament prophetic books in that it tells the story of the prophet and not just of his prophecies. In fact, only one verse is designated to Jonah's actual prophecy to Nineveh, and that is chapter 3 verse 4: "He proclaimed: 'Forty more days and Nineveh will be overturned.'" But long before Jonah's ten seconds of fame in chapter 3, is the bizarre story of what it took to get him there. If Jonah had submitted to God's instruction that was given to him from the beginning, the book of Jonah would only be two verses long. Verse 1 of chapter 1 says that a word of the Lord came to Jonah, son of Amittai, and verse 2 tells what that word was: "Go to the city of Ninevah and tell them that their wickedness has come before Me". Pretty simple. Unfortunately, verse 3 says that Jonah got up and went in the opposite direction, and that is where the plot thickens.

The book of Jonah is not a story about a prophet who did not submit to God. Jonah did submit to God, just not soon enough to keep him out of a heap of trouble. His reluctant submission cost him dearly, and endangered the lives of countless others. Making the decision to rebelliously run away from God, Jonah opened the door in his life to enemy intervention, or in other words, to the confusion and disorder that Satan was just waiting for the legal right to plant in him. Jonah disregarded God's call, and conveniently, the enemy positioned a departing ship on his path and tempted him to buy a ticket. He did. It was headed towards Tarshish, one of Phoenicia's westernmost ports. Ninevah was in the east. Jonah was obviously running as far away as he could. But Jonah's escape artist career was cut short. For "suddenly the Lord flung a powerful wind over the seas, causing a violent storm that threatened to send them to the bottom" (1:4). The sailors and captain prayed to their gods for help and threw their cargo overboard to lighten the ship. Jonah meanwhile was fast asleep below deck. Now that part interests me. I have counseled many people in blatant rebellion who would blindly describe to me the peace in their hearts concerning the disobedience they were living in. It's like they are asleep in denial-ville, and like Jonah, their actions did not seem to bother their conscience one bit. I, like the captain in Jonah's story, seemed to have more sense than they did standing on the outside looking in. Rebellion blinds, and deceit deceives. So the captain grabs Jonah and tells him to get up and pray to his god. He then has everyone on board cast lots to see which one of them has offended their god, and although it was a totally superstitious test, God used it to show Jonah that he could not run. Jonah lost the toss, and the crew was furious. As they prodded him for information, Jonah recounted his sin to them and suggested they throw him overboard in order to promptly end the storm. His eventual humility gained him obvious favor with the crew, for they tried to row even harder to steady the ship in an effort to prevent tossing him. Jonah had endangered their lives the first time, but now they were endangering their own lives again for him willingly. Still, the storm raged on so they eventually gave in, and while crying and praying loudly to "Jonah's god", they threw Jonah overboard and into the raging sea. The storm stopped at once. They were so astounded by the power of God, that they offered a sacrifice and vowed to serve Him. I believe Jonah's repentance gave birth to that mass salvation. Had he chosen to run one more time, that ship would have become a sinking tomb for many, but because of his surrender and submission, it became a stairway to heaven.

"For I have not hesitated to proclaim to you the whole will of God." Acts 20:27

GOD'S SUBMARINE

Meanwhile, under the now calm sea, Jonah was sinking to an impending death. However, once again God intervened and sent salvation in the form of a whale, or what I call "a living submarine". I imagine the sub taking Jonah in and settling quietly on the bottom of the ocean floor for those three solitary days and nights, and although many people today view that whale as God's punishment to Jonah, I believe it was His merciful salvation. We serve a creative God! Jonah chapter 2 is the beautiful prayer of a finally humbled heart, and the last verse ends with God commanding the fish to spit Jonah up and onto dry land.

I am proud of Jonah, and am astonished at how many of us judge him when we ourselves have responded to God in the same way. Perhaps nobody ever wrote a book about our rebellions (thank God), but all of us have most definitely been stubborn and reluctant to the voice of God at one time or another in our lives. Once Jonah got to Ninevah and declared God's word to them, the people repented of their wickedness with sackcloth and ashes, and the change in the city was so extraordinary that the king heard of it and was moved to repentance also. He ordered a time of fasting for the whole town, stepped down from his throne and took off his royal robes to join them. God was moved to relent from His intended judgment, and so the entire city of Ninevah, some 150,000 people, were spared on that day and transformed into righteousness.

Even though the book ends with Jonah's complaints to God about all he'd gone through just to see God slap Ninevah on the wrist and let them off the hook so "easily", I still believe we ought to cut Jonah some slack. I mean, he actually wrote the book of Jonah, and so, although he could have chosen to leave out the embarrassing parts, he didn't. He was at least gut-wrenchingly honest about his mistakes and shortcomings, a quality I indubitably admire. Also, think of it: the dude had been whale chow and then had to preach all in the same day. I love to preach, but I have to admit I would have been distracted by wanting to stop in at the Ninevah Walmart to buy some new clothes. Nothing fancy, just something without whale plaque on it. If the whale wasn't Jonah's punishment, perhaps preaching in a slobber suit was.

> *"Now finish the work, so that your eager willingness to do it may be matched by your completion of it, according to your means. For if the willingness is there, the gift is acceptable according to what one has, not according to what he does not have." 2 Corinthians 8:11-12*

THE PRICE OF RELUCTANCE

Even though God is a Redeemer, we must not abuse the grace He offers by indulging in sin that we know we will just be sorry for later on. The price of reluctant submission is the risk of a hardened heart, and the eventual deafening of our ears to the wooing voice of God. God will teach us submission, even if it be by force, for it is for our own good and protection. Like Jonah inside the belly of the whale, in the sinking place of death to our own agenda, surrender gives birth to submission which then gives birth to salvation -- and to having our feet reestablished on dry ground. Still, the rule applies: Humility before visibility. If we sink, we will rise. If we die, we will live. "And Jesus said, 'No other sign will I give them except the sign of the prophet Jonah.'" Matthew 12:39. Even some 800 years later, Jesus used Jonah as an example of how He Himself would submit to His Father in death so that after three days in a tomb He might resurrect the world to eternal life.

A WILLING SPIRIT

Along with our daily prayers for food and family, etc., we ought to ask God for a willing spirit. A willing spirit will reject all reluctance to the will of God. Even David asked God for it: "Restore to me the joy of your salvation and grant me a willing spirit, to sustain me." (Psalm 51:12). A willing spirit sustains us. It will save us from the stubbornness that steals time and energy and detours our destinies. Praying for a willing spirit is like the ounce of prevention that outweighs the pound of cure -- which would be God's grace. According to David, along with the substance that comes with a willing spirit, is great joy. Imagine your life if you always heard the voice of God, were always willing to submit to it, and were always full of His joy as a result of it. That's worth stopping right now and asking God for. Don't delay! It's yours for the asking! Ask God right now for a willing spirit of submission.

"If you are willing and obedient, you will eat the best from the land." Isaiah 1:19

"Now, who is willing to consecrate himself today to the LORD?" 1 Chronicles 29:5

"The spirit is willing, but the flesh is weak." Matthew 26:41

"A man with leprosy came and knelt before Him and said, 'Lord, if you are willing, you can make me clean'. Jesus reached out his hand and touched the man. 'I am willing,'

He said. "Be clean!' Immediately he was cured of his leprosy." Matthew 8:2-3

"The people rejoiced at the willing response of their leaders, for they had given freely and wholeheartedly to the LORD." 1 Chronicles 29:9

"Keep your servant also from willful sins; may they not rule over me. Then will I be blameless, innocent of great transgression." Psalm 19:13

"Father, if you are willing, take this cup from me; yet not my will, but yours be done." Luke 22:42

The sun above has never yet
resisted God's decree
To rise and fall, on one and all,
without the tenth degree

Nor have the moon and stars rebelled
and plotted their own course
They seem to know they only glow
when yielded to His force

Nor do my lungs withhold their breath
because they are not seen
They take their place with rhythmic pace
and follow my routine

My heart and soul, with self-control
can surely do the same
Though once unfit, they now submit
their glory is His fame

Chapter 11

POUTY-FACE SUBMISSION

With my face I'll sap your strength
each time I bat my eyes
I'll sulk and frown til you wear down
and then transmit my lies

With promises to hang the moon,
my real aim is your neck
And with my smile that does beguile
you'll sign my big blank check

DELILAH

There are fewer stories in Scripture that really get my goat worse than this one does, and if I *did* own goats, I'm sure I would have none left after reading Judges 16. I don't know who is more to blame in this ping-pongish, ill-fated love affair, Samson or Delilah, but unlike the Pointer Sisters claim, it was no match made in heaven.

Samson had been set apart from birth with a Nazarite vow. His parents, who were from the tribe of Dan, were unable to have children. But one day the angel of the Lord appeared to them and told Samson's mother that she would give birth to a son who would rescue Israel from the Philistines, the major enemy force in the land and a constant threat to Israel. She was told that she must not drink wine or any other alcoholic drink or eat any forbidden food, and that once the boy was born he must abstain from the same, as well as never cutting his hair. It was a Nazarite vow, and he kept it his entire life -- until he met Delilah.

"Some time later, he fell in love with a woman in the Valley of Sorek whose name was Delilah. The rulers of the Philistines went to her and said, "See if you can lure him into showing you the secret of his great strength and how we can overpower him so we may tie him up and subdue him. Each one of us will give you eleven hundred shekels of silver." So Delilah said to Samson, "Tell me the secret of your great strength and how you can be tied up and subdued." Samson answered her, "If anyone ties me with seven fresh thongs that have not been dried, I'll become as weak as any other man." Then the rulers of the Philistines brought her seven fresh thongs that had not been dried, and she tied him with them. With men hidden in the room, she called to him, "Samson, the Philistines are upon you!" But he snapped the thongs as easily as a piece of string snaps when it comes close to a flame. So the secret of his strength was not discovered." Then Delilah said to Samson, "You have made a fool of me; you lied to me. Come now, tell me how you can be tied."He said, "If anyone ties me securely with new ropes that have never been used, I'll become as weak as any other man." So Delilah took new ropes and tied him with them. Then, with men hidden in the room, she

called to him, "Samson, the Philistines are upon you!" But he snapped the ropes off his arms as if they were threads. Delilah then said to Samson, "Until now, you have been making a fool of me and lying to me. Tell me how you can be tied." He replied, "If you weave the seven braids of my head into the fabric [on the loom] and tighten it with the pin, I'll become as weak as any other man." So while he was sleeping, Delilah took the seven braids of his head, wove them into the fabric and tightened it with the pin. Again she called to him, "Samson, the Philistines are upon you!" He awoke from his sleep and pulled up the pin and the loom, with the fabric. Then she said to him, "How can you say, 'I love you,' when you won't confide in me? This is the third time you have made a fool of me and haven't told me the secret of your great strength." Judges 16:4-15

This is pouty-face submission in action. I actually like the New Living Translation better of v. 15 which says, "Then Delilah pouted, 'How can you say you love me when you don't confide in me?' Verse 16 reads, "So day after day she nagged him until he couldn't stand it any longer." "Finally, Samson told her his secret." (v. 17). Continuing...

"So he told her everything. "No razor has ever been used on my head," he said, "because I have been a Nazirite set apart to God since birth. If my head were shaved, my strength would leave me, and I would become as weak as any other man." When Delilah saw that he had told her everything, she sent word to the rulers of the Philistines, "Come back once more; he has told me everything." So the rulers of the Philistines returned with the silver in their hands. Having put him to sleep on her lap, she called a man to shave off the seven braids of his hair, and so began to subdue him. And his strength left him. Then she called,

"Samson, the Philistines are upon you!" He awoke from his sleep and thought, "I'll go out as before and shake myself free." But he did not know that the LORD had left him. Then the Philistines seized him, gouged out his eyes and took him down to Gaza. Binding him with bronze shackles, they set him to grinding in the prison."
Judges 16:17-21

NOTHING NEW UNDER THE SUN

Many marriages today suffer from this beguiling, controlling spirit of Delilah. Not that Delilah is reembodying herself in people today, but those spirits which controlled her most certainly are. They have been around since the fall of man and are still looking for victims to fulfill their lusts through. For instance, when we have friends who judge us we refer to that as a "spirit of Job's friends", and when we are betrayed we pray against the "Judas spirit". Likewise, there are persons today, men and women, who are under the controlling influence of and employ the same disloyal magnetic forces as Delilah did. As Solomon so eloquently said, "What has been will be again, what has been done will be done again; there is nothing new under the sun." (Ecclesiastes 1:9). This spirit is also present in the corporate world as a seductive persuasion. Unlike the spirit of Jezebel which seems to control overtly with mastery and domination, the spirit of Delilah possesses a more subtle approach to rebellion: the power of personality.

I am married to a very kind man. As I have stated in previous chapters, one of the most difficult life lessons for me was to learn how to have a decision-making conversation with Chris without pressuring him with my influential, irresistible opinions. Spouses should co-labor together, but one should never mobilize an army of evidence against the other in an attempt to win. Chris is a strong man, like Samson, in the sense that he has his own spirited convictions, but like Delilah, I know where all his buttons are. Every wife knows her husband's weak spots, and is accountable before God not to use them! We can add ourselves to those weaknesses, but we should never use them against him to get our own way.

Q & A

Let me ask you a question. How do you respond when those in authority over you make requests of you, or when necessary, make decisions for you? Picture right now your boss, your spouse, your parents or your pastor. Try to remember the last time they approached you with a request or with a choice they had already made, and ask the Lord to help you recall how you responded -- not from your perspective, but from theirs. Did you comply with their ideas, or did you sourly disagree and offer ten opinions of your own? Giving you the benefit of the doubt, I'll assume that you're not stupid enough to believe that you could respond that way to your boss and not get fired, but I'll also assume that you apply the same wisdom in communicating with your pastor, spouse, parents and even your elected officials. So let's say you chose to submit to the plan they presented to you. Did you say yes with a joyful countenance? Did you go beyond yielding to them and choose to applaud the plan they'd come up with? If their arrangement did indeed need a little tweaking or fine-tuning, did you first commend what was right about it before addressing its faults? Perhaps you're not quite there yet. Perhaps you are only able to manage a nod of compliance. That's a starting place from which you can grow! The most tormenting attitude, however, is to yield with double-minded submission. If you are going to align yourself with someone and yield to their authority, do it with all your might. Submission with sulking is not submission at all. Yielding with yelling doesn't count either. "Each man should give what he has decided in his heart to give, not reluctantly or under compulsion, for God loves a cheerful giver." (2 Corinthians 9:7) The main idea is not to water down your submission and expect it to still be seen by God as true submission. You also won't get many brownie points with those who are watching over you. Encouragers are always promoted, and if you are someone who doesn't think that everyone has a little fragment of something in them worth encouraging, then you most definitely don't need to be promoted.

ABOUT FACE

"There are those who curse their fathers and do not bless their mothers; those who are pure in their own eyes and yet are not cleansed of their filth; those whose eyes are ever so haughty, whose glances are so disdainful."
Proverbs 30:11-13

Take another minute to examine yourself. Not just your heart, but your face. How do people interpret your expressions? If you're really brave, ask a few family members and very close friends. If you're super-duper gutsy, ask your pastor or your boss. Before I made a point in my life to see myself through the eyes of others, I was often misunderstood by the looks on my face. After acting since the age of three and undergoing extensive theatrical training and experience, I always thought that my expressions were crystal clear! Still, I am an intense person and so there have been times while engaged in one-on-one conversation with someone that my intense concentration has been misinterpreted as a scowl. My husband still makes a joke by reaching over and touching my wrinkled brow with the tip of his finger during a serious discussion to remind me to loosen up and not look so intense. Thanks to his accountability and a little effort, I don't experience those misunderstandings anymore. There were times in the past when I was devastated at how misjudged I was! Still, in all of those accusations were one common denominator -- me. And at that point in life, you have a choice: keep being misunderstood or reevaluate your conduct.

> *"Wisdom brightens a man's face and changes its hard appearance." Ecclesiastes 8:1*

These are profound words from Solomon. I have known many people throughout the years who are wise and unwise, submitted and unsubmitted, and there are distinct differences in their countenances. You yourself can picture the faces of those rebellious colleagues you know and see a pattern of stern, bitter tension on all of them. Rebellion makes a person appear hard, whereas submission softens a person's features. "Loyalty makes a person attractive" (Proverbs 19:22). I remember once how a woman at our church became very cynical towards our church's leadership. Refusing to be teachable and work as a team player while offering her many giftings, she would often react with sarcasm and stubbornness. She would agree to submit to decisions the leaders made when they confronted her, but then sulk and snivel to many around her afterwards. It was sad because she had every ingredient that would one day make her a great leader -- except one.

Submission. During this period of time I watched her face grow harder and harder. Once a very beautiful woman, her features literally began to shrivel and warp. I remember one Sunday morning I looked at her and her face was so contorted that I had to look away. I was made nauseous by what the enemy had done. I had actually noticed it that morning while she was smiling, but even a smile could not hide the rebellion within. As I glanced back at her one last time, I was stunned by an open vision I had of her with a shaved head. I began to intercede for her, because in the vision she looked like a cancer patient and it alarmed me, but as I prayed the Lord reminded me of what Paul said in 1 Corinthians 11 about a woman's hair being a symbol of her covering. Verse 15 says, "And every woman who prays or prophesies with her head uncovered dishonors her head --it is just as though her head were shaved. If a woman does not cover her head, she should have her hair cut off; and if it is a disgrace for a woman to have her hair cut or shaved off, she should cover her head." Verse 10 even says, "because of the angels, the woman ought to have a sign of authority on her head". While many Christians believe this is a literal commandment for long hair and head coverings during prayer (v. 13), Paul's theme in the chapter is one of submission to authority. Through this vision, the Lord revealed to me that this young sister had lost her covering due to her rebellion. Within a month she had left our church. I continued to pray for her for many months, with the belief that if God had graced her with such multiple giftings, He would surely corner her with the necessary revelations of submission that she needed to succeed.

THE GRAND FINALE

Samson also had a rebirth and experienced a dramatic comeback. Judges 16:22 says, "But the hair on his head began to grow again after it had been shaved." Knowing that he was a prisoner, the Philistine people asked for Samson to be brought into the temple to entertain them with his strength. We'll pick up the story in verse 28:

"Then Samson prayed to the LORD, "O Sovereign LORD, remember me. O God, please strengthen me just once more, and let me with one blow get revenge on the Philistines for my two eyes." Then Samson reached toward the two central pillars on which the temple stood. Bracing himself against them, his right hand on the one and his left hand on the other, Samson said, "Let me die with the Philistines!" Then he pushed with all his might, and down came the temple on the rulers and all the people in it. Thus he killed many more when he died than while he lived."
Judges 16:28-30

A prayer of dedication:

Today, oh God, I vow to put my heart into your hands
And humbly plead for you to knead it 'til it understands

That words alone cannot fulfill the duties that are mine
But conduct too, to man and You, is what I must combine

So give me eyes to see my face and ears to hear my words
That I might judge myself as pure so I can rest assured

Amen.

Chapter 12

DOORMAT SUBMISSION

> Come on in, but wipe your feet
> Not on me, that's indiscreet
> Though I won't put you on the street
> Don't put me to the test, my sweet

DOORMATS DEFINED

I guess you could say I am a neat freak. Since the first impression a visitor has of my house is my front porch, I always like to keep it tidy. Not an easy job with the traffic of six children and all their friends and toys and pets, but I am militant about it. Every flower pot in its place. The rocking chair tilted at just the right inviting angle. And then there's the doormat. I have been accused of idolizing it. I always choose something bright and cheery that will welcome my guests and help them temporarily forget any mess they may encounter once stepping over the threshhold and into the house itself. The problem is that I have actually scolded the children for getting it dirty! Whenever Chris and the kids find me scrubbing the doormat to revive it to its hallowed condition, they have to sit me down and remind me that it's "just a doormat" and that doormats are intended to catch dirt.

You are not a doormat. Any request for submission from you that leaves you feeling like one is not the heart of God, and succumbing to it is not true submission at all, but a cheap counterfeit. Keep in mind though that while submission cannot be demanded, it most certainly can be required and expected. As I write this, I am seeing the many faces of those whom I have counseled that confused the feelings associated with submission to those of being manipulated. Of course, if you are being belittled by someone else, your surrender to that misuse of authority will not produce the fruit of true unity in that relationship. However, if you are willingly yielding yourself to the authority of another for the sake of peace and advancement-- at home, at work, or at church -- then you are walking in true submission and the relationship or venture will prosper because of it. The problem is in the surrender. If a person has woundings due to previous places where their trust was abused at some point in their life, then the most simple request for submission from them may feel like outright manipulation and control. The walls go up, fear takes over, and they are paralyzed and completely incapable of trusting authority figures past certain levels. They go so far, and then no more. The hurt was too deep. The sad thing is, they stand and give testimony of how they have forgiven those people "amen", but then their lives show no lasting fruit of it. I have sat in meetings where I was called in to mediate between two parties in which one party was so convinced they were being manipulated that it was next to impossible to explain true submission to them. True submission does involve what feels like "a dying" at times. The temporary hiddenness of personal agenda for the sake of progressing the whole. It is not a permanent "death", but let's face it, death is death is death, and no matter how large the promise of resurrection is down the road, that is little solace for the deaths of today. Jesus begged God to take the cup of death from Him, but ultimately surrendered and said, "Not my will, but thine be done". In a sense, He died before He died. He was obedient unto death on a cross, and as a result, gained access to a resurrection that we can still lay hold of today. All from the submission of one person's will.

"For it is commendable if a man bears up under the pain of unjust suffering because he is conscious of God."
1 Peter 2:19

MANIPULATION UNMASKED

With the above clarifications made, we can now address "doormat submission". While it was necessary to explain that what some people label manipulation is actually the birth pangs of submission, it is also necessary to reemphasize that manipulation *is* wrong. It produces fear because it is rooted in fear. We manipulate because we are fearful of losing control. Think of the most controlling person you know and I guarantee you that behind that visage of supremacy is a fearful little boy or little girl. While it looks like pride, and often does hide behind that mask, it all originates with fear. However, "perfect love casts out fear", (1 John 4:18) and so in this is found the secret power of submission. Love the unlovable and see them changed. Judge the unlovable and that resistance only gives birth to more resistance. But by walking in the opposite spirit of the domination they themselves were once victims of and are now trying to enforce upon you, you can be their key to deliverance. It may take time, and it may take multiple-layers of healing, but it can happen. Luke 6:28 says, "Bless those who curse you, pray for those who mistreat you". Instead of playing the victim and reliving the unfairness of a person's treatment of you, why not see yourself as the one sent by God to ensure their deliverance? His secret agent with the key to their prison! Do you love this person that much? If not, then you have an even greater problem than they do. Did you love them at one time but now are hurt and unsure of your feelings?

If you are in a covenant relationship with a person and are finding yourself with "doormat" feelings, then before turning and running, ask God to give you the bigger picture. Why do they act the way they do? Why do they feel the need to control and manipulate you? Have you merely failed to communicate your needs in the relationship, or does it go much deeper? When I use the phrase, "walk in the opposite spirit", I am describing where the true war lies, which is not at all in the realm seen with our eyes. Ephesians 6:12 says, "For our struggle is not against flesh and blood, but against the rulers, against the authorities, against the powers of this dark world and against the spiritual forces of evil in the heavenly realms." This proves that when we encounter struggle with another person, in any shape or form and on any scale whether it be personal or corporate, we are not dealing with mere men but with the spirits and forces which control them. So if your "spirit of control" tries to tame my "spirit of defiance", then World War III is bound to occur. If you want to control but I refuse to be controlled, then it's the immovable object meeting the unstoppable force. But what if one of us is brave enough to temporarily forfeit so that both of us might live and get on the peaceful path to wholeness? If one of us has the necessary revelation of love and patience, then who is the real champion in our union? God did not intend for you to be a doormat, but you may indeed be someone's threshold to breakthrough.

> "Nobody can make you feel inferior without your permission." -Eleanor Roosevelt-

"DON'T TREAD ON ME" - ABUSIVE RELATIONSHIPS

One of America's first Colonial Flags with thirteen stripes was the 1775 Navy Jack flag which sported a hissing snake along with the motto: "Don't Tread on Me". Not quite as inspirational as "In God We Trust", but still, a piece of our nation's history. Although I've seen pictures of the flag and it's not worth writing home about, I will say that it might need to hang over some people's doorposts to remind them that they should not allow themselves to be walked upon.

There are many "doormat relationships" these days, and they are not just confined to marriages, nor to just women. Many men are doormats to the whims of their wives, and for the sake of keeping peace, give in to their influential "discernments". Jesus said blessed are the peacemakers, not the peace keepers. There's a difference. The Jezebel spirit that still exists today with the intent of neutering men and reducing their authority in their own homes and fields, is fueled all the more by a weak-man spirit referred to as "the Ahab spirit". King Ahab, of course, was husband to the wicked Jezebel during the prophet Elijah's day. Husband and slave. "There was never a man like Ahab, who sold himself to do evil in the eyes of the LORD, urged on by Jezebel his wife." 1 Kings 21:25

This same doormat mentality permeates the marketplace today with overbearing bosses who overwork and underpay their employees. It is also present in our families in a day and age like never before with children, fueled by television's portrayals of fading parental authority, who neglect the respect due their mothers and fathers and instead, use and abuse them. Of course, it goes without saying that the problem goes both ways. In a study completed by the Third National Incidence Study of Child Abuse and Neglect conducted by Westat, Inc., an estimated 1,553,800 children in the United States were abused or neglected under the Harm Standard in 1993. Using the Endangerment Standard and counting neglected children too, over 2,815,600 American children were abused or neglected, a 98% increase from the study done just seven years before. America needs to shake out their doormats, take out the trash, and repent for its accumulated filth.

"And whoever welcomes a little child like this in my name welcomes me. But if anyone causes one of these little ones who believe in me to sin, it would be better for him to have a large millstone hung around his neck and to be drowned in the depths of the sea. "Woe to the world because of the things that cause people to sin! Such things must come, but woe to the man through whom they come! "See that you do not look down on one of these little ones. For I tell you that their angels in heaven always see the face of my Father in heaven." Matthew 18:5-7, 10

SHAME

"Scorn has broken my heart and has left me helpless" Psalm 69:20

"Those who look to him are radiant; their faces are never covered with shame." Psalm 34:5

"Why did I ever come out of the womb to see trouble and sorrow and to end my days in shame?" Jeremiah 20:18

"My disgrace is before me all day long, and my face is covered with shame." Psalm 44:15

"He who robs his father and drives out his mother is a son who brings shame and disgrace." Proverbs 19:26

"For I endure scorn for your sake, and shame covers my face." Psalm 69:7

"In you, O LORD, I have taken refuge; let me never be put to shame." Psalm 71:1

"Instead of their shame my people will receive a double portion, and instead of disgrace they will rejoice in their inheritance; and so they will inherit a double portion in their land, and everlasting joy will be theirs." Isaiah 61:7

"As the Scripture says, "Anyone who trusts in him will never be put to shame." Romans 10:11

The Lord does not intend for His children to endure shame. We are to be more than conquerors, overcomers, and a royal priesthood set apart for Himself. If you are in any relationship, at home at work or elsewhere, where you feel endangered emotionally or physically, follow the Lord's design given in Matthew 18:15: "If your brother sins against you, go and show him his fault, just between the two of you. If he listens to you, you have won your brother over." Go to the person who has sinned against you and lay your heart out before them. Verse 16 then defines step two, which is, "But if he will not listen, take one or two others along, so that 'every matter may be established by the testimony of two or three witnesses.'" So, we learn here that God intends for you to seek the help of mediation if step one does not work. However, before you consider employing the impersonal intervention of an attorney or government assistance, first try someone who holds some more personal ownership with the parties involved, like a pastor or a family member. I have seen many devastations resolved and redeemed through the power of prayerful mediation.

WHEN ALL ELSE FAILS

God's word, however, does address those "when all else fails" situations, particularly concerning marriage:

"To the rest I say this (I, not the Lord): If any brother has a wife who is not a believer and she is willing to live with him, he must not divorce her. And if a woman has a husband who is not a believer and he is willing to live with her, she must not divorce him. For the unbelieving husband has been sanctified through his wife, and the unbelieving wife has been sanctified through her believing husband. Otherwise your children would be unclean, but as it is, they are holy. But if the unbeliever leaves, let him do so. A believing man or woman is not bound in such

circumstances; God has called us to live in peace. How do you know, wife, whether you will save your husband? Or, how do you know, husband, whether you will save your wife?" 1 Corinthians 7:12-16

Perhaps you will still choose to loyally hold out hope for your spouse. Once, an elder from my church had a interesting teaching that pertains to these type of decisions. Romans 12:2 says, "Do not conform any longer to the pattern of this world, but be transformed by the renewing of your mind. Then you will be able to test and approve what God's will is --his good, pleasing and perfect will." Another translation says His "good, acceptable and perfect will". Elder Bob Zide's teaching describes how this indicates that God's will allows for three levels of fulfillment, and that we get to choose which one we will shoot for. All are pleasing to the Lord, but you still have the choice of aiming for His "good" will, His "acceptable" will, or His "perfect will". It's the same thrust behind Jesus' parable of the sower teaching in which He indicates the different levels at which people sow, thus resulting in varied harvest of 30, 60 or 100 fold. Of course, we can't forget how the Lord led the prophet Ezekiel to carry out the prophetic enactment of walking into the river, first at ankle deep, then waist deep, and then entirely over his head in the waters that no man could cross. Life feels that way many times. At that point, high faith is activated. I personally think that God is looking for more of those perfect will, over their heads, 100-fold kind of people.

"But without faith it is impossible to please Him, for he who comes to God must believe that He is, and that He is a rewarder of those who diligently seek Him." Hebrews 11:6

THE WORDS OF LIFE

As you patiently submit to the pledges you've made in your covenant relationships, know that God is working on your behalf night and day. Listen intently to His instruction, and be comforted by His word as you wait for Him to transform the relationships in your life through love.

"You have seen, O LORD, the wrong done to me. Uphold my cause! " Lamentations 3:59

"Make sure that nobody pays back wrong for wrong, but always try to be kind to each other and to everyone else." 1 Thessalonians 5:15

"Who is going to harm you if you are eager to do good?" 1 Peter 3:13

"...your father has cheated me by changing my wages ten times. However, God has not allowed him to harm me." Genesis 31:7

"You intended to harm me, but God intended it for good to accomplish what is now being done, the saving of many lives." Genesis 50:20

"From six calamities he will rescue you; in seven no harm will befall you." Job 5:19

"And perhaps the Lord will see that I am being wronged and will bless me because of these curses." 2 Samuel 16:12

"For I know the plans I have for you," declares the LORD,

"plans to prosper you and not to harm you, plans to give you hope and a future." Jeremiah 29:11

"Fathers, do not exasperate your children; instead, bring them up in the training and instruction of the Lord." Ephesians 6:4

"Blessed are you when men hate you, when they exclude you and insult you and reject your name as evil, because of the Son of Man." Luke 6:22

"Sometimes you were publicly exposed to insult and persecution; at other times you stood side by side with those who were so treated. So do not throw away your confidence; it will be richly rewarded." Hebrews 10:33 & 35

"Why do you tolerate wrong?" Habakkuk 1:3

"But how is it to your credit if you receive a beating for doing wrong and endure it? But if you suffer for doing good and you endure it, this is commendable before God." 1 Peter 2:20

IF YOU'RE NOT THE DOORMAT, WHO IS?

Satan is under your feet. He may occasionally bruise your heel, but you were created to crush his head (Genesis 3:15). Being a doormat is part of his job description, so whatever you do, make sure that in all of your relationships in life -- business, ministry and family -- that you let Satan do his job and fulfill his destiny by remaining under your feet.

"The God of peace will soon crush Satan under your feet." Romans 16:20

"Let your sharp arrows pierce the hearts of the king's enemies; let the nations fall beneath your feet." Psalm 45:5

"`The Lord said to my Lord: "Sit at my right hand until I put your enemies under your feet." ' Matthew 22:44

Check your baggage at the door,
if you have ego, drop it
It took 10 years to sweep this floor
and 7 more to mop it

I wouldn't make you stay outside
and risk a cold or cough
But loud and clear, once you're in here,
those shoes are comin' off!

"If anyone will not welcome you or listen to your words, shake the dust off your feet when you leave that home or town." Matthew 10:14

Chapter 13

DECEITFUL SUBMISSION

Yes sir, I will take this job
your wish is my command!
But when you're gone I'll ramble on
and take the upper-hand

You'll notice as we talk
that I am able to ad lib
But what you've heard, in other words
is more or less a fib

Perhaps in time you'll note my crime
and orders incomplete
But until then, tough-luck my friend
you're subject to deceit

TRICK OR TREAT?

Better to be the object of overt rebellion than to have someone commit to obedience with the intent of dishonor.

It turns my stomach how many people these days half-heartedly obey and yet expect to get blessed for it. Slipping by with the bare requirements for submission, they somehow think that going through the motions will gain them reward. The sad part is, when it doesn't, they complain all the more, leave that port and move on with their dirty laundry in search of another "harbor" (pun intended). They store up their accumulated record of wrongs against others with bitter contempt as they leave, and each time their life-long expectations for advancement are not met, they build even more of a case in their minds that they are exempt from submission. What's odd is they accuse those they are leaving of being deceitful. After all, they've tried being truthful and it only got them overlooked and underpaid, right? The enemy's argument is so convincing. What has become of patience these days? What has become of truth? Why have people written their own rules to fit the hurt in their hearts instead of entrusting them in faith to the Almighty God for vindication? His vindication is much more fun than our revenge. I do realize that most people who try to lie and connive their way into leadership were at some point the victims of unspeakable abuses. No matter how proud their masks look, underneath is a fear that drives them to trust no one but themselves. The difficulty comes when they are faced with a decision to trust and obey. Because of their God-given desire to trust, they say yes, but eventually their "voices" convince them to take the reigns quickly before they are disappointed one more time. Churches have split, corporations have sunk, and marriages have failed because of such double-minded treachery. God help the pastor upon whom a fourth or fifth generation wounding is unleashed, and God bless the pastor who finally confronts it. I suppose we should also bless the bosses, spouses and parents who stand up for truth, and love the unlovely by "speaking the truth in love." Its power should never be underestimated. Although it might seem to bear no fruit in a person's life, it is a seed planted that will spring up at some point, even though God may have to break the person and the topsoil of their heart for it take root. Those who despise the chastening of the Lord and cannot discipline themselves to stay put during such challenges will never see lasting promotion in their lives.

> "A malicious man disguises himself with his lips, but in his heart he harbors deceit." Proverbs 26:24

> "Like a coating of glaze over earthenware are fervent lips with an evil heart." Proverbs 26:23

THE RICH YOUNG RULER

I know everybody always rags on the rich young ruler mentioned in Matthew 19:16-22 because he seemingly refused to obey Christ, sell his goods, and give them to the poor. We all accuse him of being more loyal to his riches than to Christ, and perhaps he was. But after dealing with people over the years who vow they are going to do one thing and then do another, I actually read this story and have to commend the young ruler for not making promises he couldn't keep. I'd like to think he went away, spent many sleepless nights testing his heart concerning Jesus' challenge, and then chased Him down later as one of the 5000 that got fed on the miraculous hill that day. Better the man who says no and means it, than the man who says yes and doesn't. Or as Solomon put it: "It is better not to vow than to make a vow and not fulfill it." Ecclesiastes 5:5

So why is it that someone would make a vow, particularly a vow of submission, and then not keep it? Well, those in the vow-breaking bracket usually fall into one of two categories. There are those who make vows they never intend to keep, and those who make them with good intentions but become convinced along the way that they are exempt from fulfilling them. You see it in the marketplace, in churches, in politics and in marriages. I realize there is grace from heaven in situations where an unbelieving husband or wife leaves a Christian spouse at which point Scripture says to let them go (1 Corinthians 7:15). But God is not writing a blank check with that passage and authorizing people to forsake their oaths left and right. So for the sake of argument as it pertains to this chapter, let's determine what can and cannot be defined as "deceitful submission".

INSIDE THE HEART

Perhaps you do not consider it deceitful when someone tells you they are in submission to you but then along the way find reasons not to be. Perhaps you yourself have told someone you are on board and committed to a particular cause, but then have decided to recant. I suppose all of us who've ever quit a job would fall in that category. I have quit jobs that God told me to quit and I knew my time was up and so did my boss, but then there have been a few regretful memories where the break wasn't so clean. I remember once before I was married I took a job and let the manager spend a whole week of her time training me, and then I up and bailed. In my opinion that is deceitful submission. Choosing not to count the costs more soberly, I instead took the job with the "try it and see if I like it" mentality without telling my employer that was what I was doing. She thought I was eagerly stepping on board as a team member, when actually I was just testing the waters. That was deceitful, and cost both of us precious time. Believe it or not (and most of you will) there are people who enter into marriages, churches and friendships the same way. Covenant has become so diluted that once we find our way back to its true design it seems impossible to keep. So then if it is so impossible, why are so many of us still making vows?

> *"Jesus replied, "No one who puts his hand to the plow and looks back is fit for service in the kingdom of God."*
> *Luke 9:62*

Perhaps what is in the man or woman's heart at the time of the vow is what should be judged. Chris and I had been married just a few years when I hired a calligrapher to print a very large copy of our wedding vows and then mat and frame them for us. We made it poster size and hung it in a high traffic area so that we were under the constant influence of its glare. I literally remember passing by it after an altercation and hearing the words, "for better or for worse", or having my eyes mysteriously land on "for richer or poorer". Despite the ignorance and feeble-minded foolishness of our youth, those vows were always the bungee cord that jerked us back into proper alignment with each other. Whenever I didn't understand Chris, I at least understood the vow. I didn't like it, but I understood I had made it. Sometimes I plain old didn't like *him*, but I at least liked myself enough to keep my word and save my reputation. When I didn't want to submit to him I at least submitted to the vow. What I didn't realize was that in the midst of that contorted decision to be true to my word and myself, God was actually using that to have me stick around long enough to see Chris' view of things. That's what He was after, and that's what the vow was for. Without a doubt, the vow is the bridge in between trouble and triumph.

But again, what is in the heart at the time of the vow is what is important. I have heard many husbands and wives negate their responsibilities and totally disregard their vows due to the excuse that they were young and naive when they made them. Give me a break! If *any* of us knew all that we were in for when we committed to marriage, we never would have said yes! That's what the commitment was for. That's the purpose of the vow, regardless of how naive you were when you made it. When I am counseling a couple on the brink of divorce and hear that line I ask, "well, were you at least in love, and if not, was there anything at all you liked about them?". If you can somehow stir up those original feelings in a person, you have something to work with. Then they can remember the foundation for the vow. When I hear someone discounting it because of the lack of information they had when they made it, I can't help but nail them to the wall. Leviticus 5:4 basically says even if you make a rash vow you are responsible for keeping it. So their problem is not the other person's true colors, but their own lack of discerning them before they signed the dotted line. Once they've signed, they enter into a covenant that cannot be reversed. It can by law, but it cannot in the Spirit, which is a higher law.

IRREVOCABLE BONDS

"I will give you what you deserve, for you have taken your solemn vows lightly by breaking your covenant."
Ezekiel 16:59

We've talked about Isaac's blessing of Jacob in a previous chapter already, but consider again how that story shows the importance of a pledge. When Isaac blessed the wrong son, albeit through the trickery of the one being blessed, he said it was impossible to take it back. His word was spoken and it was irreversible. When Isaac realized the mistake he had made, Genesis 27:33 says, "Isaac began to tremble uncontrollably and said...I blessed him with an irrevocable blessing before you came." Genesis 27:34-35 continues: "When Esau heard his father's words, he burst out with a loud and bitter cry and said to his father, "Bless me --me too, my father!" But he said, "Your brother came deceitfully and took your blessing".

Many covenant relationships, including marriages, are in this same devastating place today. You wake up and are trembling uncontrollably because you realize you are perhaps even in the wrong relationship. But what if both parties are willing, or can be convinced, to trust God to bring the missing feelings of love as you honor your vow and decide it is irreversible? "Irrevocable". I understand there are times when both parties are not willing and in that case, "let the unbeliever leave" as Paul commanded in 1 Corinthians. And what about other covenant relationships we enter into in life? What about taking responsibility for the children we give birth to? And what about staying at a church you've vowed your membership to and taking that commitment seriously through thick and thin? What about staying on a job instead of bailing when the boss insults you? So the question is, is there ever a time when it's ok to move on? Is every vow an irrevocable bond? Yes in perfection, but no because of God's grace.

I'll give you a for instance: I have been in a church where I felt called to serve and submit, but then felt released to leave when the church leadership's constant quenching of the spirit was drying the church up. Although I felt the release of God to leave, I remember one instance that I still wish I had handled with more maturity, and I eventually went back to the pastor and told him so. Like a fireball, I had rushed in before I left with all of my fresh revelations and dumped them out in the pastor's lap, instead of patiently and calmly relaying my heart to him and being honest about my concern for the church. It wasn't really his fault anyway because the democratic design of our church's leadership put everything in the hands of the deacons, and he, at times, felt like a lame duck I am sure. So here I was, freshly baptized in the Holy Spirit and didn't know what to call it but only knew I was having massive visitations from the Lord during which He would speak to me and I could hear His words, and yet His manifest presence was so strong I was actually unable to get up off the floor. I remember hearing the charismatic term, "slain in the spirit", but in trying to test everything by the Word of God, couldn't find anything in my concordance on the word "slain" except in reference to bulls and goats. Then I began finding passages like the one in Revelation where John describes his encounter with Jesus (1:17) and says, "And when I saw Him, I fell at His feet as dead.", or the one in Daniel when Daniel described his visitation from the Lord by saying, "no strength remained within me; for my vigor was turned to frailty in me and I retained no strength. Yet I heard the sound of his words; and while I heard the sound of his words I was in a deep sleep on my face, with my face to the ground." (10:8-9). Well, because my level of maturity did not match my level of zeal, I blurted all this out to the pastor one night and ended up later getting myself accused of seeing an angel of light. (2 Corinthians 11:14 describes

Satan masquerading as an angel of light to deceive us.) It hurt, but all these years later I don't blame that pastor. On a scale of 1-10 my faith was at about a 55, but my maturity was at a sub-zero level. Again, perhaps it was God's will for us to move on out of that church, but if I'd left with more respect for the authority in that house, then perhaps I wouldn't have given the very Holy Spirit I wanted to exemplify such a bad name.

DECEITFULNESS VS. IMMATURITY

God has forgiven me for many "lack of submissions", but part of that release involved me going back to people and asking their forgiveness. It was hard but it sure felt good afterwards. Sometimes God has had me move on from certain places during which I thought it was to bless me because of how "held back" I had felt there, when in truth it was to take me somewhere new where He could answer my dangerous prayers and discipline me into a greater maturity. How shocking to discover that a departure was less about them and more about you. And even though I don't feel like those "lack of submissions" were "deceitful submissions" on my behalf, I do see how those watching could have perceived it as such. Trusting that if you are reading this book you want to be a person who lives above reproach and above even every appearance of evil, let's end this chapter by defining what is truly deceitful submission, in the eyes of all parties involved.

Consider the following two groupings:

1. Those who make vows of submission and covenant they never intend to keep, which is deceitful.

2. And those who are so immature when they make commitments that they do not know how to keep them, and then in breaking them are labeled as "deceitful".

Do we want to be in either breed? Is it really o.k. to seek amnesty by claiming we are part of the second group and yet never strive to grow beyond our immaturities? Perhaps if we could grow up, there'd be fewer arguments from sideline unbelievers about the "hypocrites in the church". They accuse us of talking the talk but not walking the walk, and rightly so. Perhaps with proper maturation in marriages, we could do away with the fear in singles that no commitment is lasting anymore. And maybe if we'd stop badgering our public officials and started praying for them, (even those undeserving of our loyalty), perhaps more of the good-hearted guys wouldn't be so afraid to run for office in the future.

Of course, if you fit the D.N.A. description of group one and are a bold-face manipulator with no intention of giving submission anything more than your lip-service -- the way Judas did to Jesus -- you need to take a look at the Word of God. Only then can you take a true look at your heart. Ask God to heal you from the hurts that have caused you to trust no one but yourself. Ask Him to help you submit with your words, but more importantly with your whole heart. Ask him to rid your mouth of all flattery for the sole purposes of promotion, and of all lies against the righteous. Ask Him to fasten His belt of truth around your waist without which you will not carry the full armor of God. Read through His Word, and your life will line up with it before your very eyes, and the eyes of those watching you.

"Therefore, rid yourselves of all malice and all deceit,

hypocrisy, envy, and slander of every kind." 1 Peter 2:1

"The heart is deceitful above all things and beyond cure. Who can understand it?" Jeremiah 17:9

"These are rebellious people, deceitful children, children unwilling to listen to the LORD's instruction." Isaiah 30:9

""You are a child of the devil and an enemy of everything that is right! You are full of all kinds of deceit and trickery. Will you never stop perverting the right ways of the Lord?" Acts 13:10

"He committed no sin, and no deceit was found in his mouth." 1 Peter 2:22

"You belong to your father, the devil, and you want to carry out your father's desire. He was a murderer from the beginning, not holding to the truth, for there is no truth in him. When he lies, he speaks his native language, for he is a liar and the father of lies." John 8:44

"My lips will not speak wickedness, and my tongue will utter no deceit." Job 27:4

"Nothing impure will ever enter it, nor will anyone who does what is shameful or deceitful, but only those whose names are written in the Lamb's book of life." Revelation 21:27

David and Solomon, father and son, knew a great deal about the treachery of deceitfulness. Weigh their words from Psalms and Proverbs:

"I do not sit with deceitful men, nor do I consort with hypocrites." Psalm 26:4

"The tongue that brings healing is a tree of life, but a deceitful tongue crushes the spirit." Proverbs 15:4

"Not a word from their mouth can be trusted; their heart is filled with destruction. Their throat is an open grave; with their tongue they speak deceit." Psalm 5:9

"Blessed is the man whose sin the LORD does not count against him and in whose spirit is no deceit." Psalm 32:2

"You use your mouth for evil and harness your tongue to deceit." Psalm 50:19

"Let their lying lips be silenced, for with pride and contempt they speak arrogantly against the righteous." Psalm 31:18

"But then they would flatter him with their mouths, lying to him with their tongues." Psalm 78:36

"If you keep your mouth shut, you will stay out of trouble" Proverbs 21:23

"He who rebukes a man will in the end gain more favor than he who has a flattering tongue. Proverbs 28:23

"For wicked and deceitful men have opened their mouths against me; they have spoken against me with lying tongues." Psalm 109:2

"He who conceals his hatred has lying lips, and whoever spreads slander is a fool." Proverbs 10:18

"Truthful lips endure forever, but a lying tongue lasts only a moment." Proverbs 12:19

"The LORD detests lying lips, but he delights in men who are truthful." Proverbs 12:22

"Arrogant lips are unsuited to a fool-- how much worse lying lips to a ruler!" Proverbs 17:7

"A fortune made by a lying tongue is a fleeting vapor and a deadly snare." Proverbs 21:6

"A lying tongue hates those it hurts, and a flattering mouth works ruin" Proverbs 26:28 .

"You destroy those who tell lies; bloodthirsty and deceitful men the LORD abhors." Psalm 5:6

"They fully intend to topple him from his lofty place; they take delight in lies. With their mouths they bless, but in their hearts they curse. Selah" Psalm 62:4

"A false witness will not go unpunished, and he who pours out lies will not go free." Proverbs 19:5

"If a ruler listens to lies, all his officials become wicked." Proverbs 29:12

"Save me, O LORD, from lying lips and from deceitful tongues." Psalm 120:2

"Keep your tongue from evil and your lips from speaking lies." Psalm 34:13

Guide my heart within me Lord
and don't forget my tongue
For though my heart is seasoning
my mouth is very young

And please, oh God, what'er the cost
please make me patient now!
So I can stand, despite demand
beside my every vow

Amen.

Chapter 14

LET'S MAKE A DEAL SUBMISSION

Kinda, sorta, well... o.k.
It won't matter either way
I guess I'll do it as I should
if the pay is pretty good

Maybe I will and maybe I won't
Can't say I do when I know I don't
Perhaps I'll do it on one condition
If we can stop all this talk on submission

NO COMPROMISE

When starting the study for this chapter, I typed the word "compromise" into my Bible concordance software to see if I could make some correlation between compromise and trying to "make a deal" with authority. There was nothing in the NIV translation software I was using with that root word, but the funny thing was that because I have talking alerts on my computer, I discovered this when the voice blurted out, "THE WORD COMPROMISE CANNOT BE FOUND". Oh Lord, let it be so in our lives!

I suppose "Let's Make a Deal Submission" could be closely linked with the previous chapter on "Pouty-Face Submission", except for the fact that not everyone who tries to strike a deal with authority to avoid submission does so with a pout. Sometimes we bargain with the persuasion of another genre. Sometimes laughter, sometimes logic. Most of the time it's an unoffensive brainwashing. I used to do it all the time. The verdict was given or the request was made, and by coming up with slight alterations here and there, I would eventually dilute the mandate down to a more digestible level that I could swallow. Little did I know then that dilution is delusion! Sometimes God is testing your heart and isn't concerned about how high the fence is you are being asked to jump, but about seeing if you will try! It's not in the legs but in the heart!

My son, Julian, is a master strategist. Of course, he's also a master guitarist, but behind that creative right brain genius is a left-brain diversion engineer. When he was younger he used to get himself in trouble with the very gift God gave him. We'd specifically spell out a certain rule we had made for him after much prayer about a certain situation, and he'd calmly agree. Then after a predictable 10 seconds of silence, he'd kindly present to us a better idea. Julian always has better ideas. I'm not being sarcastic -- he is an idea machine! The problem is that in submission to authority, God's not always as concerned with the "best idea" as we are. In fact, many times He goes for the no-brainers mind-boggling brain teasers in an attempt to test the heart. He'll put those illogical directions in front of us just to see if we will follow them. He did it with Abraham.

He did it with Noah by telling him to build a boat in the middle of a drought. He did it with Peter, with Paul and with His very own Son. So why do we try to convince ourselves that He'll do any less with us?

TWO CENTS WORTH

The widow put in two cents and got praised for it, but when you put in your two cents worth to maneuver your way into an easier submission, you will not. How often do you carry out marching orders only after putting in your two cents worth? How often does your compliance have stipulations? The Bible is full of such stories. Remember when Thomas said he'd believe Christ had been resurrected only if he could see for himself and touch the holes in His hands? Stipulated submission. Trust, with terms. Faith, with conditions. Or what about when Saul disobeyed the Prophet Samuel by slightly altering his orders with logic? In 1 Samuel 15, we see where Samuel relays God's message to King Saul that he must make war on the Amalekites and wipe out every trace of them -- men, women, children, even their cattle, sheep and other specifically mentioned livestock. However, when Saul decided that it would be better to save the fatted calves and sheep in order to perform an impressive burnt offering before the Lord, it cost him his kingdom It sounds not only logical, but kind of sweet, but no matter how you turn it upside and shake it it still reveals Saul's heart of rebellion. When Samuel approached the city the next day and Saul greeted him with the words, "The LORD bless you! I have carried out the LORD's instructions" (v. 13), Samuel answered, "What then is this bleating of sheep in my ears? What is this lowing of cattle that I hear?" (v. 14). When Saul tried to explain to him his reasons for disobedience, Samuel said,

"Stop!"..."Let me tell you what the LORD said to me last night." "Tell me," Saul replied. Listen to Samuel's answer, which reveals God's view of Saul's actions:

"Samuel said, "Although you were once small in your own eyes, did you not become the head of the tribes of Israel? The LORD anointed you king over Israel. And he sent you on a mission, saying, 'Go and completely destroy those wicked people, the Amalekites; make war on them until you have wiped them out.' Why did you not obey the LORD? Why did you pounce on the plunder and do evil in the eyes of the LORD?" "But I did obey the LORD," Saul said. "I went on the mission the LORD assigned me. I completely destroyed the Amalekites and brought back Agag their king. The soldiers took sheep and cattle from the plunder, the best of what was devoted to God, in order to sacrifice them to the LORD your God at Gilgal." But Samuel replied: "Does the LORD delight in burnt offerings and sacrifices as much as in obeying the voice of the LORD? To obey is better than sacrifice, and to heed is better than the fat of rams." (1 Samuel 15:16-22)

Samuel went on to explain that rebellion is as the sin of witchcraft, and stubbornness as of the sin of idolatry, ending with the edict that God had rejected Saul as king forever.

"HELPING GOD OUT"

That story is a sobering wake-up call to get us to see how seriously God takes submission. Our obedience to the authority of those whom He speaks to us through is judged by the immediate and exact action we take with their words. Notice how even good intentions do not impress the Lord when they don't line up with His commands. The same exact lesson can be learned from the story of Abraham and Sarah, and Sarah's impatience in waiting for the son God had promised them. By getting ahead of God and devising a logical plan to "help God out", she was actually creating a solution that would come back to haunt her and endanger the life of the true promise once it was fulfilled. In a moment that she would regret for the rest of her life, she told Abraham to sleep with her servant Hagar in order that God's promise might be fulfilled and they would finally have a son. They "birthed an Ishmael", and it is a term still used today to describe hearts that get ahead of God. Not only did Ishmael resent Isaac, the promised son that Abraham and Sarah eventually had, but he also meant such harm to him that Abraham had to send him away to protect Isaac's life. What Sarah meant for good eventually meant much harm for everyone. What is most interesting about Ishmael is that he went on to have twelve sons and start the Arab nation, out of which came the Muslim faith. So Sarah's decision to negotiate the terms of her obedience to God's promise not only resulted in her own personal battles, but in the present battles that exist still today between the Jews and Muslims. Yes, the Christian faith has its own resistance from Muslims, but nothing can compare to the age-old battle between Jews and Muslims. Consider the constant warring between Israel and Palestine still today. Had Sarah only known what she was getting herself, and us, into, perhaps she would have submitted with a little more patience. The interesting thing is that the word "muslim" is an Arabic word that means "one who submits to God", and the word "islam", which is the name given to the message preached by Muslims, is Arabic for "submission".

So how are we so easily swayed by logic when we know we should be submitting in blind faith? Well, consider the craftiness of the enemy, Satan, as he approached Eve in the garden with his "let's make a deal" plan.

> *"Now the serpent was more crafty than any of the wild animals the LORD God had made. He said to the woman, "Did God really say, `You must not eat from any tree in the garden'?" The woman said to the serpent, "We may eat fruit from the trees in the garden, but God did say, `You must not eat fruit from the tree that is in the middle of the garden, and you must not touch it, or you will die.'" "You will not surely die," the serpent said to the woman. "For God knows that when you eat of it your eyes will be opened, and you will be like God, knowing good and evil. "When the woman saw that the fruit of the tree was good for food and pleasing to the eye, and also desirable for gaining wisdom, she took some and ate it. She also gave some to her husband, who was with her, and he ate it. Then the eyes of both of them were opened, and they realized they were naked; so they sewed fig leaves together and made coverings for themselves." Genesis 3:1-7*

Resisting the enemy is the key. He comes in with persuasive words, which many times end up coming into our minds and then straight out of our mouths. Next time you are tempted to negotiate the terms of your submission, consider that the enemy may be the very author of those terms. Also consider the plan God gives us for resisting him: "Therefore submit to God. Resist the devil and he will flee from you." James 4:7. How much clearer can God make it that we can best resist the enemy through submission?

"IF"

There are no "ifs" in submission. When you find yourself bargaining with your authority figures in an attempt to make it easier on yourself, you can be sure that you have entered the Monty Hall of fame called "Let's Make a Deal" submission. You cannot negotiate the terms of obedience. Hopefully, you haven't placed yourself under the authority of anyone who has nothing in them worth trusting, but even if you do find yourself there, it could be that God has placed you as His secret agent in that person's life to help transfigure them by your radical obedience. You've heard of "killing them with kindness"? Well, get even more radical and try slaying them with your submission.

I have not only tried to negotiate the terms of my submission to various authority figures in my life, but before I knew any better I also used to negotiate directly with God. Take my advice and don't try either. Once I was actually arguing with God over submitting to my husband, and because I loved Chris and knew I was caught in that valley of decision, I blurted out something stupid like, "I can NOT follow imperfection Lord! Nobody ever told me that submission would include trusting fallible people!" His comeback was priceless. "Laura, if I can run an entire universe by trusting fallible people, then surely you can manage one household under the direction of an imperfect leader in progress. Do you know what your problem is? You want to be married to yourself!!!"

"How then can I dispute with him? How can I find words to argue with him?" Job 9:14

"Do everything without complaining or arguing,"
Philippians 2:14

"Will your long-winded speeches never end? What ails you that you keep on arguing?" Job 16:3

"Resist the devil and he will flee"
So far so good, I'm off scott-free!
But the terms that strike me as really odd
Is the part about "submit to God"

When I submerge, does Satan drown?
Can one choice truly take him down?
Submitting, he cannot conceive
So when I do, he has to leave

Chapter 15

JUNE CLEAVER SUBMISSION

June and Ward were sittin' in a tree
S.-L.-A.-V.-I.-N.-G
First June's tired
Then June's trash
Then June's lawyer's suing Ward for cash

SERVANTHOOD VS. SLAVERY

Ok, so I couldn't resist the title or the sappy limerick, but perhaps through both you are already grasping the theme for this chapter. We will take an in depth look at the difference between servanthood and slavery, and as usual, that distinction lies in the heart.

Take two different people. Give them both the same jobs and lists of tasks. Depending on attitude and gratitude, one will be a co-laborer and the other a slave. Take me for example: I do things in a day's time that would astound people if they only knew. I don't even tell family and friends or they would worry about me. There is a supernatural grace upon me during this season of my life to work, pray, clean, love on my husband, fix boo-boos, clean some more, write (there's never a day I don't), change diapers, follow through with business/ministry contacts, encourage many via phone or email, clean-up one more time, prepare twenty-four plates of food a day for a family of eight, homeschool the kids, and oh yeh, squeeze in five to six hours of sleep. I do those things every day of my life without fail; that's the baseline, and some days there is more. That grace may not always be on my life in later seasons as things change, but for now, I am milking it for all it's worth. I wake up every day to a full plate and go to bed every night poured out with a sense of great satisfaction and success.

"But even if I am being poured out like a drink offering on the sacrifice and service coming from your faith, I am glad and rejoice with all of you." Philippians 2:17

Take another woman who does some or all of those same things. But perhaps she does them because she has a husband or an employer who does not fully know the gift he has in her, and since she doesn't fully know herself either, she strives harder and harder until her rituals become resentments. No grace is given her and so she has no grace to give. So she is a slave, in her own eyes and in the eyes of those she serves. However, what would happen if you stirred one ounce of confidence into that woman? What would happen to her? What if through her husband's mouth, through the Lord's motivations as she meets with Him each day, and through the encouragement of her children or co-workers or friends she was transformed from a slave into a star? I tell you, she could go from a charity case to a champion in one day.

There are plenty of men who feel enslaved as well. Perhaps they are slaves to work, slaves to bondages, or slaves to women. Ahab may have been a king but he was a slave to Jezebel indeed. I began with examples of women because of the title of this chapter, but there are plenty of June Cleaver men out there too. You don't have to think very hard to name some of them in your own family or circle of friends. Both men and women degrade and feel degraded. However, no one can truly degrade you without your permission! If you know who you are, meaning that you know who Christ says you are and you believe it, then a thousand voices or demands will not be able to sway you out of your rightful place of peace. As a result, you will be able to submit and serve cheerfully with a whole heart! Your joy will be full, and your service will be reflect it.

"Serve wholeheartedly, as if you were serving the Lord, not men." Ephesians 6:7

"Since you know that you will receive an inheritance from the Lord as a reward. It is the Lord Christ you are serving." Colossians 3:24

FEAR OF MAN

Psalm 56:11, Psalm 118:6 and Hebrews 13:6 all say the same thing:

*"In God I trust; I will not be afraid.
What can man do to me?"*

It is not easy to be fearless, but it is possible. 2 Timothy 2:17 teaches us that "God has not given us a spirit of fear, but of love, power and a sound mind". Again, although we are using June Cleaver as an example of an enslavement -- a counterfeit submission -- I suppose the truth is that June loved her job and so she wasn't a slave at all. In fact, she seemed fearless; like she truly had a spirit of love, power and a sound mind. She loved making Wally's tuna salad and pouring Ward's coffee. She didn't mind running the vacuum in a dress and heels. But if Ward had been a heavy-handed tyrant, or if her own heart had been tainted by animosity, indignation or even envy of other women, then she would have done all the same daily duties and been a slave. That's the true problem with today's homes. Distorted perspectives. Warped self-images that have lead to embellished fantasy lives for the sake of "sanity". However, once those fantasies become more tangible than the drudgery of the real world a person lives in, they eventually become reality.

But what if every man and woman knew who they were in Christ? Or to be more specific, what if every one of us knew we were created by an all-seeing Creator with a distinct purpose that the world's success was dependent on? What if every man, woman and child knew such perfect love that it cast out all fear? (1 John 4:18). What if each individual confidently took his or her place in the course of history with such individually fulfilling destinies that providence couldn't help but prevail? It'd be like a visit to Jiffy Lube for the earth's axis!

If we will fear the Lord, and not man, then we can serve our fellow man with joy. Any service outside that joyful love is shallow and futile.

> *"Fear of man will prove to be a snare, but whoever trusts in the LORD is kept safe."*
> *Proverbs 29:25*

M.B.A. DEGREE

Dave Thomas, founder of the Wendy's restaurant chain, had an interesting perspective about service. He wouldn't hire anyone who didn't have an M.B.A. In fact, he himself said he had an M.B.A. before he had a high school diploma. But to Dave, an M.B.A. was a "mop-bucket attitude". I've heard that his perspective of service was second to none. You can see it in the commercials! Believing that everyone should be willing to mop the floor before they are entrusted with more, he also believed it should never be beneath you to come back and mop it no matter how high up the chain of command you go! Servanthood with promotion. Humility before visibility. A good lesson for the home, for the workplace, for the church, and for life itself. Thanks Dave. I always knew there was an M.B.A. in me somewhere.

> *"This service that you perform is not only supplying the needs of God's people but is also overflowing in many expressions of thanks to God. Because of the service by which you have proved yourselves, men will praise God for the obedience that accompanies your confession of the gospel of Christ, and for your generosity in sharing with them and with everyone else."*
> *2 Corinthians 9:12-13*

On another funny note, I knew a couple who are in pastoral ministry that tell of an interesting interval in their marriage concerning this type of submission and service. They were newly married at the time, and were experiencing the clash of the two different worlds in which they were raised. The husband had been brought up in a home where the mother was indeed a June Cleaver. No glass at the dinner table was ever allowed to go empty without her taking notice and filling it. However, this husband's young wife had been raised in a home where everyone pitched in and helped. She had a mom who served her family but who also was very involved in ministry and teaching, and as a result, her dad was always willing to pinch hit. Well, when the new young couple was wed, some interesting things began to take place at the dinner table. He would look at his glass, then at his wife, and then back at his glass trying to drop hints. She would wonder what was going on, would ask, and then be frustrated at such controversy over such a simple issue. The next thing they knew she'd be telling him to get his own drink and he'd be reminding her that Sarah called Abraham "Lord". She laughs now when telling the story! The funniest part is that God used that simple matter to begin working into their hearts a vision for co-laboring together in all things -- home and ministry. Today, they are co-pastors of a thriving international ministry!

SARAH VS. HAGAR

"For it is written that Abraham had two sons, one by the slave woman and the other by the free woman. His son by the slave woman was born in the ordinary way; but his son by the free woman was born as the result of a promise. These things may be taken figuratively, for the women represent two covenants. One covenant is from Mount Sinai

> *and bears children who are to be slaves: This is Hagar. Now Hagar stands for Mount Sinai in Arabia and corresponds to the present city of Jerusalem, because she is in slavery with her children. But the Jerusalem that is above is free, and she is our mother. For it is written: "Be glad, O barren woman, who bears no children; break forth and cry aloud, you who have no labor pains; because more are the children of the desolate woman than of her who has a husband." Now you, brothers, like Isaac, are children of promise. At that time the son born in the ordinary way persecuted the son born by the power of the Spirit. It is the same now. But what does the Scripture say? "Get rid of the slave woman and her son, for the slave woman's son will never share in the inheritance with the free woman's son." Therefore, brothers, we are not children of the slave woman, but of the free woman."* Galatians 4:22-31

We talked about Sarah and Hagar in the previous chapter and how Sarah struck a deal with God in order to expedite His promise. But look at the story on the flip side now: Not just at the two leading ladies in the saga, but at the fruit they bore because of who they were. Women today, and men for that matter, have eternal impact on their children due to attitude. Heart. If parents don't know who they are then their children won't either. Many times in everyday life we have to choose if we will be a Sarah or a Hagar in our actions and attitudes. We must decide, when everything hits the fan, if we are free or slave. With the proper alignment, we can conquer anything.

I mentioned in chapter one about a time in my life when God asked me if I was willing to make the sacrifices to build an empire. Well, one year, two weeks and one day later, I discovered what I was made of. I thought I had made sacrifices before, and trust me, I had actually made some whoppers, but this was "sacrifice" with a capital "S". In chapter seven I spoke of it when I eluded to the time when Chris sacrificed his position at Reunion Records at the instruction of the Lord to come home and regain a ministry-driven mindset towards his work. He immediately began forming a business with a large vision for various art forms being managed in one "house", where musicians, actors, photographers, sculptors and even architects could be taught to "minister" with their gifts and broaden their soul-scopes from hundreds to millions. It was a noble endeavor, one that he continues on with today, but as we look back on that time, that decision God had asked Chris to make was less about ministry and more about family. Little did we know we were entering into four year period of utter dependence on God. No income, one house, two car payments, and five kids (at the time). We had no idea the emotional and spiritual alignment we were in for. Our perspectives had checked in for cosmetic surgery without our consent. We went from six digits (Chris' job plus some other ventures) down to zero, zippo, nada. He'd be offered other lucrative offers but doors would be slammed and no peace would be present to kick them open. So we waited. And waited and waited and waited. Creditors called. One car was repossessed and the other was demolished by a drunk driver. We almost lost the house twice, once on October 24, 1999 and again on July 31st, 2000. The dates are still fresh in my memory. We received food from the government, state-aid insurance to pay for the delivery of our sixth child, and went without toilet paper for two months one time. My dad repurchased our car for us, our church and its Master's Hands Ministry run by an angel named Peggy Zide fed us, and my mom kept me stocked in a free supply of Mary Kay cosmetics which she will never know how important that was to my "self-image" during that hard season. God provided for us, but it was manna that had to be collected daily without complaint.

Somewhere in the midst of that, we realized the importance of perspective. Instead of going to the pantry everyday and dreading trying to get creative again with beans and rice (and rice and beans), I began to appreciate the fact that my family ate three meals a day together. Mom and Dad and all kids present, thanks to tutoring the kids at home. Other kids would visit our home and tell us that they hadn't even eaten a dinner with their parents in months. There was a prayer that we always prayed over our meals as a family, and it was the verse from Exodus 23:25 where God promises to "bless your bread and your water and take sickness away from the midst of you." Well, one particular morning I went to the kitchen, to once again put all of my creative skills to use in making breakfast out of what was available to me. I looked in the refrigerator and all that was there was a can of biscuits. No juice, no eggs, no cereal, and no milk to put on it even if we'd had any. I admit, I sighed heavily and had to pray for an attitude adjustment. But then I cooked the can of biscuits, placed a pitcher of ice-water on the table and called everyone in. There must have been a supernatural suppression on our appetites during that period. As we bowed our heads to pray, Exodus 23:25 took on a new meaning: "God, bless our BREAD and our WATER, and take sickness away from the midst of us". We cried and then laughed out loud. I can't quit crying now just thinking about it. The point is that, in that moment I had to decide if I was a free woman or a slave. Because I chose to be free, my children followed suit. They never complained, not once. They were not angels. They were humans under grace. Humans under fire under grace!

Many times they would babysit for friends and give us the money to get our lights or phones reconnected. I lost track of how many Ben Franklins my daughter gave us to pay bills, or how many piggy banks were raided for a loaf of bread. They gave extravagantly, and because they did it cheerfully, God is blessing them extravagantly. And how could they give cheerfully in the midst of such sacrifice? Because they knew they were free and not slaves. Hallelujah! Peace is not the absence of struggle. Peace is the presence of laughter in the midst of struggle. Amen.

> *"I know your deeds, your love and faith, your service and perseverance, and that you are now doing more than you did at first." Revelation 2:19*

MARY VS. MARTHA

Mary and Martha were sisters mentioned in the gospels. They are notorious typecasts of the struggle between the roles of worshiper and the worker. I have a good friend whose name is Mary Martha. I used to think that would produce more confusion than was bearable, but when I look at her life I see the beauty of both at work. Service and surrender. Although the passage in Luke 10 is known for Jesus' words to Martha about how she needed to slow down and relax in her duties, I still don't see Jesus rebuking Martha here. Look at the passage:

> *"As Jesus and his disciples were on their way, he came to a village where a woman named Martha opened her home to him. She had a sister called Mary, who sat at the Lord's feet listening to what he said. But Martha was distracted by all the preparations that had to be made. She came to him*

and asked, "Lord, don't you care that my sister has left me to do the work by myself? Tell her to help me!" "Martha, Martha," the Lord answered, "you are worried and upset about many things, but only one thing is needed. Mary has chosen what is better, and it will not be taken away from her." Luke 10:38-42

Martha had opened up her home to the ministry of Jesus. She had a gift of service and was going to use it by golly even if it killed her. Jesus understood this and even appreciated her service, but wanted her to tap into that thing which would ignite her service: Him. Mary knew how to do that. What we don't know is if Mary knew how to work hard and serve others. I wonder if Jesus ever told Mary that faith without works is dead (James 2:17). We don't see from this passage if Martha ever sat down or if Mary ever got up, but what we can glean from the story are the lessons of employing both each day of our lives.

"There are different kinds of service, but the same Lord. There are different kinds of working, but the same God works all of them in all men. Now to each one the manifestation of the Spirit is given for the common good. To one there is given through the Spirit the message of wisdom, to another the message of knowledge by means of the same Spirit, to another faith by the same Spirit, to another gifts of healing by that one Spirit, to another miraculous powers, to another prophecy, to another distinguishing between spirits, to another speaking in different kinds of tongues, and to still another the interpretation of tongues. All these are the work of one and the same Spirit, and he gives them to each one, just as he determines. 1 Corinthians 12:5-11

"Be dressed ready for service and keep your lamps burning" Luke 12:35

"Therefore I glory in Christ Jesus in my service to God." Romans 15:17

"They urgently pleaded with us for the privilege of sharing in this service to the saints." 2 Corinthians 8:4

"...to prepare God's people for works of service, so that the body of Christ may be built up." Ephesians 4:12

"I thank Christ Jesus our Lord, who has given me strength, that he considered me faithful, appointing me to his service." 1 Timothy 1:12

"We have different gifts, according to the grace given us. If a man's gift is prophesying, let him use it in proportion to his faith. If it is serving, let him serve." Romans 12:6-7

"Never be lacking in zeal, but keep your spiritual fervor, serving the Lord." Romans 12:11

June and Ward were sittin' in a tree
S-.E-.R-.V-.I-.N-.G.
First came God
Then came kin
Then came multitudes that they could win!

Chapter 16

SARCASTIC SUBMISSION

Give me a break, do you honestly think
my life is yours to live?
I'll give you some rights but I'll put up a fight
and you'd better be appreciative
Good grief, who are you, to tell me what to do?
Don't remind me I said I'd submit
Because if you do, I might come unglued
throw a tantrum or pitch a big fit!

"ALL RIGHT THEN, FINE!"

Ever said those words? If I had a dollar for every time I used to say them, I could've bought this book for you and one for each of your friends. Cynical, comical concession. Why concede at all? I mean, if God loves a cheerful giver, then why on earth would you ever give anything begrudgingly? Better to not give at all. The other person might somehow be blessed by your gift, but your reward will be nullified.

"Will your idle talk reduce men to silence? Will no one rebuke you when you mock?" Job 11:3

For some reason, television is full of sarcastic submission these days. Every night on any given channel there is some t.v. teen who is allowed to fly off at his or her parents and storm out of the room without so much as a raise of the eyebrows by mom or dad afterwards. They either don't agree with Mom or Dad at all, or they do so with a biting, snide remark. What would the Waltons think? What is so boring about discipling children, I mean, isn't it the most entertaining action sport of all times? Something that we all do and need creative help with? I have six kids and just one day at my house could be prime time action television. But I've noticed that no t.v. moms or dads discipline with righteousness or wisdom anymore. It's a forsaken art form. Humdrum. Dull. Doesn't sell. It's like parents can't be shown demonstrating their rightful authority all due to America's over-compensation towards the abuse of children. Those kids deserve compensation, yes and amen, but over-compensation which removes the administration of loving discipline will only harm them in the end. They don't need their parents below them, but above them. The mentality is that children have been mistreated (and they have), and so they now need to be given a right to dominate the home. It's the "I love you Mom and Dad but I need to make decisions for myself because, gee, I am thirteen years old now" mentality. It's a dangerous position. We're throwing out the baby with bath water, when instead we need more programs that show parents in fun-loving relationships with their kids, and children who are willing to trust Mom and Dad's judgment because of how loved, respected and adored they feel. It's not the absence of respect, but the presence of it with order and love. The antagonists in the plot would no longer be under the same roof, but on the outside coming against a united family. It would sell and I know it would. It is real life.

I watched a t.v. show recently that had been advertised as a clean family sitcom. In it, the family's oldest child, a teen, was smoking pot up in his room with a friend, and when Mom and Dad found out, they didn't scold him but instead decided to "mess with his mind". Negating all discipline, they instead thought it funny to play jokes on him and toy with his senses while he was still on the high. No discipline or consequences ever followed. Only a "talking-to" in which the dad cracked jokes. "Sit-com" stands for "situation-comedy", but trust me, not only did I not laugh during this entire program, but I came away feeling the weight of a national crisis. I challenge you to try to find one t.v. show this week where there is no trace of sarcasm and rebellion between parents and children, wives and husbands, or employers and employees. You won't find it on the major networks. I won't name names, but you know the shows. Rebellion, sarcasm, and Jezebel sells. Not to mention the other goliaths like lust, greed and rivalry. They are the staple ingredients of every soap opera, and to watch them is to become them. You are what you eat! So not only will I challenge you to try to find a t.v. show without it this week, but I challenge you to rise up as a creative artisan who can change the face of modern media. Perhaps you have no desire like I do to be in the t.v. and film making business, but even if you just own a t.v., you can at least see the need for you to be praying about what comes out of it.

"So I gave them over to their stubborn hearts to follow their own devices." Psalm 81:12

STUBBORNNESS

I know for myself, whenever I used to drag my feet and then eventually submit with my sarcastic "two-cents worth", I somehow was deceived into thinking this was true submission. Sarcastic submission is an oxymoron, just like "jumbo-shrimp" or "awfully good". Submission with sarcasm is no submission at all, for the heart has not surrendered. Once the heart surrenders, then the mouth and feet can follow. However, if the mouth concedes without the heart, it is merely lip service. "For out of the overflow of the heart the mouth speaks." Matthew 12:34. So what is at the root of this lip service? It is actually a soul in torment: one who's heart knows it should submit but who's mind is screaming no.

> *"But they did not listen or pay attention; instead, they followed the stubborn inclinations of their evil hearts. They went backward and not forward." Jeremiah 7:24*

At that moment, you have the choice to let your heart override your mind. I'm not suggesting that you just submit to John Doe on the street without discretion. It goes without saying that you should not be under the authority of just anybody. But once you are there and you know it is a relationship that God has placed you in, hard or easy, that is when you must start making the choices you know you should make. With a smile! Otherwise you are not only moving in rebellion, but stubbornness. Is there a difference? Yes. I would suggest to you that rebellion is in the heart, and stubbornness is in the will, or the mind. Therefore, if you know you are to be in relationship with and under the authority of a particular person in your life -- a boss, parent, pastor, spouse, etc.. -- and you decide that you will submit to them but that you will stomp around and throw a fit first, then you are being stubborn. If you throw a fit and then never surrender, it's rebellion. Be careful though, because they work as a team and their goal is sure destruction. Scripture speaks pretty loudly about rebellion and stubbornness, their differences and similarities, and how God feels about them both:

"For rebellion is as the sin of witchcraft, and stubbornness is as iniquity and idolatry." 1 Samuel 15:23

"But because of your stubbornness and your unrepentant heart, you are storing up wrath against yourself for the day of God's wrath, when his righteous judgment will be revealed." Romans 2:5

"They would not be like their forefathers-- a stubborn and rebellious generation, whose hearts were not loyal to God, whose spirits were not faithful to him." Psalm 78:8

"But these people have stubborn and rebellious hearts; they have turned aside and gone away." Jeremiah 5:23

"For I knew how stubborn you were; the sinews of your neck were iron, your forehead was bronze." Isaiah 48:4

"An evil man is bent only on rebellion; a merciless official will be sent against him." Proverbs 17:11

"Later Jesus appeared to the Eleven as they were eating; he rebuked them for their lack of faith and their stubborn refusal to believe those who had seen him after he had risen." Mark 16:14

"I will break down your stubborn pride and make the sky above you like iron and the ground beneath you like bronze." Leviticus 26:19

That quote from Leviticus 26:19 describes the lengths God will go to to break stubborn pride. However a few verses before this passage, He says something even more startling:

> *"However, if you do not listen to me or obey my commands, and if you break my covenant by rejecting my laws and treating my regulations with contempt, I will punish you. You will suffer from sudden terrors, with wasting diseases, and with burning fevers, causing your eyes to fail and your life to ebb away." Leviticus 26:14-16*

Your life will "ebb away?" Another translation says, "to drain away". He even makes a direct correlation between disobedience and disease. He vows that sin will give birth to sickness. We can choose to be offended at that or accept it as the Word of God and yield. Verse 17 then goes on to describe how people like this will end up running even when no one is chasing them. Better a moment of surrender and submission, than a lifetime of utter confusion!

THE CLOSING OF EARS

There is also an interesting correlation in Scripture between rebellion and deaf ears. Whether the lack of submission is sarcastic, stubborn or secretive, such people hear what they want to hear, and when they turn a deaf ear to wisdom too many times, eventually their hearts become hardened in rebellion.

> *"As has just been said: "Today, if you hear his voice, do not harden your hearts as you did in the rebellion."*
> *Hebrews 3:15*

"'But they refused to pay attention; stubbornly they turned their backs and stopped up their ears." Zechariah 7:11

"For this people's heart has become calloused; they hardly hear with their ears, and they have closed their eyes. Otherwise they might see with their eyes, hear with their ears, understand with their hearts and turn, and I would heal them.' " Matthew 13:15

"But Stephen, full of the Holy Spirit, looked up to heaven and saw the glory of God, and Jesus standing at the right hand of God. "Look," he said, "I see heaven open and the Son of Man standing at the right hand of God." At this they covered their ears and, yelling at the top of their voices, they all rushed at him, dragged him out of the city and began to stone him." Acts 7:55-58a

If sarcasm is a snare to you, you should put your hand over your mouth and not your ears!

"...keep your ears open and your mouth shut!" Ecclesiastes 5:1

"If you have been foolish in exalting yourself, or if you have devised evil, put your hand on your mouth." Proverbs 30:32

"Look at Me and be astonished; put your hand over your mouth." Job 21:5

"If you keep your mouth shut, you will stay out of trouble." Proverbs 20:23

REPENTANCE FROM SARCASM

Ask the Lord to reveal to you right now if your life is plagued by sarcasm. Websters defines it as, "an insulting or mocking statement or remark." Perhaps you've seen how sarcasm is even present in compliments, but so waters down it down that no blessing remains. For instance, I had a friend who simply could not pay a compliment if her life depended on it. She was so insecure that whenever I complimented her she wouldn't even look me in the eye. When she started making progress, her compliments sounded like a curse. For example, she'd say with a scowl, "Laura, you're so skinny it makes me sick!". Like I said, all scowl, no smile. I knew she was trying to compliment me on getting back in shape after the baby was born, but she just couldn't bring herself to say what she meant. That is another form of sarcastic submission, because keep in mind that submission also includes "mutual submission", which is the principal behind "submitting ye one to another". There will be certain groups of people where that sarcastic spirit will flourish. You will notice it running rampant sometimes as you sit with family members, or perhaps in certain circles of friends. What does it feed on? Surrender. Not to the Lord, but to that spirit. As someone starts up a critical conversation about someone else behind their back or to their face, you will soon hear others chiming in with the same spirit. At that moment, you have the ability to change the whole atmosphere in the room by finding something about that person to bless. As you ask God to turn your heart, you will find yourself unable to sit by and let sarcasm rule. Ask God right now to show you who you are so that you can recognize who others are and bless them verbally for it. As you do, you will see your own heart turning away from sarcastic mockery, and running towards the rewards of submission.

"He mocks proud mockers but gives grace to the humble."
Proverbs 3:34

"Whom are you mocking? At whom do you sneer and stick out your tongue? Are you not a brood of rebels, the offspring of liars?" Isaiah 57:4

"The eye that mocks a father, that scorns obedience to a mother, will be pecked out by the ravens of the valley, will be eaten by the vultures." Proverbs 30:17

"Oh what joy for those whose rebellion is forgiven, whose sin is put out of sight!" Psalm 32:1

Lips be thoughtful, mouth be wise
Tongue be fully circumcised
Words be whittled with a knife
Censor all that is not life

Hand be ready to move in
Cover death from nose to chin
Mouth be moistened, smile don't frown!
Blessings flow where curses drown

" In him you were also circumcised, in the putting off of the sinful nature, not with a circumcision done by the hands of men but with the circumcision done by Christ, having been buried with him in baptism and raised with him through your faith in the power of God, who raised him from the dead. " Colossians 2:11-12

Chapter 17

MURMURING SUBMISSION

Peter Griper tricked a trek of fickle helpers
A trek of fickle helpers Peter Griper tricked
If Peter Griper tricked a trek of fickle helpers
How many fickle helpers ever learned to submit?

CAUTION! WARNING! HOT CONTENTS!

Ok, you have been given fair warning and now you can't sue me. You are about to be asked to take a test. If you have no desire to find out what's really in your heart concerning those in authority over you, you might want to rip this part out of the book. Actually, that won't help, because you'll just hear it again before the end anyway! Are you ready?

Give yourself 5 points for each of the following you can truthfully answer yes to:

1. I have never talked poorly about my spouse behind his or her back (or parents if not married).
2. I have never rolled my eyes at my spouse during a conversation (or parents if not married).
3. I always honor my parents in person, and especially with my words when they are not present (honor: Strong's Greek Concordance "kabed" means to "promote" / Websters "honor" means to "praise, credit, elevate, love, salute, prize.")
4. I have never defaced or spoken ill of my government leaders (even if they deserved it).
5. I have never eaten fried Preacher for Sunday dinner, or spoken badly about him or her (nor jokingly exposed his or her weaknesses).
6. I have never talked about my friends behind their backs in a way that would hurt them in person.
7. I have never demeaned my boss to other employees, or even suggested that he or she is not capable of doing the job (even if he or she isn't).

Ok, so that just about rules all of us out. If your score was in the single digits you have a lot of people to go to and ask forgiveness from. If your score was on the low end of the double digits, then you need to keep reading. If you scored 20 or higher, you're in pretty good shape, but there's room for improvement. And if your score is a perfect 35, then your name is probably Jesus.

> *"I the LORD search the heart and examine the mind, to reward a man according to his conduct, according to what his deeds deserve." Jeremiah 17:10*

Now let's be realistic and give credit where credit is due. If you're thinking, "I can't say I've NEVER done those things, but I can say that I don't anymore", then give yourself 4 points for each question you can apply that to. If your score is 20 or higher, then you're on the right road. If it's under 20, but your true desire is to learn how to better respect those in authority over you, even if it means praying for the ones who don't deserve respect, then ask God to give you grace in this area. With God and this book, you've got a fighting chance!

I am not afraid to say that this book will help people. God said to write it and so I believe that He wants to use it to set people free from rebellion. Subtle or overt, it is all a stench in God's nostrils. God has given me a message, and so I have no doubt He will supply the megaphone.

Just as Tiger Woods made golf look fun again, and Charlotte Church revived classical opera in a modernized world, my desire is to take the topic of submission and give it the colorful credit it is finally due.

"For we are righteous when we obey." Deuteronomy 6:25

GRIPE, GRIPE, GRIPE

So what's the moral behind Peter Griper? Put one loose tongue in a crowd and everyone who's wavering will go along with him. Yes, Peter Griper is at fault for demeaning leadership behind their backs, but equally at fault are all the fickle helpers that gave him an ear. Are you a fickle helper, a Peter Griper, or maybe the person in leadership who's the object of their whining? I hope you are none. If you are, there are some truths you need to weigh.

If you are Peter Griper, I have a question to ask you. Have you never read James 1:26?

> *"If anyone considers himself religious and yet does not keep a tight rein on his tongue, he deceives himself and his religion is worthless."*

Now you have no excuse. If you gripe and grumble against a parent, a spouse, a boss or a pastor, you have willingly packed your bags and moved into a dangerous place called, "outside of the will of God". If you are miserable with a situation you have two choices, neither of which is to murmur (nor is one of them to just leave if it is a covenant relationship). Choice number one is to go directly to the person and work hard to work it out. Do it more than once if you have to, taking a third party in to help mediate if they did not "hear" you the first time. Love does not quit. "It always protects, always trusts, always hopes, always perseveres. Love never fails." 1 Corinthians 13:7-8 Bringing in a mediator means finding someone whom both parties trust, and planning a meeting where you both sit and tell your sides, humbly willing to submit to the authority of the person you've called in to "judge". It's basic Matthew 18. We studied it before in earlier chapters but it is worth repeating again: "If your brother sins against you, go and show him his fault, just between the two of you. If he listens to you, you have won your brother over. But if he will not listen, take one or two others along, so that 'every matter may be established by the testimony of two or three witnesses.'" (v. 15-16). If that still does not work, there is actually more to that passage that you should study for instruction, and it involves taking your issue before the church. You need to rest assured that God does not tell you to blindly submit and endanger yourself, but that He has designed all authority with the proper checks and balances. If the checks and balances are out of whack too, well, then I can assure you it is an establishment that will fall. I have a dear friend right now in another city who is in the middle of a falling, failing church, all because the Pastor has refused any checks and balances in his ministry. He has an international board worldwide, but no accountability locally. He has two elders at his church, but they are not given right to speak into his life. As a result he began moving in deceit and improperly spending the church's money. It was a sticky situation that left the Elders feeling like lame ducks and the staff feeling like there was no where to go for justice. I have watched my friend submit through everything, but now he sees his church disintegrating and a pastor who needs to be confronted in love. I am proud of him for doing this and for including the elders in the meetings. I have total peace that God will either get the spirits out of the pastor or get the pastor out of that church! "Do not be deceived! God is not mocked! A man will reap what he sows!" Galatians 6:7

Let's now move on however to Peter Griper's second choice. It is found in Proverbs 19:11, and frankly, I have seen it solve many more messes than Matthew 18.

"A man's wisdom gives him patience; it is to his glory to overlook an offense."

God is not saying to just overlook it when a visible leader is involved in substantial sin. The debate, however, is usually over what is substantial and what is not. Some people take personality molehills and make mountains out of them. Let's describe "substantial". Let's say the leader in question is a pastor. Your pastor. And let's say that he has, in your opinion, some major personality flaws. Is there fruit in your church? Are souls being won and discipled? Is there fruit in his personal life? Are his children obedient? No child obeys all the time, and I am not asking if you've seen his kids running in the church. There is training involved in raising a child, but is this man's household in order? After being in a church where I have seen complaints come against leadership, especially the pastor, I have cornered God and begged Him -- wrestled, if you will -- to explain to me how it is this happens when both parties seem so obviously dedicated to the Lord. I felt they were all false accusations, but I wanted to be willing to take these criticisms to God and ask Him what He thought. Wouldn't that be best? Not ungodly introspection, but a vulnerable trust in whatever God shows you about you and the leaders you are following. I am going to share with you what the Lord told me, and if it at all strikes your spirit as truthful, I urge you to "corner Him" in the same way concerning any situation you might be in the middle of right now. Being in leadership at this particular church, and being the wife of one of the elders who had to mediate many meetings, I knew all the details of the complaints inside and out. Not because we sat around and gossiped about them (who has time for such stupidity?) but because when you choose to bring an accusation against an elder or a pastor you set yourself up for becoming an item of church business in the flock they are called to protect.

WHERE'S THE BEEF?

So concerning these complaints, there were many things said that were just downright not true concerning church matters and we had the documentation to prove it. But then there were the other "beefs". Taking a person's individual demeanor and labeling it a "demon". Because of our pastor's heart for seeing our whole church pursue revival and all that means, he's been known to do what most pastors will not do from a pulpit: Outright ask that all members be at certain functions that he felt were strategic for such outpourings. He tried not to lay that card down too often, but come on, is it a pastor's fault when the Spirit starts moving? When he did this he would passionately and strongly urge that everyone show up. Show up prayed up, and those pleas were sometimes mistaken as being controlling. We Americans couldn't make it in third world countries where people walk eight miles to get to church and then sit through six hour meetings with heat-waves and no refreshments afterwards. The gospel is all they have. I applauded my pastor for being unafraid to continue kindly challenging the people to let God order their Americanized, independent schedules. It was gusto tempered with gentleness. Still, it stepped on toes. It revealed hearts. Personally, my obedience to Pastor's "pleas" have brought revival to my own life and deposited massive ministry into me. I would obey at this local level, and suddenly start receiving national and international opportunities to minister abroad by various ministries. There were other accusations against Pastor too, all of which eventually evaporated. That's not to say they never resurfaced, but I have seen each one ultimately perish with patience and prayer. So what was it God showed me about it all that was so profound? It was from Matthew 7:

"By their fruit you will recognize them. Do people pick grapes from thorn bushes, or figs from thistles? Likewise every good tree bears good fruit, but a bad tree bears bad fruit. A good tree cannot bear bad fruit, and a bad tree cannot bear good fruit. Every tree that does not bear good fruit is cut down and thrown into the fire. Thus, by their fruit you will recognize them."
Matthew 7:16-20

What followed was a conversation with the Lord that went something like this:

He asked me pointblank if I saw good fruit in my pastor's life and ministry.

"Yes Sir."

"Describe it to Me."

"He loves his wife. He's a gentle daddy. People get saved almost every week as a result of his teachings, and yet he doesn't rest until he sees those "babies" growing up into their destinies. He's not satisfied with fruit until it is "lasting" fruit. And oh yeh, he's a good friend to me."

God then asked me, "Is he perfect?".

"No Sir. He is a man, made of dust".

"Is he filled with the power of My Holy Spirit?"

"Yes Sir, and with the fruits of your Holy Spirit".

"Well then, let me ask you another question. What's the worst thing you can think of that he does?"

I thought a moment. "Well, he seems to lose his keys a lot".

"Anything else?"

I thought back over years of walking with him and pondered his idiosyncrasies. Before I could dwell too long on them I heard another question from the Lord.

"Now name a few of your own imperfections..... or are you perfect?"

"No Sir, I am most certainly not."

"Does your pastor expect you to be? Didn't he place you in leadership over many people fully knowing that you had not reach full maturity in My character?"

I answered an obvious yes.

"Well then, let My man be My man to raise up in My image. He is young in years but seasoned in My Spirit. Do not regard him according to the flesh. I will make him into all he needs to be. Do you trust me to do that?"

I was stunned at how logically God saw it all. If the accusations against Pastor had been adultery or fraud or some sort of foul play, that would have been reason to investigate. But what had been brought to the table -- the personal issues, not church matters in which all documentation was solid -- seemed so puny to God that I wondered how anyone could waste time on it. Kingdom time. Time to work towards a full heaven and an empty hell. Time to spend in prayer. Time to feed the poor and heal the sick. Time to visit with God. I suddenly saw the ploy of the enemy.

MURMURING SUBMISSIONS

Such murmurings, usually mouthed by people who are appearing to submit and stay planted in a place so that they can try and "make things better", are no more than Satan's way of stealing time from both parties. Perhaps eating away at our time is the best he can do. Perhaps he can't find a road in otherwise, I mean, most of these altercations I have experienced have been between strong Christians who are all in ministry together. I've noticed that the accusing parties are usually strong in giftings but weak in submission. So strong in their giftings in fact that it seems they have a hard time submitting them to someone's leadership when asked to in circumstances that may cause them to be a little less visible for a season. God says that to whom much is given, much is required (Luke 12:48). I am noticing therefore that the stronger a person's call is on their life and the more submitted they are to it, God will begin to test their hearts to see how submitted they can be to the leaders He has set in place to train them. Strong call, strong tests. He already knows He can entrust the gift to them, but now He needs to see if He can entrust them to the gift. Heart vs. hands. Submission to authority, in fact, is such a priority to the Lord that He might put someone in leadership over you who knows less than you do or is less gifted than you are *just* to test your faithfulness and submission to covenant! If you can trust God through that person then you can trust God through anything! Well, as I studied these lives, I really couldn't find many other weaknesses except that one, but unfortunately the omission of submission is a sure downfall in the life of any man. It was the death of Absolom, Korah and Judas (guys you don't catch people naming their kids after, hint hint), but submission brought the promotion of such still-honored heroes like David, Paul and Esther. As I sat and further contemplated Satan's attempts to divide and conquer, the Lord let me in on a little secret: He'd had a part in setting it all up too. I was shocked! I heard Him say that He had seen us all stand in church and cry out for unity, and so He had put us in the middle of certain situations to see just how badly we wanted it. I then realized we can't cry out for unity amongst other churches unless we are willing to pay the price for it within our own. God wasn't the author of these attacks, but if what I was hearing was correct then He was telling me that He had allowed these fiery darts to leave Satan's hand just to see just how unified we would be when they struck the ground and started blazing a trail. I suddenly gained a new affection and admiration for all those who had stayed on board, and a thankfulness to God for letting me be one of them.

FICKLE HELPERS

Perhaps you do not consider yourself a Peter Griper. But, if you are a "fickle helper", ask yourself why you are remaining at a place that you are so unsure of. I mean, if you're wavering instead of leaving, you must know in your gut somehow that you're not supposed to leave. So, if you're not supposed to leave, then why not change your attitude and believe you are the key to helping things improve? It might be a marriage. It might be your church. It might be a relationship with a boss or a parent. But whatever the reason you are there, *you are there,* and are subject to the authority in that house. Wavering. Inconsistent. Erratic. Flighty. Unsteady. Unstable. Wayward. These are the definitions of "fickle". Try not to epitomize them.

Peter Griper is attracted to fickle helpers. He knows where they live and which buttons he can push to get inside. He is dependent upon them to keep his "ministry" going! I remember during the time when our church had some angry people who were leaving us and going elsewhere, it seemed many of them were not satisfied unless they took others with them. Some who left I was very proud of; they left to go on to other ministries God was calling them to and did it in peace and integrity. But there were others, as hard as it was to watch, who seemed to find pleasure in talking to as many people as they could on their way out the door. I had one person tell me during that time that they could not come to church without one of these people cornering them or at least firing snide remarks at them about someone in leadership. When they asked me why I thought that was, I shot from the hip.

> *"Their throats are open graves; their tongues practice deceit." "The poison of vipers is on their lips." "Their mouths are full of cursing and bitterness." "Their feet are swift to shed blood; ruin and misery mark their ways, and the way of peace they do not know." "There is no fear of God before their eyes." Romans 3:13-18*

I wasn't familiar enough with that verse to quote it when asked why I thought these murmurers were attracted to my friend, but I did still give my thoughts on the matter. I could tell that my friend was also wavering inside concerning our church and some of the circulating rumors. Although this person was in no way contributing to their spreading, they were still in a weak place of uncertainty and Satan knew it. Perhaps those grumblers had no idea why their mouths were attracted to my friend's ears, but that spirit within them was crouching at the door waiting to find a fickle helper to fulfill its lusts through, and I was determined that my friend was not going to be its next victim.

How did my friend overcome? By submission to authority. Submission to my advice, and to the leadership in their home. When feelings were swaying, they relied upon those over them to steady the boat, and as a result, those Peter Gripers left them alone and left the church entirely. Had they given that spirit audience for even one more day, it would have actually prolonged the predicament for the entire church.

"Warn a divisive person once, and then warn him a second time. After that, have nothing to do with him." Titus 3:10

THE END OF THE ROAD

This is the end of the section on The Counterfeits of Submission. As we close out this chapter on Murmuring Submission -- a heart which is disqualified by a mouth -- take some time to chew on and digest the following scriptures. They may challenge your flesh, but if you'll let them, they will change your heart!

"The crucible for silver and the furnace for gold, but the LORD tests the heart." Proverbs 17:3

"Must you rebel forever?" Isaiah 1:5

"LORD, who may dwell in your sanctuary? Who may live on your holy hill? He whose walk is blameless and who does what is righteous, who speaks the truth from his heart and has no slander on his tongue, who does his neighbor no wrong and casts no slur on his fellow man, who despises a vile man but honors those who fear the LORD, who keeps his oath even when it hurts, who lends his money without usury and does not accept a bribe against the innocent. He

who does these things will never be shaken" Psalm 15:1-5

"I the LORD search the heart and examine the mind, to reward a man according to his conduct, according to what his deeds deserve." Jeremiah 17:10

"The man who shows contempt for the judge or for the priest who stands ministering there to the LORD your God must be put to death. You must purge the evil from Israel. All the people will hear and be afraid, and will not be contemptuous again." Deuteronomy 17:12-13

"Woe to them! They have taken the way of Cain; they have rushed for profit into Balaam's error; they have been destroyed in Korah's rebellion. These men are blemishes at your love feasts, eating with you without the slightest qualm --shepherds who feed only themselves. They are clouds without rain, blown along by the wind; autumn trees, without fruit and uprooted --twice dead. They are wild waves of the sea, foaming up their shame; wandering stars, for whom blackest darkness has been reserved forever. Enoch, the seventh from Adam, prophesied about these men: "See, the Lord is coming with thousands upon thousands of his holy ones to judge everyone, and to convict all the ungodly of all the ungodly acts they have done in the ungodly way, and of all the harsh words ungodly sinners have spoken against him." These men are grumblers and faultfinders; they follow their own evil desires; they boast about themselves and flatter others for their own advantage." Jude 11-16

"He who is pregnant with evil and conceives trouble gives birth to disillusionment." Psalm 7:14

"Do not entertain an accusation against an elder unless it is brought by two or three witnesses." 1 Timothy 5:19

"For there are many who rebel against right teaching; they engage in useless talk and deceive people...They must be silenced. By their wrong teaching, they have already turned whole families away from the truth." Titus 1:10-11

"Snatch me back from the jaws of death!" Psalm 9:13

"Set a guard over my mouth, O LORD; keep watch over the door of my lips." Psalm 141:3

Above the chin, beneath the eyes
There the vile volcano lies
Spewing toxic undertones
Murder with a megaphone

Cast your lots to dabble on
Mumble, mutter, babble on
Mountains made from small faux pas
"Blah, blah, blah, blah, blah, blah, blahs"

Whisper, chatter, gush and spout
Poison and malignant doubt
Venom verified by hate
Greedy for a double-date

Guard the gap and close the spout
Let no deadly thing come out
Lest I wake in the abyss
Prisoner to its crafty kiss

Section Four ~

SUBMISSION: THE CLOUT

"Praise the LORD, O my soul, and forget not all his benefits..." Psalm 103:2

In this world's submission drought
Where rules have been turned inside out
Surrender is not free of doubt
And searches for another route

But drizzles from a few devout
Who know they cannot thrive without
Are breaking ground with each loud shout
"Sow submission, reap the clout!"

"Wisdom, like an inheritance, is a good thing and benefits those who see the sun."
Ecclesiastes 7:11

Chapter 18

FEARLESS SUBMISSION

Yes dear, yes sir, yes your honor!
Without faith I'd be a goner
So I'll trust your given right
To exercise divine foresight

MAKE A LIST AND CHECK IT TWICE

Make a list of everyone in your life who deserves your submission to their authority. Bosses. Pastors. Spouses. Government Leaders. Friends. Parents. Go for it, and once you finish the list, go back and jot down beside each name some ideas on how you can better serve and encourage them in their roles. Remember that the Hebrew word for "honor" means to "promote", so in essence, take a minute and plan how you can give each of these people a promotion, deserved or undeserved. You may be God's tool in their lives to change unhealthy behaviors that no one else has been willing to love them through.

So far, we've spent this book talking about what submission is and what it is not. In this last section we're going to spend some time talking about the perks! Obedience has benefits! I told you in section one that you would be building a structure in your life by reading this book, and that if you could make it through that portion you'd have a humble abode. If you stomached sections two and three you'd get the mansion! Well guess what? After reading this last segment on The Clout, you will get the fully furnished palatial estate! I applaud you for being willing to stick it out and take it all in. God has some wonderful things in store for you as you apply them to your life.

"All these blessings will come upon you and accompany you if you obey the LORD your God." Deuteronomy 28:2

Since you just finished a long section on the counterfeits and studying what submission is not, I thought that before we dove into the perks in this section we'd spend this chapter taking a really daring look at what obedience looks like in its highest and purest form: *fearless submission.* Section one may have been Submission 101, but since you have hung in there and completed your elementary, jr. high and high school education on the topic, I figured it was now time to go to college. You can do it! Although not everyone goes to obedience school, I urge you to turn God's head and make the decision to go all the way with this thing. Hopefully if I've done my job right, you are no longer looking at submission as toil but as treasure. Not as causing slavery but as gaining seniority! Privilege not pain. Rewarding not ridiculous! Gratifying not degrading! Worthwhile not worthless!

"Dear friends, if our hearts do not condemn us, we have confidence before God and receive from him anything we ask, because we obey his commands and do what pleases him." 1 John 3:21-22

SERVICE WITH A SMILE

Use that list you just made and imagine yourself interacting with each of those people. Picture yourself having optimum relationships everywhere you go in your life-- at work, at home or at your desired place of worship. Strive for excellence in everything you do, or I should say, with everyone you know. Don't settle for the status-quo or the independent Americanized way of thinking which reduces relationships to disposable diapers. Don't "throw someone away" just because they loused up or because you are ashamed of how much you've loused up in front of them. Ecclesiastes 10:4 is worth quoting again: "If your boss is angry with you don't quit! A quiet spirit can overcome even great mistakes". Or what about 1 Corinthians 13:4-5 and 7? "Love is patient and kind. Love is not jealous or boastful or proud or rude. Love does not demand its own way. Love is not irritable, and it keeps no record of when it has been wronged. Love never gives up, never loses faith, is always hopeful, and endures through every circumstance." So you see, submission is summed up, wrapped up and all tangled up in love. Seeing submission as a way to love someone takes covenant commitment to a whole new height. Go lower, grow higher. It is kingdom upside down. "Whoever finds his life will lose it, and whoever loses his life for my sake will find it" (Matthew 10:39). Be a loser! Love your spiritual leaders, your spouse and your parents by giving them the respect and honor they are due. You may not think you should "love" your boss, but as long as you're going to be spending so much time with him you might as well learn to like him!

Are you able to "serve the Lord with gladness?" (Psalm 100:2) Do you find yourself grumbling at work, or enjoying the day despite the obstacles that present themselves? And what about at home? Do you serve your family with complaints and a stern face, or are you able to smile at the unpredictabilities of family life? And finally, how do you worship the Lord? Do you come into his presence with singing or sighing? It goes without saying that from time to time we're all going to have a bad day. But if you're finding yourself having day after day after day of feeling like your face would break if you cracked a smile, then something is wrong. Something is wrong and you have two choices: Change where you are or change *who* you are. If it is a covenant relationship, then number one is not an option! Instead, I challenge you to be daring enough to ask God for an attitude adjustment. The truth is, many people don't want to actually leave where they are, they just want to stick around and complain. Make up your mind today that that is not an option! What good will that do? As long as you're going to do a job, why not enjoy it? Many people in ministry today are giving God a bad name with their perpetual griping about how impossible their job is. Many parents today are so tired and worn out trying to make enough money to pay for things they never should have bought in the first place that they are grieving their way through basic parenthood and making their children feel like liabilities instead of blessings. Remember: Children need your presence not your presents! If you don't make up your mind now to make parenthood look more appealing, you may never have grandchildren! So whether your place of employment is at home, in an office or in ministry, ask God to help you submit to those you love with a smile. If you're happy and you know it.... inform your face!

"Wisdom lights up a person's face, softening its hardness"
Ecclesiastes 8:1

DELAYED OBEDIENCE

If part of fearless submission is service with a smile, then an equally important ingredient would be the speed at which you submit. Delayed obedience is not obedience at all. Dragging your feet will never get you anywhere with your boss, your spouse, your friends, children or spiritual leaders. You will only gain yourself the reputation of being untrustable and uncooperative. Do yourself a favor and have feet that are quick to obey!

"...and immediately they left the boat and their father and followed him." Matthew 4:22

If you find yourself continuously practicing "Reluctant Submission", then ask God to give you a willing spirit. Remember 51:12? "Restore to me the joy of your salvation and grant me a willing spirit, to sustain me". Our human flesh, or our will, desires to fight to the bitter end to maintain control in every situation. If we can determine it within ourselves that submission is a choice, not a feeling, then we will always make the right decisions to obey cheerfully and actually get pleasure out of it. Once you begin to experience that pleasure, that's the sign that you have made the supernatural shift which has changed submission from a hard choice to beautiful feeling. At that point you realize you don't have to submit, but you *get* to.

When you wake up in the morning, chances are that even though you are "awake" in the bed, it's the getting up part that actually helps you shake the sleepy feelings. You don't just wake up feeling awake. My dad grew up on a farm and has always risen with the sun. I did not inherit that gene. Even though I've had six children who all wake me up promptly for a 6 a.m. feeding, I still would just plop them in the bed with me and rest during it, technically not having to "get up" until an hour or so later. When I wake up in the morning (after having been up til after midnight), I have to make the choice to surrender to the day that is calling me and get going. Once I am up, it takes another few minutes to lose that sleepy feeling. Submission is the same way. You make the choice to do it before you ever feel like it. Your flesh will *never* want to submit. It is a decision you make *for* your flesh ahead of time, and when the moment arises, you remind your flesh who's boss. Having fearlessly vowed ahead of time that you will greet each request for obedience with a smile, you make the choice to rise to the occasion and do it just like you have to make the choice to rise each morning to the sound of your alarm clock. Pressing snooze is not an option in obedience!

"The spirit is willing, but the flesh is weak." Matthew 26:41

FEAR OF GOD VS. FEAR OF MAN

If you can settle it within your heart that your submission, regardless of whom you are giving it to, is an act that you do unto the Lord, then you will be filled with a fearlessness that will allow you to obey your leaders without hesitation. You will no longer waste hours wondering if the person's judgment is sound or not. That's a decision that should have been made before you entered into any kind of relationship with them. They will not always make perfect decisions, and you certainly should be able to exchange ideas with them and make suggestions, but when it counts and it's down to the wire and someone must make the final decision, that is when submission must step up to the plate. That is what keeps peace. Better to go down together than to succeed with separation. Success with separation is no success at all.

"Am I now trying to win the approval of men, or of God? Or am I trying to please men? If I were still trying to please men, I would not be a servant of Christ." Galatians 1:10

In order to see your submission to others as unto the Lord, you must not have any fear of man within you. So you see, this is the mystery of submission: many think it is birthed out of fear, when in truth real submission must be fearless. Submission with fear is slavery. Fearless submission brings liberation.

"Then you will lift up your face without shame; you will stand firm and without fear." Job 11:15

If you truly trust God as much as you say you do, then why are you so afraid of obeying someone He has put in authority over you? Even if you don't think that God put them in place over you -- say for instance if it was a marriage that you entered into before you were truly walking the Lord -- then can you still not summon up enough faith to believe that the Lord will chase that person down on your behalf? If the fear of the Lord is in your life -- which is a healthy reverence for the trustworthiness of our God -- then you will never again fear any man.

Consider what God's word says about it:

"Fear of man will prove to be a snare, but whoever trusts in the LORD is kept safe."
Proverbs 29:25

"The fear of the LORD is the beginning of wisdom, and knowledge of the Holy One is understanding."
Proverbs 9:10

"Fear the LORD your God, serve him only and take your oaths in his name." Deuteronomy 6:13

"Now fear the LORD and serve him with all faithfulness."
Joshua 24:14

"Now let the fear of the LORD be upon you."
2 Chronicles 19:7

"He gave them these orders: "You must serve faithfully and wholeheartedly in the fear of the LORD."
2 Chronicles 19:9

"Their homes are safe and free from fear; the rod of God is not upon them." Job 21:9

"Who despises a vile man but honors those who fear the LORD, who keeps his oath even when it hurts....he who does these things will never be shaken." Psalm 15:4 -5

"He laughs at fear, afraid of nothing; he does not shy away from the sword." Job 39:22

THE GOOD BOOK

You'll notice in this book that a few Scriptures on submission are listed more than once. They are worth repeating, and sometimes I chose a particular Scripture not because I couldn't find another one, but because I wanted to repeat it and have you really grab hold of it. God often repeated himself too for emphasis, even giving people dreams twice in an attempt to really get their attention (Joseph and Pharaoh). Even still, there are over 1000 scriptures in this book. Over 600 passages, but when broken down into verses there are, like I said, over 1000. Think of it like getting 1000 quotes from the most inspired authors in the world -- the 40-plus authors of the Bible! As I spoke about in chapter eight, prior to writing this book the Lord instructed me to read entirely through the Bible from cover to cover in five days looking for verses which dealt with submission or related topics. By His grace I did it, and it resulted in a week in which I was absolutely saturated and dripping with God's perspective on obedience and submission. Oh, to live there! But this book, I firmly believe, is the fruit of that solitude. Read it and reap! Don't forget to make your list of how you can better love and serve those who lead you. The written Word of God, or the "logos" (Greek), combined with "rhema", which is the spoken Word of God, is an unconquerable team. We don't just need to know the Word of God but also the God of the Word. So as you canvass these pages, I pray that both the logos and rhema would spring up within you with practical application. May we not just be hearers of the Word, but doers. May God add His super to your natural and grant you interludes of your own to meditate on His goodness -- part of which includes an adventurous life complete with fearless obedience and all of its winnings.

"I press on toward the goal to win the prize for which God has called me heavenward in Christ Jesus. All of us who are mature should take such a view of things. And if on some point you think differently, that too God will make clear to you. Only let us live up to what we have already attained. "
Philippians 3:14-16

Makin' a list, checking it twice
Gonna submit whatever the price
This, my cause, will gain me a crown

Chapter 19

BEING WORTHY TO BE SUBMITTED TO

What an honor to be esteemed
To lead the pack and guide the team
To set the pace and find a theme
And know that others will follow

But am I just to head the line?
Don't strength and kindness intertwine?
How do I rule yet still resign
To serve those I am leading?

Within my sphere I oversee
God keep me from all tyranny
And help me steer this company
And slave to be worthy to lead them

TAKING INVENTORY

You're going to make another list now. On this one, I want you to chart everyone you can think of who submits to *you*. They may be children, employees, church members, a spouse, or your friends. Everyone is a leader in some capacity. Now beside each name, write the ways in which you let this person know how much you care for them. List the tangible ways in which you communicate your covering for them. Put checks beside each name that you think really believes you are trustworthy enough to be submitted to; those people who serve you with their hearts and not just their hands.

Relationships take time. It may be that your intentions are good but that you just don't take enough time to let people know how much you appreciate them. When's the last time you told your kids all the things you like about them? Or how often do you do the same for your spouse? When's the last time you sowed a couple of hours into those who work for you -- at church or at your job -- and had an informal get-together where you just got to know them as people?

Some of the most beautiful memories we have in our home have been the casual gatherings we've had for those we lead at our church. Trust me, we've had more fiery prayer meetings than parties, but the moments worth writing home about have been those laugh 'til your belly hurts encounters. The ones where you sit around and bear your most appalling secrets, knowing that everyone in the room loves you enough to laugh along with you at your former stupidities.

TRUSTWORTHINESS

If you are reading this book and you are a leader, there is a passage in Scripture that can help you lead with excellence, whether you are in charge of many or a few, children or adults, submitted or rebellious individuals. In it are twenty qualities that make up a good leader -- a leader who is worthy to be trusted and submitted to. Even if you are not an "overseer" in a church, you oversee people in your care in other arenas of life. Apply these qualities to your personal character and watch your areas of authority grow! It is found in 1 Timothy 3:1-13:

> "Here is a trustworthy saying: If anyone sets his heart on being an overseer, he desires a noble task. Now the overseer must be above reproach, the husband of but one wife, temperate, self-controlled, respectable, hospitable, able to teach, not given to drunkenness, not violent but gentle, not quarrelsome, not a lover of money. He must manage his own family well and see that his children obey him with proper respect. (If anyone does not know how to manage his own family, how can he take care of God's church?) He must not be a recent convert, or he may become conceited and fall under the same judgment as the devil. He must also have a good reputation with outsiders, so that he will not fall into disgrace and into the devil's trap. Deacons, likewise, are to be men worthy of respect, sincere, not indulging in much wine, and not pursuing dishonest gain. They must keep hold of the deep truths of the faith with a clear conscience. They must first be tested; and then if there is nothing against them, let them serve as deacons. In the same way, their wives are to be women worthy of respect, not malicious talkers but temperate and trustworthy in everything. A deacon must be the husband of but one wife and must manage his children and his household well. Those who have served well gain an excellent standing and great assurance in their faith in Christ Jesus."

1. LIVE ABOVE REPROACH
2. ONE SPOUSE (LOYALTY)
3. TEMPERATE (pleasant, level-headed, reasonable)
4. SELF-CONTROLLED
5. RESPECTABLE
6. HOSPITABLE
7. ABLE TO TEACH
8. NOT GIVEN TO DRUNKENNESS (or other addictions)
9. NOT VIOLENT BUT GENTLE
10. NOT QUARRELSOME
11. NOT A LOVER OF MONEY
12. MANAGE FAMILY WELL
13. NOT INEXPERIENCED
14. NOT CONCEITED
15. GOOD REPUTATION
16. SINCERE (transparent)
17. DISHONEST GAIN
18. HOLD DEEP TRUTHS with FAITH
19. A GOOD CONSCIENCE
20. TESTED

Out of those twenty qualities that make any leader a good overseer, I believe that three of them epitomize the entire person: Judge the heart, the hands and the home of any individual and you will unmask what they are truly made of:

THE HEART: #16 ~ "SINCERE" (TRANSPARENCY)

Transparency is a dying art, don't you think? I remember when Billy Joel came out with his "Glass Houses" album in 1980 when I was in high school. I thought that was the greatest concept ever thought of for an album title. Of course, the picture on the front cover was of him with rock in hand ready to shatter one side of the house, and so I remember thinking that perhaps living in glass houses wasn't all it was "cracked" up to be. But now I disagree. I believe transparency has great perks. Of course, only the brave build such lives. Only someone who is totally secure is gutsy enough to walk around in their daily lives totally unafraid to let others peek inside without any given notice. I'm not talking about a life with no boundaries to others, but a life with no fear of others. Imagine living in a house where you were on display at all times and people could see every intimate detail of your life. They could see your emotions, your pain and even your nakedness. Then imagine the opposite: a life with so many masks that no one can see enough of the real you to help, befriend or encourage. Why do people live such lives? Do parents think they teach their children anything by hiding their fears and their flaws from them? Do politicians and presidents honestly think that Americans can't discern they guy behind the suit? Do pastors think that in their stoic heroism for Christ that they will model what true Christianity should be? Jesus hung on a cross naked and bled in front of others. Strangers and family. Enemies and friends. He was unafraid to let the world come close and watch Him suffer. In utter humility he was obedient to the point of death, and already dead enough to His reputation to not care who watched. If we are truly made in His image then why do we try to display something He is not? Just because many abuse this concept and walk around in a constant state of pessimism in the name of honesty, we should not throw the baby out with the bath water. Transparency is a valuable asset to every leader. Again, not a life with no boundaries to those you lead, but a life with no fear of them or what they think of you. That's where freedom is to become all that God wants you to be. Liberation from all fear of man.

I actually made a vow to the Lord once to live like this. It was more like I just begged Him to please never let me get so wrapped up in pride that I fell into the lie of independence. If you find yourself falling into the "it's just me and Jesus and I don't need anybody else" trap, especially when you are hurting or experiencing the need for encouragement, then you need to quickly reconsider being a leader of any kind. This must be where the phrase, "it's lonely at the top" comes from. It does not have to be lonely at the top. Of course, there does have to be healthy boundaries between leaders and followers so that familiarity doesn't cause people to regard their leaders according to the flesh and eventually disregard their authority, but again, I am not talking about removing those boundaries. I am talking about boundaries and walls made out of glass. Segregation without separation. Fences without facades. Moses went up on the mountain and talked with God, but then he came back down and spoke with the people. Real counsel comes from real life, and hurting people know who to go to to get the real deal. Joyce Meyer, perhaps the world's most successful woman minister who is seen in two-thirds of the world every day to a viewing audience of over 1 billion, is known for being able to teach the hard truth by admitting, "I'm not dishin' out anything to you that God hasn't made me eat first!" You hear realism and fearlessness in her voice and know you can trust what she says and reap from her wisdom. She is so gut-wrenchingly honest that it makes you laugh out loud, and after just a little while of listening you come to the conclusion that the enemy has no place in her. You can't imagine any scandal that could creep up against her that couldn't be disarmed.

Not because she's perfect, but because she's not afraid of being imperfect. It's the kingdom upside down again! Lose your life and find it! (Matthew 10:39). Transparency breeds trust. Let those you lead see your imperfections as you strive toward perfection in Christ and you will lay down a bridge for them to cross over and attain it with you.

Those you lead can never learn from you if they think you are perfect. They will either see you as a fake, or see your lifestyle as unattainable. Either way, you won't win much trust. Jesus, being fully God and the epitome of perfection, was also fully human in front of others. He didn't just declare the mysterious kingdom of God, but used life parables and simplicity to teach the people how to seize it. He built bridges instead of walls. Perhaps you agree that you are not perfect, but do you display that to your followers? Are you all God but not human? Or like Jesus, do you understand the importance of being both? David was a man, a king, who was unafraid to get real with God in front of people. He once disrobed himself in public and danced wildly before the Lord because he was so full of thanksgiving to Him for bringing the Ark back to the Israelites. Scripture says that when he was made fun of by his wife he said, "I will become even more undignified than this!" (2 Samuel 6:22). David proved that being undignified won't cost you your throne. It also proved that manners have nothing to do with the anointing!

TRANSPARENCY TEST

To discover if you are lacking in transparency as a leader (an employer, a parent, a pastor, a church leader, a spouse, etc.) ask yourself the following questions. Be transparent and truthful!

1) When someone brings up something I've done wrong, even in a joking manner, I feel the need to set the record straight and defend myself, even if I am laughing along with them.

2) When trouble arises or discouragement sets in, I take everything to God in prayer but never/rarely call others for support. If I do, I have waited first to regain composure so that I don't give them the wrong impression of who I "really am".

3) I have little accountability with people in my life (other than family) who I can share my weaknesses and sin struggles with.

4) I am a person of authority but am not really under the direct authority of those older / wiser / above me in rank who speak into my life directionally.

5) I go to painstakingly great lengths to ensure that people understand my motives so that they do not/have not wrongly judged me.

6) When I speak with people, I am more comfortable talking about my revelations or strengths than I am with my weaknesses. Caution usually causes me to not share my weaknesses, unless I am speaking of them after already moving past them.

7) Although I don't believe it's good to worry, I do spend a good chunk of time wondering how I could have/can say things in such a way that will better explain myself, justify myself, or win others over.

8) Concerning character, I am one person in public and another in private.

9) I long to have more people whom I can be transparent with without the fear of betrayal.

10) I'd rather appear right than real.

If you answered yes to three or more of the previous questions, then consider the following verses as you ask God to give you a transparent heart that is free of all false testimony. Ask him to help you die to reputation and all fear of man, trusting that in the end it will only increase your esteem among others. Many will look into your life and see God's strengths covering your weaknesses, and then hearing you give Him all the glory, will feel hope for their own lives and gladly submit to your sincere authority for the sake of their own freedom.

> *"Let us draw near to God with a sincere heart in full assurance of faith, having our hearts sprinkled to cleanse us from a guilty conscience and having our bodies washed with pure water." Hebrews 10:22*

> *"He who speaks on his own does so to gain honor for himself, but he who works for the honor of the One who sent him is a man of truth; there is nothing false about him. John 7:18*

> *"Love must be sincere. Hate what is evil; cling to what is good." Romans 12:9*

> *"A truthful witness gives honest testimony, but a false witness tells lies." Proverbs 12:17*

"But the wisdom that comes from heaven is first of all pure; then peace-loving, considerate, submissive, full of mercy and good fruit, impartial and sincere." James 3:17
"The goal of this command is love, which comes from a pure heart and a good conscience and a sincere faith." 1 Timothy 1:5

"They overcame him by the blood of the Lamb and by the word of their testimony; they did not love their lives so much as to shrink from death." Revelation 12:11

"Now that you have purified yourselves by obeying the truth so that you have sincere love for your brothers, love one another deeply, from the heart." 1 Peter 1:22

Remember: Your life is a living epistle; a letter. People read you everyday. Your face. Your actions. Your motives and intentions. Make sure as you lead those intrusted to your care that you end every letter with "sincerely yours".

THE HOME: #12 ~ MANAGE FAMILY WELL

You can tell a lot about a leader by looking inside the walls of his or her home. Many won't invite you into their homes for that very reason! We've all heard horror stories about "PK's" or "preacher's kids", but the truth is that a pastor's children, like anyone's children, should be under loving training which allows a steady development in discipline and maturity. All children will misbehave at times, in public and in private, because "foolishness is bound up in the heart of a child" (Proverbs 22:15). Therefore, we shouldn't judge a leader's home life based entirely on the behavior of his or her children per se, but on how he or she disciplines that behavior.

With six children, getting out is always an interesting adventure. Isn't there a scripture that says, "pandemonium and mayhem resound in the tents with many children"? Everything seems to take longer for our family than a "normal" size family, thus requiring a head start to avoid all miscommunications and clamor. Getting out of the house takes longer, getting into the car takes longer, getting out and into our next stop takes longer, and then keeping everyone from getting separated while looking for a whole row of open seats is usually the final test of each outing. Once when attending a city-wide gathering in downtown Nashville to hear South African Prophet Kim Clement speak, we successfully arrived at the War Memorial Auditorium in tact and proceeded to the front to claim a row of seats that had been reserved for all of campsmith. As we were getting seated, the kids started in: "Mom, can't we go sit with some of our church friends just this once?". We were in the middle of a very difficult season in our family concerning health and finances, and Chris and I had felt it was very important for the eight of us to stick together and worship the Lord side by side as a family and call on His name with one voice. I immediately said no. Unfortunately, the favor of the Lord was on my children and every friend they had in the building was begging. Our kids were persistent, not disrespectful, but still I had given them an answer and they needed to abide by it. So they did and they promptly sat down, although they didn't seem overjoyed about it. I reminded them it was just for a season, and they reminded me this "season" had been going on for four years. Good point God. (At least they were gaining incentive to pray!) Right at that moment, mercy met submission. Chris looked at them, then at me, and decided it would be fine if they went and found their friends just this once. After all, any kid who had turned out to hear a prophet speak couldn't be all that bad. That's when the next test of submission presented itself -- to me. I saw most of the kids get up from my perfect little Partridge family row and scatter throughout the building. We had all of them in eye shot, but still I couldn't understand Chris' decision. Understanding or no, he had made it and I decided the world would keep spinning even if I didn't have all my chicks under-wing. Sincerely, the secret desire of my discouraged heart that night had been to catch the eye of the prophet ("Hark! Who art thou that thou taketh up an entire row?"), and receive some encouraging word from God. Knocking down the sides of my box, God was setting me up for even more of an encouragement than I could ask for or imagine, *if* I would cooperate and trust Him.

The music began, and ministry followed suit, as Prophet Clement is a radically rock-in-roll classically trained pianist who often prophesies with music as well as the spoken word of God. Very early in the meeting, he stood, turned to his far left and pointed up into the balcony and said, "You there! The young boy with the spikey hair, stand to your feet!" We quickly perceived he was speaking to Julian, our teenage son. After prophesying to him about how God was going to "change everybody's life because of him" and that He would "prophesy with song to many nations" (Julian is a guitarist) and because he had an "antagonistic spirit which would torment darkness and raise millions into the Kingdom", he then ministered to a few others and then turned to his far right and pointed into the balcony again, this time toward the other side of the auditorium. "Little Miss Primrose!... That little girl there in the blue dress with the little roses, stand up." We saw our eight year old daughter, Jeorgi, stand up shyly. "You will write poems, songs and books and it will go into the secular arena, and the brain that God has given you will torment the powers of darkness!" He then remarked, "do you have a brother?". The audience began laughing and cheering because many of them knew us, and as he turned back to the crowd they were all pointing at Julian. "What? Aha! I see! Obviously God's got something to do with this!" He then added, "there's another brother over here somewhere isn't there?", and pointed to a totally different area of the balcony that our second son, Jhason, was sitting in. Turning sharply he shouted, "Where is the mother and father? Please tell me this!" Back down on the floor, Chris and I stepped out of our seats with the younger ones, and again, the audience went wild. "My God, you have some anointed children! You have some anointed children, MY GOD!" He proceeded: "Your family is going to ROCK and destroy the powers of darkness over Politics, the Arts, Education and the Legal system. Four arenas! YOUR FAMILY WILL GO IN AND SHAKE THEM SAYS THE LORD!!!". The Spirit of the God was so thick and the cheers of the crowd were so loud that I couldn't even hear myself sobbing. Some of those arenas seemed obvious, but "politics?" Within six months, we found our worlds engaging themselves in all of those arenas, including an invitation from a U.S. Congressman to visit the U.S. Capitol in Washington D.C. with my prayer team and pray for him. Within another six months, I was standing in the home of the Governor and delivering a prophetic word of encouragement to him. Within another three months, I saw a return to the secular entertainment arena for me in the form of television commercials, an arena I had started out in at age 3 and yet laid down many years later to have a family. Being an artistic person who understands artisans and their frequent woundings and sensativities, I do indeed feel like a rock now wherever God sends me in that industry. At times I feel like the "Rev. 007", and there has not been one production set I've been on or one audition I have gone to since that prophecy where God didn't allow me to minister to someone or even lead them to the Lord.

So you see, God had obviously wanted to strengthen and encourage us that night individually and as a family, but in His usual dramatic fashion He wanted to go "out of His way" to do it, a part of the blessing that I would have missed out on had I not submitted to my husband and let the children spread out throughout the building. I couldn't have penned anything that theatrical if I had tried! I firmly believe that through the power released through obedience and submission -- from the children to me and then from me to my husband -- that the Prophet was then able to be in full submission to God and to His perfect plan for that perfect word to be released. Had even one link in the chain been missing -- or had my husband's heart not been tender towards his children God gave him to lead -- the evening would have had an entirely different ending.

God uses the family structure as a means by which to train us and develop His character in us. We cannot claim to be religious and neglect our parents or children. Consider the following related verses carefully:

> *"Listen, my son, to your father's instruction and do not forsake your mother's teaching." Proverbs 1:8*

> *"But if a widow has children or grandchildren, these should learn first of all to put their religion into practice by caring for their own family and so repaying their parents and grandparents, for this is pleasing to God." 1 Timothy 5:4*

"He will turn the hearts of the fathers to their children, and the hearts of the children to their fathers; or else I will come and strike the land with a curse." Malachi 4:6

"If anyone does not provide for his relatives, and especially for his immediate family, he has denied the faith and is worse than an unbeliever." 1 Timothy 5:8

"By faith Noah, when warned about things not yet seen, in holy fear built an ark to save his family." Hebrews 11:7

"Our fathers disciplined us for a little while as they thought best; but God disciplines us for our good, that we may share in his holiness." Hebrews 12:10

"Fathers, do not exasperate your children; instead, bring them up in the training and instruction of the Lord." Ephesians 6:4

"Even though you have ten thousand guardians in Christ, you do not have many fathers, for in Christ Jesus I became your father through the gospel." 1 Corinthians 4:15

"Like mother, like daughter." Ezekiel 16:44

"A wise servant will rule over a disgraceful son, and will share the inheritance as one of the brothers." Proverbs 17:2

"But we were gentle among you, like a mother caring for her little children." 1 Thessalonians 2:7

*"Which of you fathers, if your son asks for a fish, will give

him a snake instead?" Luke 11:11

"Fathers, do not embitter your children, or they will become discouraged." Colossians 3:21

"I have been reminded of your sincere faith, which first lived in your grandmother Lois and in your mother Eunice and, I am persuaded, now lives in you also." 2 Timothy 1:5

"He who brings trouble on his family will inherit only wind, and the fool will be servant to the wise." Proverbs 11:29

"She gets up while it is still dark; she provides food for her family and portions for her servant girls." Proverbs 31:15

THE HANDS: #7 ~ "ABLE TO TEACH"

"Diligent hands will rule, but laziness ends in slave labor." Proverbs 12:24

"Bless all his skills, O LORD, and be pleased with the work of his hands." Deuteronomy 33:11

"From the fruit of his lips a man is filled with good things as surely as the work of his hands rewards him." Proverbs 12:14

I learn best by example. Most of us do, whether you're discussing textbooks or people. I can learn from a book, but I can learn faster by application. For me, it's that way with cooking, with driving, and with watching my leaders. They are able to teach me best when they live out their lives -- as managers and as mortals -- in front of me, no-holds-barred as living epistles.

"You are manifestly an epistle of Christ, ministered by us, written not with ink but by the Spirit of the living God, not on tablets of stone but on tablets of flesh, that is, of the heart." 2 Corinthians 3:3

You may not consider yourself a leader in any area, and you may not think you have many people watching you, but I guarantee you that even if you aren't an apostle you are an epistle! Someone is watching you! Someone is reading the script of your life! Your actions are speaking louder than your words, and the work of your hands -- in ministry, in business, in parenthood, in marriage -- is forever being examined and judged by many more than you'd care to know about. It sways the decisions for their lives. What if you could always be a clear well-written letter inscribed with the hand of God for others to read? What if your marriage so evidenced joy that it diminished fear of commitment in others' minds? What if people saw your intimate relationship with God, felt a holy jealousy, and ran after Him with a new hunger? All of that without a word! St. Francis of Assisi is quoted as saying, "Preach the gospel. Use words if necessary." Amen!

"Watch me," he told them. "Follow my lead. When I get to the edge of the camp, do exactly as I do." Judges 7:17

Peruse these scriptures and discover what God has to say about the importance of teaching. These are lessons that could be learned by all teachers everywhere.

"He said to them, "Therefore every teacher of the law who has been instructed about the kingdom of heaven is like the owner of a house who brings out of his storeroom new

treasures as well as old." Matthew 13:52

"Not only was the Teacher wise, but also he imparted knowledge to the people. He pondered and searched out and set in order many proverbs. The Teacher searched to find just the right words, and what he wrote was upright and true." Ecclesiastes 12:9-10

"They sent their disciples to him along with the Herodians. "Teacher," they said, "we know you are a man of integrity and that you teach the way of God in accordance with the truth. You aren't swayed by men, because you pay no attention to who they are." Matthew 22:16

"A student is not above his teacher, but everyone who is fully trained will be like his teacher." Luke 6:40

"When Jesus had finished saying these things, the crowds were amazed at his teaching, because he taught as one who had authority, and not as their teachers of the law. When he came down from the mountainside, large crowds followed him." Matthew 7:28

"Some of the teachers of the law responded, "Well said, teacher!"" Luke 20:39

"And in the church God has appointed first of all apostles, second prophets, third teachers."
1 Corinthians 12:28

"It was he who gave some to be apostles, some to be prophets, some to be evangelists, and some to be pastors and teachers." Ephesians 4:11

More crucial is the volume of Scripture devoted to forewarning teachers to practice what they preach!

"Not many of you should presume to be teachers, my brothers, because you know that we who teach will be judged more strictly." James 3:1

"You, then, who teach others, do you not teach yourself? You who preach against stealing, do you steal? You who say that people should not commit adultery, do you commit adultery? You who abhor idols, do you rob temples? You who brag about the law, do you dishonor God by breaking the law? " Romans 2:21-23

"Nor are you to be called 'teacher,' for you have one Teacher, the Christ." Matthew 23:10
"As he taught, Jesus said, "Watch out for the teachers of the law. They like to walk around in flowing robes and be greeted in the marketplaces, and have the most important seats in the synagogues and the places of honor at banquets. They devour widows' houses and for a show make lengthy prayers. Such men will be punished most severely."
Mark 12:38-40

"Anyone who breaks one of the least of these commandments and teaches others to do the same will be called least in the kingdom of heaven, but whoever practices and teaches these commands will be called great in the kingdom of heaven. For I tell you that unless your righteousness surpasses that of the Pharisees and the teachers of the law, you will certainly not enter the kingdom of heaven." Matthew 5:19-20

"In fact, though by this time you ought to be teachers, you

need someone to teach you the elementary truths of God's word all over again. You need milk, not solid food!"
Hebrews 5:12

"Who is it he is trying to teach? To whom is he explaining his message? To children weaned from their milk, to those just taken from the breast?" For it is: Do and do, do and do, rule on rule, rule on rule; a little here, a little there."
Isaiah 28:9-10

"For the time will come when men will not put up with sound doctrine. Instead, to suit their own desires, they will gather around them a great number of teachers to say what their itching ears want to hear." 2 Timothy 4:3

"But there were also false prophets among the people, just as there will be false teachers among you. They will secretly introduce destructive heresies, even denying the sovereign Lord who bought them --bringing swift destruction on themselves." 2 Peter 2:1

Before moving on, I'd like to comment on the last scripture noted: 2 Peter 2:1. It is a very serious thing to be a false prophet, but it is an equally serious thing to falsely accuse someone of being a false prophet! I remember once many years ago I was called a false prophet. I didn't even know at the time that I had a call upon my life into prophetic ministry or that I would eventually be ordained as Prophet. But I lost a lot of sleep over it fearing the accusation might be true, all because I had explicitly stated something for myself personally that did not come true when I thought it would. I had moved in presumption and birthed an "Ishmael", but when I went to the Lord He reassured me of the purity of my heart in testing my wings. He used it to train me in ministry, and He used it to test my character, but in the end here is what He left me with. "You may have been a wrong prophet, but you will never be a false prophet". He also reminded me, that we "know in part and we prophesy in part" (1 Corinthians 13:9), so He did not condemn me for having to learn to hear Him better. False prophets "secretly introduce destructive heresies, even denying the sovereign Lord" (2 Peter 2:1), and that is something I had not, and never will do.

God sees the heart. If we err as leaders, may we err on the side of faith! Better to be a wrong prophet with a small audience but with a tender heart trying to better hear the voice of God, than a proud teacher with a large audience and a hard heart that maddens the Almighty.

"Then Jesus said to the crowds and to his disciples: "The teachers of the law and the Pharisees sit in Moses' seat. So you must obey them and do everything they tell you. But do not do what they do, for they do not practice what they preach. They tie up heavy loads and put them on men's shoulders, but they themselves are not willing to lift a finger to move them. "Everything they do is done for men to see: They make their phylacteries wide and the tassels on their garments long; they love the place of honor at banquets and the most important seats in the synagogues; they love to be greeted in the marketplaces and to have men call them `Rabbi.' "But you are not to be called `Rabbi,' for you have only one Master and you are all brothers. And do not call anyone on earth `father,' for you have one Father, and he is in heaven. Nor are you to be called `teacher,' for you have one Teacher, the Christ. The greatest among you will be your servant. For whoever exalts himself will be humbled,

and whoever humbles himself will be exalted. "Woe to you, teachers of the law and Pharisees, you hypocrites! You shut the kingdom of heaven in men's faces. You yourselves do not enter, nor will you let those enter who are trying to.

"Woe to you, teachers of the law and Pharisees, you hypocrites! You travel over land and sea to win a single convert, and when he becomes one, you make him twice as much a son of hell as you are. "Woe to you, blind guides! You say, `If anyone swears by the temple, it means nothing; but if anyone swears by the gold of the temple, he is bound by his oath.' You blind fools! Which is greater: the gold, or the temple that makes the gold sacred? You also say, `If anyone swears by the altar, it means nothing; but if anyone swears by the gift on it, he is bound by his oath.' You blind men! Which is greater: the gift, or the altar that makes the gift sacred? Therefore, he who swears by the altar swears by it and by everything on it. And he who swears by the temple swears by it and by the one who dwells in it. And he who swears by heaven swears by God's throne and by the one who sits on it. "Woe to you, teachers of the law and Pharisees, you hypocrites! You give a tenth of your spices -- mint, dill and cummin. But you have neglected the more important matters of the law --justice, mercy and faithfulness. You should have practiced the latter, without neglecting the former. You blind guides! You strain out a gnat but swallow a camel. "Woe to you, teachers of the law and Pharisees, you hypocrites! You clean the outside of the cup and dish, but inside they are full of greed and self-indulgence. Blind Pharisee! First clean the inside of the cup and dish, and then the outside also will be clean. "Woe to you, teachers of the law and Pharisees, you hypocrites! You are like whitewashed tombs, which look beautiful on the outside but on the inside are full of dead men's bones and everything unclean. In the same way, on the outside you *appear to people as righteous but on the inside you are full of hypocrisy and wickedness." Matthew 23:1-28*

CONCLUSION

Perhaps you should keep that second list you made before you -- the one which details the people under your care and the ways in which you should better serve them. Revisit and revise it often, praying through this last grouping of Scriptures as you do.

"Give me wisdom and knowledge, that I may lead this people, for who is able to govern this great people of yours?"" 2 Chronicles 1:10

"Then I will give you shepherds after my own heart, who will lead you with knowledge and understanding." Jeremiah 3:15

"He also told them this parable: "Can a blind man lead a blind man? Will they not both fall into a pit? A student is not above his teacher, but everyone who is fully trained will be like his teacher." Luke 6:39-40

"By me princes govern, and all nobles who rule on earth." Proverbs 8:16

"When the righteous thrive, the people rejoice; when the wicked rule, the people groan." Proverbs 29:2

"See, a king will reign in righteousness and rulers will rule with justice." Isaiah 32:1

"Do not rule over them ruthlessly, but fear your God." Leviticus 25:43

A Prayer for Leaders:

Take false caution out of me
Fill me with transparency
Clean my heart, my home, my hands
As my leadership expands

Govern, guide and promise me
Strict accountability
Test me, try my wherewithal
Or don't let me lead at all

"Now that I, your Lord and Teacher, have washed your feet, you also should wash one another's feet. I have set you an example that you should do as I have done for you."
John 13:14-15

Chapter 20

FREQUENT TRYER MILES

The Trophies of Trying Submission!

I've won the Nobel Peace Prize
The Twenty-one Gun Salute
A Grammy, Tony, Oscar
And a Pulitzer to boot

Olympic medals everywhere
An Eagle-Scout Badge too
The Heisman and the Winston Cup
With Wimbledon in view

I've won the People's Choice Award
On People Magazine
Been decorated by a King
And crowned Homecoming Queen

My Superbowl Ring flashes
Like the medals on my chest
But though my trophy case is full
My laurels cannot rest

I still chase after one prize
That no accolades can bring
With that award: *Submission's Sword*
The victory song I'll sing!

EISENHOWER

The week before starting this chapter, I awoke to an interesting vision. Actually, I awoke that morning to a deluge of warfare, a warfare that I will describe later on herein, but the vision God brought helped me put in perspective this particular battle -- a battle I had been fighting for twenty-three years. I saw a man, Dwight D. Eisenhower, and he was in full military dress uniform. Not camouflage, but the commander's suit. He was so highly decorated that the normal left lapel that usually sports ranks and honors couldn't contain all his medals. His ENTIRE jacket, from collar to hem, top to bottom, was covered in colorful pins and war medals. I'd never seen anything like it! That was it. I opened my eyes and felt encouraged that the Lord would answer my heart's question in this sweet way. My heart's questions were the same ones I'd been asking for years: "Why must I awake every morning to war, Lord?" ..."I understand that you have fashioned me for war, and have trained me up as a warrior, but isn't every warrior entitled to a cave every once in a while? What on earth requires this much training?" Then came the vision I just described. I knew then that God saw my battle scars and would reward me accordingly. But what puzzled me was why he used Eisenhower, a man who I and most of the nation just view as another President. I got up and studied "Ike's" life.

I had no idea how decorated Dwight D. Eisenhower was as a military leader with over thirty years of war experience. Raised by deeply religious parents with six children, he was the third child (as am I). His parents strongly opposed war, and he respected their wishes but entered military school after high school only because tuition was free and he had given all his money to send his older brother to college. Without itemizing his entire military career, suffice it to say that he rose quickly to the highest rank in the Army, a four star general, and had so much more success afterwards that he was awarded a newly created rank of "five star general". He changed the course of history with his direct combat leadership in many battles, and in both World Wars. He was often promoted by Presidents over other officers who were older and had more seniority. In about one year's time, he was the Commanding General of U.S. Forces, was named Supreme commander of the World Allied Forces, and then created and executed a war plan that resulted in Nazi Germany's surrender in 1945, ending World War II. One year! He then became Supreme Commander of NATO. He planned military defenses that amazed the world. He was a man of great discipline and organization, but felt that good leadership was not a matter of issuing orders and enforcing obedience, but of inspiring others to cooperate to use their own talents to the fullest. When he was finally "talked into" running for President, he was so popular that both the Republican and Democratic tickets were begging him to be their candidate. He chose the Republican ticket. Over and over, his is a story of a soldier in the White House, acquainted with war, but a diplomat who had learned to keep the world at peace. He was so able to bring unity amongst both parties to work together that by 1956, the U.S. Treasury actually had a small surplus and there was no national debt.

Famous Eisenhower quotes:

"...in the final choice, a soldier's pack is not so heavy a burden as a prisoner's chains"
    (1st Inaugural Address, 1953)

"...what counts is not necessarily the size of the dog in the fight -- it's the size of the fight in the dog."
(Speech to the Republican National Committee, 1958)

THE DRAFT

What an honor to be compared to this war hero by God. Some people, especially other women, may not understand my love of combat and conquering, but then, I do not understand most people's love of passivity and indifference. I do not see war as the absence of peace, but instead find my greatest peace on the frontlines of God's battle, fully engaged in progressing His army and kingdom. Faith involves risk. I love living on that edge -- not moving out in presumption -- but fully willing to pick up in a moment's notice and fight off the hordes of hell that oppose God's will being done on earth as it is in heaven. People are quick to call Jesus the Lamb of God, but fail to remember He is also the Lion of the Tribe of Judah. Exodus 15:3 says, "The LORD is a warrior; the LORD is his name", so if I am praying to be made into God's image, then that is a dangerous prayer that will inevitably result in my recruitment into battle.

As we close out this book with a section called "The Clout" in a chapter about my trophies of submission, I am obligated to share with you one of those dangers I have lived through. A danger which has nearly cost me my life, a danger which qualifies me to pen this book, and a danger which was dismantled through submission and submission alone.

I guess you could say I was drafted into this war that I have fought for over two decades. I certainly did not sign up voluntarily. Not knowingly anyhow. I did sign up for

God's army of course, becoming a Christian when I was just ten years old and having experienced sweet visitations from the Holy Spirit in my bedroom as a little girl even years before that. But I had no idea that God was trying to do anything more than give me the basics: love, joy, and peace. I remember hearing that if you were really brave you prayed for patience, and so I did. Bad decision. Bad for the flesh, but of course, advantageous for the spirit.

In 1978 I was diagnosed with petit mal epilepsy. I was just thirteen years old, and had started experiencing short absences in consciousness in which I would be engaged in conversation one minute, and then next, sort of drifting off for a few moments, totally unaware of anything around me. I couldn't hear; I couldn't speak; I sort of just "left" and went somewhere else for a few seconds. Not knowing what these episodes were, I called them "Big Mac attacks", since McDonalds had just launched their new big mac campaign! When my parents took me to a pediatric neurologist, he quickly recognized it as a form of epilepsy called petit mal, or "small seizures". I was put on medication, and went about my life without any interruptions.

The diagnosis didn't really rock my boat, since my focus was on other things at the time. Two things in particular: cheerleading and Jesus. Funny, since that has seemed to sum up my purpose in ministry all of these years! I was a kingdom zealot even then, not really understanding the full gospel by any means, but definitely set on helping purchase tickets to heaven for all of my jr. high friends. I held a weekly Bible study in my neighborhood for kids whose parents didn't take them to church. I remember one day when seven teenagers got saved in my front yard all at once. It is without arrogance that I can now say that I was most definitely a threat to the kingdom of darkness. Even if I didn't know it, Satan did. I think that is the point in time when God drafted me, and sort of like the unknowing vow I took which I described back in chapter one, I signed up having no idea what I was really in for.

> "You do not test the resources of God until you attempt the impossible" ~ F. B. Meyer

THE FRIDAY NIGHT BIBLE STUDIES

The next twelve years were seemingly peaceful, and were only interrupted by an occasional visit to the neurologist when an adjustment needed to be made in my medication. By now I was married and a mother of two, and we enjoyed a quiet Christian life which included a Friday night Bible study where a dozen of our closest friends would congregate in our home to dig into the word of God for buried treasure. That's when the trouble started. We were stirring up hornets' nests in the spirit, totally unaware of the threat we were to an enemy that some of us weren't totally comfortable discussing to begin with. We were a group who didn't let any grass grow under our feet, spiritually speaking, and when you got us all together in one room we would challenge each other to the highest places our faith could go. We were iron sharpening iron, young -- barely in our twenties -- and just green enough to believe that if we could find something in God's word, we should be able to find it in our lives. We had no idea the destiny-packed lives that were about to embarked upon. We are all in our late thirties or forties now, but are all still intricately involved in each other's journeys, even though it be from a bit more afar. The holy anointing of God that was upon that Friday Night Group has transcended all time, still showing up on street corners, in offices and in each other's homes as we run into each other from time to time after months or even years of being apart.

One particular Friday night, I put out an unusual prayer request to the gang. I had recently given birth to our third child and second son, Jhason, and he had remained jaundiced for so many weeks after his birth that the specialists we'd brought in were now talking total blood transfusions. Jhason and I both had the same blood type, and so I volunteered, but when the doctors learned that I was on anti-convulsants for absence seizures, they declined my request to be the donor. For the first time in twelve years, my epilepsy was now an inconvenience. It was officially interfering with my life. Doctors at Vanderbilt Medical Center were telling me that perhaps my medicine was even causing the prolonged jaundice, since I was breast feeding Jhason and was his sole source of nourishment at the time. They told me I should stop nursing. Another inconvenience that brought me to a crossroad. Stop nursing, something I believed firmly in and was an advocate to other mothers for, or dig deep inside God's Word and see if all my Friday night buddies were right in saying that God was a healing God. I subconsciously skirted the issue one last time and instead begged Vanderbilt to make me a case study by testing my breast milk to discover the effects of such anti-convulsants upon it. The study was successful, stating that "only trace amounts of the drug were found, therefore breast feeding is not contraindicated", and so I continued nursing and felt temporary victory. Still, Jhason got worse. He had already been a month premature, and now doctors were telling me that if this went on any longer his little liver would be in grave danger. With a blood transfusion scheduled for the next Monday morning and my mother lined up as the donor, I entered Friday night Bible study that week with a heavy, somber heart.

THE FLEECE

My desperation, mixed with my friends' love and convincing arguments from the Word of God, sparked a bit of faith in my heart concerning healing. I think that was the night God gave me my mustard seed. It was June 1990. I'd really never had a need to trust in God as a Healer before then, as ludicrous as that seems after twelve years of seizures. But now, God was up in my face forcing me to study His Word and decide. I didn't want to do it. The arguments in my mind as to why God didn't heal -- all the relatives and friends I had lost or seen struggle with various infirmities -- were no match for the Word of God. That's the honest truth, as much as I hate to admit it. I was much more comfortable preaching my experiences on the matter than God's Word, for if I began to find Scriptures that plainly stated God's desire was to heal the sick, then I would have no choice but to rearrange my whole world. As a test that night, I allowed the gang to pray over me and told God I would ask Him for healing -- for Jhason and maybe for me if He had time -- but that my "fleece" in testing Him about all this healing stuff would be if Jhason would be healed by Monday morning in time to cancel his blood transfusion. That is exactly what happened.

I was stunned. After two long months, Jhason's billirubin count was suddenly normal. His skin regained perfect color and his little body seemed stronger than ever. It was during that time that I discovered the meaning to Jhason's name: "healer". All added up together, I found myself engaged in a supernatural curiosity to take God at His Word, and so I waited in faith for my own breakthrough for healing. Satan, afraid of my newfound faith in healing but seeing that I had no awareness of spiritual warfare, decided to butt in in a crafty way that would steal every ounce of faith that I had. That very week, I had my first grand mal convulsion.

Not grounded well enough yet in the healing scriptures, I assumed this was God's answer to me. He did not want me well. In some warped religious way, I felt like it was all right to pray "thy will be done" prayers without first asking God to reveal His will. Now I know though that Ephesians 5:17 says, "Do not be unwise, but understand what the will of the Lord is". Once you find out the will of God -- through prayers and open ears -- you are then cornered into warring for it in prayer despite what demonic opposition you may face. It is much easier just to not ask and not know, but God can't answer your prayers to grow you up in Him if you are never willing to go there. At the time, I was not willing. It just didn't seem logical to me yet. So, not understanding that faith bypasses logic, I told my Friday Night friends that this must be God's answer: God wanted Jhason well, but not me. They told me He was no respecter of persons, but somehow I could not be swayed. I'm sure once again all of Heaven sighed and waited for my will to fully submit to the God it claimed to belong to. A few more hard years would have to pass first.

"The sinful mind is hostile to God. It does not submit to God's law, nor can it do so."
Romans 8:7

BABY #4

There's a rumor in our family that our fourth child, Jeorgi, owes her life to me since I was the one who talked her well-budgeted father into breaking outside of the then popular 3-child family norm and trusting God enough to have another baby (after #4, no more convincing was necessary!). Proud to say I trusted God and was full of faith for this child, I somehow failed to see my deficit of faith for what I really needed: healing. Those two worlds were about to collide. Pregnant once again, the medication I was on -- now a new one -- presented problems to the pregnancy we had not foreseen. There were risks of neurotube defects in the baby such as spina bifoda. We were overwhelmed and outraged at how we'd never been told this. Having already been on the medicine for the first few weeks of the pregnancy, we decided to pursue a quick change. The neurologist did just that, but we would not find out until three months later that the medication he had placed me on was a barbiturate. I spent my first trimester in a drug-induced stupor, sleeping about twenty-two hours every day. Our church helped care for us and brought food to the house regularly. Chris and the kids pitched in and did laundry and kept the house running. With all that time on my hands -- sleeping or resting -- God dealt with me inside and out. There is nothing more tormenting than a soul that is chasing God and running away from Him all at the same time.

God was chasing me down to believe him for healing. Little by little I trusted Him for more and more details in my health, and at this juncture it would be to trust Him enough to get back on the normal medication so I could get out of bed, and then entrust the unborn baby's health to him. I did, and Jeorgi Anna was born right on time and in perfect health. You may remember she was also our first child born with her Daddy's blue eyes, and thus came the family joke that my genes had finally started submitting to Chris'. Boy was God dealing with me on the issue! Stride for stride with my ability to give my whole heart to him, I began to give Him my whole body too. Wasn't I made up of three parts just like God? Could I really be entirely His if I believed Him for spiritual and emotional healings but not for physical ones? Could I really live anymore with a "que sera, sera, whatever will be, will be" attitude, or was it up to me -- as it is with salvation -- to believe it before I could receive it? Didn't Isaiah say, "surely He took up our infirmities and carried our sorrows, yet we considered him stricken by God, smitten by him, and afflicted"? (Isaiah 53:4) Wasn't He "pierced for our transgressions, he was crushed for our iniquities; the punishment that brought us peace was upon him, and by his wounds we are healed."? (Isaiah 53:5) Didn't Matthew say the exact same thing too after seeing Jesus perform healings?

> *"This was to fulfill what was spoken through the prophet Isaiah: "He took up our infirmities and carried our diseases.""* Matthew 8:17

I began to devour the Word of God and discovered that from Genesis to Revelation, healing wasn't just something God does it's who He is. Within a few months I was clinging to God with full faith for healing, and I went to the pastor of the church I was in at the time and asked to be prayed over for healing with the anointing of oil according to James 5:14. There had only been one other woman in the history of the church who had done this, and she had died. I was jumping across chasms that had never been jumped across before by any people in my circle, and as a result I gained myself a reputation for being quite out of my mind! Again, faith involves risk, and sometimes it just looks downright irresponsible. Within a few more months we were leaving that precious congregation and joining another that would give us fuel for the fight we were in. At that church, Harvest International Church, we were stuffed full of a side of God's Word we had never heard taught from a pulpit before. It's as if we had totally neglected certain portions of God's word, and allowed the enemy to convince us that those sections were just not a living and active part of modern Christianity. Make no mistake, I knew God *could* heal, I just never understood that He *would*. We have not because we ask not.

"Bless the Lord, O my soul; and all that is within me, bless His holy name! Bless the Lord, O my soul, and forget not all His benefits: who forgives all your iniquities and who heals all your diseases." Psalm 103: 1-3

BY DUE PROCESS

On January 26th, 1993 -- it was a Tuesday -- I sat on my living room sofa and met God. Having walked with Him for almost twenty years by this point, and having received the baptism of His Holy Spirit just a few months before -- the same baptism that John the Baptist prophesied when he said, "I baptize you with water for repentance. But after me will come one who is more powerful than I, whose sandals I am not fit to carry. He will baptize you with the Holy Spirit and with fire." Matthew 3:11 -- on that day all my questions to God about healing for my body were all answered. I thought I had finally reached the end of this long search, but little did I know then it was just the beginning -- literally. I heard God speak: "Yes I want to heal you, in fact, I have already begun to, but it will be by process". He was referring to the seizures. He would later show me the verse in Exodus 23:30 which says, "Little by little I will drive them out from before you, until you have increased enough to take possession of the land." I remember thinking "by process" meant four or five days. Well, those four or five days turned into four or five months, then four or five years and then double that! I began to see that getting me to believe in healing was not God's main objective here as I had thought. His pinnacle plan was to get me to believe in it so entirely that I would keep believing no matter what I saw... or didn't see. With that measure of faith, He could then heal me but then go beyond healing to wholeness, hereby depositing healing ministry into me. In essence, God had brought me full circle and plopped me right back down in the same spot in the road I was before. However, I was no longer "under" attack, but over it. I had wanted to conquer, but Jesus wanted me to be *more* than a conqueror. I was still sick. Only now, it was with a holy inoculation. Before, the seizures were a thorn. Now, each one actually served as an immunization against the disease as a whole. It would just be a matter of time. Just like a doctor wisely injects just enough of the virus in an attempt to help the body grow in resistance against the real thing that may come along one day, God was allowing these seizures to remain in my life for a season in an attempt to draw me into my destiny as a warrior against this spirit as a whole. A spirit that Jesus identifies in Mark 9 as a "deaf and dumb" spirit.

"Then one from the multitude answered and said, 'Teacher, I brought You my son, who has a mute spirit. And wherever he seizes him, he throws him down; he foams at the mouth, gnashes his teeth, and becomes rigid. So I spoke to Your disciples, that they should cast him out, but they could not.' He answered him and said, 'O faithless generation, how long shall I be with you? How long shall I bear with you? Bring him to Me.' Then they brought him to Him. And

when he saw Him, immediately the spirit convulsed him, and he fell on the ground and wallowed, foaming at the mouth. So He asked his father, 'How long has this been happening to him?' And he said, 'From childhood. And often he has thrown him both into the fire and into the water to destroy him. But if You can do anything, have compassion on us and help us.' Jesus said to him, 'If you can believe, all things are possible to him who believe.' Immediately, the father of the child cried out and said with tears, 'Lord, I believe; help my unbelief!' When Jesus saw that the people came running together, He rebuked the unclean spirit, saying to him, 'You deaf and dumb spirit, I command you, come out of him, and enter him no more!' Then the spirit cried out, convulsed him greatly, and came out of him. And he became as one dead, so that many said, 'He is dead.' But Jesus took him by the hand and lifted him up, and he arose. And when He had come into the house, His disciples asked Him privately, 'Why could we not cast him out?' So He said to them, 'This kind can come out by nothing but prayer and fasting,'" Mark 9:14-29

"ONE HEALING TO GO PLEASE"

Get a miracle instantly and you'll have healing put into you. Get a miracle by process and you'll have healing *ministry* put into you. One brings passion, the other brings compassion.... and extra passion too! Although I wanted the drive-thru version, God's mission was to draw my faith out for something greater. I wanted healing for my body, and He wanted healing for a city. A city which I would soon learn was under the sway of this same deaf and dumb spirit. My home city, Nashville, Tennessee, is a wonderful place full of God's work. It is home to Gideon's International (the largest distributor of Bibles in the world), the Baptist Sunday School Board (world's largest producer of Sunday school material), "The Upper Room" (a Methodist publication and one of the most widely circulated Christian devotionals ever), Thomas Nelson Publishers (the world's largest Bible producers), and countless, countless denominational headquarters and Christian colleges. We have more churches per capita than any other American city, with more than one per square mile throughout the region. All of this looks wonderful from the outside, but on the inside produces much confusion and disunity. Each church has its own camp and stays there, while God's purposes for the city as a whole are never realized. Relationship is replaced with religion. Change is in a constant battle with tradition. Competition and pride take the place of humility, and as a result, God resists us. "For God resists the proud, but gives favor to the humble" 1 Peter 5:5. As a result of God's resistance -- especially to a people who are working so hard "for" Him -- faith eventually succumbs to unbelief. So what does all this have to do with a deaf and dumb spirit?

In the winter of 1994, Rabbi Richard Glickstein, a Christian Jew and Prophet who was visiting from Russia and speaking at our church, approached me after the Sunday morning service and began to pray over me, releasing the following prophecy: "That which hinders you hinders the city, and when he falls many under him will fall and widespread healing will be released." He had no idea what all had been climaxing in my health. As if it wasn't enough that I didn't understand how what hindered me could hinder the city, I also was stumped by how he was referring to it as a "he". When I got home and studied the Mark 9 passage, I understood that Nashville must be suffering from the sway of a deaf and dumb territorial spirit. Jesus even refers to the spirit as a "he" or a "him" 5 times in the passage. Territorial spirits are described all over the Bible, in passages like Daniel 10 where Daniel has been fasting for his people and region for twenty-one days and finally an angel (who some believe was the Lord) comes and tells him that his prayers have been heard but that there is a fierce battle going on in the heavenlies. He tells Daniel that he has been trying to get to him for twenty-one days, but that he has had to "withstand the Prince of Persia", which was a demonic territorial spirit laying claim to that area. Before leaving he assures Daniel that he will return to the battle where Michael the archangel will now assist him, and that there will be victory through Daniel's prayers. He wasn't merely fighting off a demon, but a territorial spirit that had been given legal claim to that area due to sin. It would take time, and it would also take prayer and fasting.

"The seventy-two returned with joy and said, 'Lord, even the demons submit to us in Your name.'" Luke 10:17

In a region where a deaf and dumb spirit rules (which we just saw in Mark 9:29 only comes out through prayer and fasting), the people there will seem to have a spiritual deafness as well as an inability to boldly speak the whole Word of God, or the "full gospel". Like the deaf and dumb spirit did to the little boy, and to me, that spirit manifesting in a city or nation will make the Body (of Christ) rigid and seek to destroy it entirely. As a result of the Body of Christ being unable to "hear" the voice of the Lord and His fresh mandates for winning today's world, that deafness produces a people which cling to dead tradition. In their defense, they are clinging to what they at least know God spoke yesterday, because they sincerely cannot hear His rhema voice today. This territorial spirit's influence on unbelievers is such that it causes them to not hear the gospel at all. Not only are their ears clogged, but the muted mouths of Christians imprisoned to dead tradition fails to win them at all. It is an endless cycle of the deaf and dumb spirit, and results in the eventual dissemination of the thriving Church. Why? "Faith comes by hearing and hearing by the word of God" (Romans 10:17). Where there is no hearing, there can be no faith.

MY MISSION: SUBMISSION

As I began to get the big picture, I got excited about submitting to it. God didn't just want me to pray for my healing, but for my people's healing. It was the beginning of prophetic ministry. Prophetic embodiment. God had told Hosea to marry a prostitute to embody His heartache over Israel's disloyalty to him. He'd afflicted Jacob with a wound because he wrestled with God for something that God wanted him to have to begin with, but used the struggle to draw passion and submission out of Jacob to maintain it. That struggle resulted in more than a blessed man. It gave birth to a blessed people. "For our struggle is not against flesh and blood, but against the rulers, against the authorities, against the powers of this dark world and against the spiritual forces of evil in the heavenly realms." Ephesians 6:12.

Still, I didn't understand how God could say no one was listening in Nashville -- a city where the gospel was so promoted and taught, but then I found verses like Matthew 13:13: "Though seeing, they do not see; though hearing, they do not hear or understand." He then commissioned me with Acts 28:26: "'Go to this people and say, "You will be ever hearing but never understanding; you will be ever seeing but never perceiving.", but He also put the words of

Jeremiah in my mouth: "Oh land, land, land, hear the word of the Lord!" (Jeremiah 22:29). Realizing that in Matthew 12:29 Jesus said about prayer that if we "bind the strongman" we can go in and "plunder his whole house", I came to grips with the truth that God was calling me into a warfare in which he would have me pray and rally others to pray against the deaf and dumb spirit over our precious city, thereby causing "many under him to fall" (as was prophesied by Rabbi Glickstein). I saw those underneath him as Pride, Tradition, Religion and Unbelief. This was no skirmish. God was going to plunder Satan's whole house.

"For the eyes of the Lord run to and fro throughout the whole earth, to show Himself strong on behalf of those whose heart is loyal to Him." 2 Chronicles 16:9

Suddenly, with the submission to what God was doing, Chris and I began to notice that God was sending various speakers into the city to confirm His work. I remember once when sitting in the first conference that Prophet Jim Goll taught at in the city, his wife, Michal Ann, stopped in the middle of her teaching and said, "There is a deaf and dumb spirit over this area!". I suppose she could tell by the way people were responding -- or not responding -- to the raw meat she was laying on our plates that day. I bless the Golls for their role in pioneering prophetic ministry. I fully believe God moved them to Nashville just for me! I began to notice a real shift in the heavenlies over Nashville from then on, and from Jim's constant weekly teachings throughout the city emerged a faithful group of intercessors to help in the hand to hand combat of this prayer effort.

THE BEE'S NEST

One night while in one of Jim's weekly classes, he called me forward to be prayed over. I was so glad, as I had been undergoing tremendous warfare in my health which he did not know about. After much prayer and fasting during 1993, God had spoken to me about coming off of my medication, not because He is anti-medicine or because He desires everyone to do that, but because He saw in my heart the unhealthy trust I had put in doctors and in my medication -- a trust that I didn't realize was competing with my trust in God. It was as if it was my only lifeline to health. When you are diagnosed with something as a child and taught to be responsible with a daily medication, it is hard once an adult to ever view life without it. That is what God needed to break down in my mind, and for me, the stronghold was so great that it was in direct conflict with the faith God was trying to build in me. As a result, on October 31st, 1993 -- after ten months and five days of intense prayer and fasting -- God released me to lay down my anti-convulsants. Chris agreed and so we had unity in our house and proceeded. Everything was fine in the months ahead. No major seizures but the same amount of usual small absence ones. And then the plot thickened. As soon as I began to speak out publicly about this battle and rally others to pray along with me, it's like a wanted poster went up in hell with my face and name on it.

Several years went by and I was still praying and getting the word out. I was also being raised up into higher places of leadership around the city and country and so my platform to mobilize intercessors grew. Suddenly my health worsened. What had happened? Why was God allowing this? Wasn't I doing exactly what He told me to do? Hadn't I prayed and fasted and rallied others to do so? Weren't we all remaining humble? "What on earth had I done wrong?!!!" Nothing. Nada. Zippo. I can say that now, although in the midst of such warfare the temptation is to scrape the sides of your heart clean 100 times looking for the hidden sin that's causing everything. I was not in secret sin. I was, however in secret ignorance. Ignorance to the effectiveness of a stealth weapon called submission.

So while at Jim Goll's class that Monday night, he called me forward and prayed. He began to cry, stating, "She has stirred up such a bee's nest! Such a bee's nest!". He was tearful as he prophesied, as if God's heart was breaking over it. Could something I was doing be reducing God to a spectator in the whole event? Maybe something I was *not* doing? Why was I now suffering memory loss? On many days I was having over 100 petit mal seizures just while awake, more while asleep, and then of course there were the unpredictable convulsions.

> "Vindicate me, O LORD, for I have led a blameless life; I have trusted in the LORD without wavering. Test me, O LORD, and try me, examine my heart and my mind."
> Psalm 26:1-2

THE DESERT

The years that followed were hard ones. I had to learn to praise God with thanks for things I'd never seen. During this time, we had another baby boy, our fifth child, and named him Jude, which means "praise". As if the battle wasn't hard enough, there were few people who truly understood why I wanted to be there. I had walked away from one camp that didn't believe in God's divine health, and now been quite misunderstood by another that believed in it so strongly that they just knew I must be lacking in faith since I wasn't receiving it. Right in the middle was my loving church family at Harvest International Church, and had it not been for them I would probably be dead in a gutter somewhere today. I am forever indebted to those who held my hands in the air *for years* when the fighting got too hard to bear alone -- the Andersons, the Barrys, Dena Fields, the Frosts, the Gees, the Gwinns, the Harmons, the Humphreys, the Marreros, Jennifer Middleman, the Mullins, Christy Ray Pugh, Nancy Sharpes, Sandy Smith, the Smiths, Fiona Soltes, the Svoltos, the Watsons, the Withers, the Zides -- whew! From A to Z God had us covered! Add to that the core of the former Friday Night Bible Study gang -- the Peters, the Barrys, the Sandifers, and wow!: True Aarons and Hurs just like Moses had! You must understand, these people became covenant family. Of course, because of our growing ministry around the nation I also had the undying support of many others. God brought them out of the woodworks to keep me going. So keep me going they did, but still, none of these people -- or their amazing prayer coverage -- seemed to be able to stay the hand of the treacherous warfare against my life. It only increased.

> *"My son, pay attention to what I say; listen closely to my words. Do not let them out of your sight, keep them within your heart; for they are life to those who find them and health to a man's whole body. Proverbs 4:20-22*

At the crux of all of this I began to ponder the question that so many others had asked since the beginning of time. Why do the good suffer? David asked it. Paul asked it. We are all still asking today! It certainly can do harm to the faith of those watching, and almost helps explain why so many Christians believe it is the will of God to not heal some. They see sickness on a "godly" man or woman and assume it to be the will of God, not taking into account that he or she may be prime target by Satan in a long line of generational curses. It may not be his sin eating away at the health of his body, but the penalizing sins of his forefathers. Exodus 34:7 says, "Yet He does not leave the guilty unpunished; He punishes the children and their children for the sin of the fathers to the third and fourth generation." Praise God, these curses can be broken! The question is, how many of us pray those lineage prayers? Even Jesus, after healing someone, would say, "Your sins are forgiven you", which obviously shows the correlation between sin and sickness. That's not judgment, that's the truth. We must see this link between the two -- not so we can become perfect and attain healing -- but so we can be cleansed and maintain it!

"Because of your wrath there is no health in my body; my bones have no soundness because of my sin." Psalm 38:3

Even knowing all this I still wondered if there was another key I was not factoring in. Not a hidden sin, but a hidden ignorance. An ignorance concerning submission. Once again, God began to set me up for the upcoming revelation. It was something that could not be learned on the padded chair of a conference, but that must be experienced with the blood, sweat and tears of life. It could not be imparted through the mere laying on of hands, anymore than patience could be received in such ways. As I asked and asked God for directions on this journey that He Himself had put me on, I felt as if I was wandering around the same mountain over and over again. I kept praying. I kept rallying the troops. We kept fighting in the heavenlies, but finally I was at the end of my rope physically and could not go on unless the Lord moved.

By now I had exhausted every prayer I had, and stood in every healing line for prayer at every service I could find to attend. God actually told me to quit going! He told me that the rest of my healing would not come in a healing line, although I'd seen Him do that for many others -- even through my own hands in many gatherings. He told me it would come another way. My health grew increasingly worse and I was now pregnant with our sixth child and having countless petit mal seizures every day -- in the hundreds -- and waking most mornings to an awaiting war. I had about one convulsion each week in which I would lay unconscious for several hours afterwards. I fell through glass, fell down stairs, almost drowned, and oh, I cannot recount all the episodes of fear. I almost think it was harder on those watching me though -- my husband and children -- and yet somehow they bravely cared for me dozens and dozens and dozens of times when I was unable to care for myself. It turned my children into prayer mercenaries; intercessory troopers of war determined to see Satan pay. My husband too emerged quite a warrior, and before my very eyes I saw this calm, quiet man become Satan's worst enemy! So there we were, all looking like Hulk Hogans in the spirit, yet feeling like puny Gumbies in the natural. It was a strenuous time. We prayed and prayed, then would emerge revived and ready. For what? To pray some more! It tested our hearts for prayer. We went from "can you not watch with Me for one hour" to "Lord, can we not just have one hour off?". Having done all else though, we stood (Ephesians 6:13), eventually growing unashamed that we were "praying through to the breakthrough" even if the whole world got tired of hearing us pray the same things!

"Once more He went away and prayed the same thing."
Mark 14:39

"theWAIT"

It goes without saying this was written in that desert time:

I've got a problem; Maybe you have the same
Mine searches me out and it knows me by name
Its goal is to use me and leave me ashamed
To kill, steal and destroy

It met no resistance, once upon a time
For years I allowed it, for years I was blind
And then I awoke and saw what was mine
Although I have still yet to hold it

I've asked believing; I've fasted; I've prayed
I've heard God's instruction and learned to obey
I've seen others get what I want in one day
And learned to love without envy

I've spoke to the mountain; I've named and I've claimed
I've bound and I've loosed and had things stay the same
I've warred with the name that's above all names
While it seemed to profit me nothing

Through visions and dreams my instruction's been sealed
Hearing more than can ever be shared or revealed
Staying quiet so God's secret plans are concealed
And released then at just the right moment

I've trusted, rested, hoped for and doubted
I've ached with self-pity, I've grieved and I've pouted
I've seen power come when I whispered or shouted
For I've learned it's not your volume, but your authority

I've seen my protection in prayer as I kneeled
I've seen with my eyes His great buckler and shield

*Discovering wholeness as you wait to be healed
And dwelling in the shelter of the Most High*

*I've drank from a fountain, in gulps and in sips
I've seen the Son shine in a total eclipse
I've tasted sweet praise pouring over bruised lips
and I've felt Him inhabit that praise*

*Hungry for more, I've tasted some power
I've drank from a cup that is sweet, and still sour
I've starved my flesh hoping to feast at some hour
Only to feast once again on the fruit of patience*

*I've swam upstream in water that's muddy
I've knocked and I've knocked til my knuckles are bloody
I've heard people say without words that I'm nutty
And can honestly say I've died to all reputation*

*I've suffered through wisdom that's not from above
I've heard it come straight out of mouths that I love
I've talked with Job's friends, who were jury and judge
And learned that I'll never act that way to anybody again in my whole life...*

*People tell me where to go but don't know where I am
"Try these herbs", "Take this pill", "Eat more fat, and less ham"!
But looking deep into their eyes, I saw the love of the Lamb
and realized they meant no harm, but simply wanted me well*

*Blessed is he who does not see, yet believes
Perhaps it's an office we all should achieve
The price though, is more than we ever perceive
When we start praying those dangerous prayers for patience*

Does faith say this is the day, if it's not?
Can God stretch a scene if He's building a plot?
Do you judge those who wait, or want what they've got?
Knowing that it's through faith & patience we receive God's promises

We can't live without it, we can barely live through it
It's a fruit of God's Spirit, and there's no shortcuts to it
If you find one, it only reveals that you blew it
Cause King James said it best when he called it "long suffering".

Are you willing to wait? Are you able to learn?
Is getting an answer your only concern?
Can anything hide your impatience that burns
From a God who is a consuming fire and knows your heart?

Those who wait on the Lord, they will find great strength
Strength that cannot be owned by the proud, but the meek
It's the joy of the Lord without which you're weak
Strength by which you can run against a troop and defeat your enemies

Your waiting is precious; Your trials are gold;
Your tears: liquid praise when the battle gets old
Though the waters rise and the rivers overflow;
You're winning! You're winning! You're winning!

Though others may laugh and call you a fool
Though despised, rejected, judged; ridiculed
Never forget this one tiny rule:
"Do not be deceived; God is not mocked; A man will reap what he sows."
(Galatians 6:17)

THE TEST

Near the end of this rugged pregnancy, the sixth, Chris suggested that I return to a neurologist to determine what was going on in my body. It was as if the illness was different than before, and it now seemed too dangerous to ignore. However, I knew that going to a doctor meant more medication, and I was sticking to my guns and was totally unwilling to return to a medication that God had told me to come off of. Still, with just a few months left on the insurance plan we were on, I saw a window of time to have this testing covered, and so I consented and made an appointment. The doctor set me up for a series of neurological tests that proved shocking. We discovered that the epilepsy -- that deaf and dumb spirit -- had grown more hostile than we'd known. I was told that day that there were four main forms of epilepsy and that I had them all. Unlike partialized seizures in which just a certain damaged area of the brain has the seizures, I had what was called "generalized" seizures, which meant that my entire brain was damaged and under constant fire. In essence, epilepsy is merely an overactive brain in which there are over-firings and mis-firings from the neurons within, and in my case, constant misfirings. The neurologist read the E.E.G. results and told me that I was having constant seizure activity in all regions of my brain at all times -- whether I was aware of it or not. This explained the memory loss, confusion and even difficulty in basic communication at times -- not something a public speaker wants to hear.

I am sure it was during this season that my "Eisenhower coat" got full. By the power of God's strong grace, I stood firm and never once wanted to quit. Where would I go? I had entered the land of all or nothing. To walk away from my healing at this point would have been to walk away from God. The two were so tangled up together that I had finally reached that place where God could do a miracle. I wanted victory for Nashville too, but it was a pursuit that would run me into the ground if I didn't stay close to God and get the right keys from Him. This diagnosis now left me standing at a door that was so massive I could not ignore it, and yet the tiny key He was trying to put in my hand to open it seemed so insignificant that I discounted it. It was the key of submission. I think there are many more than just me who disregard it.

My take on the matter was, "Give me liberty or give me death!". I was on a mission from God against that deaf and dumb spirit and would not back away from it. Chris' view of the whole thing however was, "Uh, honey... your brain cells are frying and the kids and I have to run in the room every time we hear you drop something in fear that you're having a convulsion!". I couldn't drive, I couldn't bathe alone without Chris hanging around pretending to have something to fix in the bathroom, and I couldn't stay up late at night to write like I wanted because the convulsions always seemed to come with sleep loss. As a result, my creativity suffered a bit and I felt unfulfilled at times. All that in the name of obedience. How ridiculous I now see! Jesus said His yoke was light and easy! Not always simple, because once you begin chasing God all hell will chase *you*, but certainly it should have been easier than the drudgery I was persisting through. I will say however that I/we had tapped into such a joy that it fueled us with an invincible strength. We were winning individual battles as a result, but somehow off track as to winning the whole war.

That was difficult to see however when the neurologist all

but demanded I go back on anti-convulsants. It was a new drug with fewer side effects to the patient, but upon investigation we discovered that it had a risk of still born births or fetal death in unborn babies when administered to their mothers in later gestation. I was six months pregnant. I hated the idea of the medicine, not just for the obvious reasons, but mainly because I considered it in direct opposition to the word God had given me to lay the medicine down -- *a word from 1993*. Little did I know I was clinging to yesterday's word! Here I was, an advocate who was teaching people everywhere that the deaf and dumb spirit would plug up their ears and cause them to cling to yesterday's words since they could not hear God today, and yet I myself was guilty as charged! I was so unable to understand why God would require me to go "backwards" that I even became angry at Him. Determined to obey Him, yet indignant about how He wanted me to do it! It was as if I was using the very spirit of endurance that God had put within me to endure against God. How tormenting! Still, I saw my persistence as obedience and rejected the advice about going on the medication. Advice that Chris seemed to favor. That's when everything hit the fan.

THE POWER OF PERSUASION

I can mark the day it happened. Submission left the camp and my protection left with it. It was not a rude lack of submission or any other overt disagreement, in fact, there was no disagreement at all. So how had submission left the camp? Through my ability to persuade Chris over to my view of things -- a view that unfortunately was so emotionally tied to the situation that it could not see clearly. Oh what a fine line lays between persuasion and coercion! And the closer a couple are in marriage the easier it can be for the one leading to lose his head and make decisions based on feeling and not faith. Swaying Chris with my desire to check out some nutritional and herbal remedies, he gave in and I began seeing a nutritionist and was quickly put on a regimented herbal/dietary routine. He even went with me, and we had a form of peace in our home as a result. I was so excited about the nutritionist's findings and suggestions! It all made perfect sense! We had come to a logical speculation as to why I was having the seizures and now I would not have to take the dreaded anti-convulsant pill every day. Hurray! The funny thing is that I ended up taking fourteen supplements and vitamin tablets each day, plus a cream to balance my hormones in case their deficiency which was causing the seizures! What I was calling freedom was actually a bondage. I began having more and more seizures, and even more convulsions which resulted in injuries I'd never sustained before. My tongue was so marred and scarred from all the bitings that it hardly looked like a tongue anymore. I cried so much and so hard during this time that I had constant speckled bruises under my eyes. I was so perplexed. I had seen proper nutrition work and solve mysteries in the lives of so many others, and so it puzzled me. It puzzled those who had encouraged me to do it! It made no sense to any of us who had fasted and prayed about it, especially since the only route left was to go on the anti-convulsants. But that's when I started seeing the pattern. A pattern in the past in which God would take something totally irrational, totally illogical, and then have me apply all of my faith to it. I was going to have to lay down everything that I had gathered in my arms on this healing journey prior to this point: Every promise. Every prophetic word. Every dream. Every pain. Even every instruction by God He'd told me to wage war with.

This obedience felt like disobedience, and yet God was trying to save my life. It was a surprise attack on the enemy. Like Abraham, I was going to have to take the very promise of God and lay it on an altar.

> *"...God tested Abraham. He said to him, "Abraham!" "Here I am," he replied. Then God said, "Take your son, your only son, Isaac, whom you love, and go to the region of Moriah. Sacrifice him there as a burnt offering on one of the mountains I will tell you about.""*
> Genesis 22:1-2

I remember during this time frame one of the hardest tests of submission I had was to my pastor. The two most godly men I walked with on a daily basis, Chris and Pastor Brad, and they were both ganging up on me it felt like! I had returned from a neurologist's visit and felt I needed prayer on whether or not I would begin the medication again. Since this medication was so dangerous, I decided to send out an email to my closest circle (which was about 60 people in my case), and ask them to pray and seek the Lord for me. Something inside told me to let two people read it first. Chris and Brad. I immediately got a call from Pastor telling me to reconsider sending it. He would never order me not to, but I could hear the urgency in his voice. "Laura, what you do not need right now are countless, conflicting prophetic "words" from the Lord. You need to listen carefully to your husband and submit to the authority and wisdom that God will give him for the task." It was the words of Paul in 1 Corinthians 4:15: "Even though you have ten thousand guardians in Christ, you do not have many fathers, for in Christ Jesus I became your father through the gospel." I was so mad! I cried incoherently while on the phone with him and told him I could not do without the prayer coverage of these people! I gave him an earful of Reluctant Submission! However, I knew by Pastor's urging he was saying that God would bring my answer from the top down, and not from side to side. If I would give up the lateral God would give me the literal. I decided to not send the well-written email, but instead decided to take it to God via knee-mail. That night I asked God to shoot straight with me, and shoot He did.

THE HARD TRUTH

When I asked the Lord why the nutritional route had not worked for me, He made it very clear what I was dealing with: "This is not a health issue, Laura. It is a submission issue. You are trying to submit to Me without submitting forthright and undesigningly to your husband, but Chris and I are so tangled up together over you that you cannot separate us. Do as he says." My whole world got an instant front and rear end alignment. I realized that although my heart had been pure, I had unknowingly run off the road somewhere. "In his heart a man plans his course, but the LORD determines his steps." Proverbs 16:9 How true! Proverbs 20:24 echoes this by adding: "A man's steps are directed by the LORD. How then can anyone understand his own way?". I could no longer "understand my way". I was so emotionally spent that I was nearing a nervous breakdown. Add to this all we were going through financially in the now four years since Chris had stepped away from his job, and campsmith was in a heavy-duty pressure cooker!

After many, many, many years of working on my strong will, God had finally gotten the best of me. All those years that I was serving Him with gusto and sincerity with all the gifts He'd given me suddenly seemed like filthy rags. Hear me: I have served the Lord my *whole* life, been a spirit-filled worshiper who desired to see Him face to face and a servant who humbly sought to be entrusted with the biggest of jobs He needed doing. I have always given God my best! The best of the best, in heart, body and soul. But here I sat with the hard-earned understanding that even that didn't cut it. God doesn't want our best, he wants our worst so He can give us better than best! Best is just filthy rags! Just when I felt like I was at my worst, God showed me He could finally get the best of me. I was so dead to my hopes and dreams that I was begging God not to use me anymore. "For Your own sake Lord, find someone else!" I now knew why Moses and Jeremiah told God to find somebody else. I wasn't quitting, and neither were they. We were just all trying to do God a favor. I realized there was nothing good in me, short of Jesus. Not even just a little bit. It was the sweetest most painful time of my life. I had never felt so weak, and yet so free. Nothing left to worry about. If I went crazy at least I'd be done with the battle. It was actually a very liberating place where the enemy could cause me no more torment. That's when true death to the flesh occurred. Death doesn't say, "Thank God I've died to my dreams, hallelujah amen, and now God can resurrect them!". True, all-the-way, bona fide death has no kick left, no ulterior motives, no plans and no hope in anything short of the love of God. There, it and you are totally at rest. There, God is Your portion. I was dead indeed and begging God to be smart and not raise me.

But raise me He did! I remember waking up in the middle of the night one night during this time and deciding to get up and pray. When I got to the living room, Chris was already there, pacing back and forth in prayer. We sat down together and talked about how dead we were. We decided there was nothing "good" in us, and finally we understood Jesus' words:

> "Why do you call me good?" Jesus answered. "No one is good --except God alone." Mark 10:18

It was not a weak place of concession or termination to our vows that night, it was a place even the Son of God had been willing to go. It was the same revelation Paul had when he said, "I know that nothing good lives in me, that is, in my sinful nature." Romans 7:18. It was my heart saying, " I am nothing without you God. "I can do nothing *for* you... But you can do everything *through* me now". It was decreasing so He could increase. It was an unshackling emancipation.

A NEW BEGINNING

On Passover 2000 baby #6 arrived. Due on Resurrection Easter Sunday, she came instead three days early on the day in which Israel celebrates how a Sovereign God saved them from a spirit of death that passed over their homes as they rested safely inside having applied the blood of the lamb. It was so with campsmith. With eighteen people in the delivery room that night, we celebrated and wept, and even won a hospital award that landed us on the news with all local networks. All of Nashville celebrated her birth with us. "Jenesis", our new beginning. Change began to come to every area of our lives. After the pregnancy ended, I started on the new medication. The neurologist told me not to put too much hope in it totally taking away all the various kinds of seizures, but we were greatly surprised.

Immediately, almost overnight, I went from having more than a hundred absence seizures a day to none. On a bad day, maybe one or two. I went from having weekly convulsions to none at all, and that has remained the case since the day I accepted this call to submission. Not one grand mal seizure! But the surprising thing is that due to nursing the baby, I was only put on half the normal adult dosage and yet it has had complete success and amazed the neurologists. I have obviously already attained another level of my healing. Another step in the "by process" healing that God promised me on my sofa that day in 1993. And while a few say that this is the entire healing that God has for me, I disagree. I am dead to the dreams of man and the enemy has no place in me. I am Teflon to his schemes of strife. I have been fully resurrected by the Lord Jesus Christ and when He raised me up from the pit of despair His promise for healing was still alive within my womb. It has not yet been birthed and held, and therefore it would be sin for me to abort it. Besides, God did not promise me the absence of seizures only but the presence of health! He didn't say he would just prevent my seizures but that He would heal them. And He will. You watch and see!

GO FIGURE

I once sat down and tallied an average number of all the seizures I suppose I've had over the course of the 23 years. That's 8400 days of embodying this affliction. Times 1,440 minutes in each day that totals 12,096,000 minutes. Prior to this last season of my life, I can count the days on two hands in which I've had no seizures at all during the 23 years. Some days having 2 or 3 each minute, sometimes even more. Sometimes less though-- only experiencing 1 or 2 each hour, and with that average, the Lord helped me do the math and count up all the enemy had stolen. One or more seizures per hour -- or at least 30 seizures per day every day -- times the 8400 days equals 252,000 absence seizures. I do not understand how I have any brain cells left, nor how my creativity continues to only be sharpened. At 3 seconds each (sometimes more, sometimes less) this totals 756,000 seconds of unconsciousness or 12,600 minutes or 210 hours of battling this deaf and dumb spirit physically. Add to that the 80+ convulsions (grand mal seizures) throughout the years, which brought at least 2 hours of total loss of consciousness each (not to mention the hours and days of being out of commission afterwards), and those convulsions have stolen at least 160 hours of my God-given time. Coupled with the 210 hours from the petit mal absence seizures, that totals 370 hours or 15.4 days stolen from my life. 15.4 days where I could have been a mouthpiece for God. 15.4 days that I could have been interceding. 15.4 days where I could have been vibrant and enjoying the family and incredible life that God has given me. Therefore, I have told the Lord my God that in His promise to restore to me all that the locusts have eaten, I will accept no less than a 15.4 day visitation from Him face to face! With a double portion that's a whole month! Amen!

All these figures of course do not even come close to accounting for the hours, days, and bloody tears spent in prayer and fasting, battling this spirit in hand to hand combat. I would count all that time in prayer, but that has been my reward and shown me the face of God! Why should I hold that against the enemy?! Ha!

THE GOOD NEWS CONTINUES

Even during the writing of this book, my healing advances.

In an M.R.I. that was ordered for me by my neurologist during the writing of this very chapter, an amazing report came to us. "Mrs. Smith, your brain is "absolutely normal". "Perfectly fine". He tells me there is still activity in it that they are unable to explain, but that after 23 years of intense electrical storms, there is not one spot, clot, tumor or damage at all in my brain. It was just a year or two ago that a reputable neurologist with scientific tests in hand told me my entire brain was damaged! That alone is proof that God is at work and not finished with this story! I know beyond a shadow of anybody's doubt that I was not created to have seizures!

"Little by little I will drive them out before you, until you have increased enough to take possession of the land."
Exodus 23:30

(a word from the Lord to me in May 1994)

IT TAKES TWO, BABY

"...imitate those who through faith and patience inherit the promises." Hebrews 6:12

Abraham waited. Sarah waited. Hannah waited. Paul waited. David, Elijah, and Daniel waited. Job, Ruth and Noah waited. Even our Savior waited. It paid off, and they all saw the promise and held it in their arms. What an honor to be told in Hebrews 6:12 to imitate them. But most people preach that we should imitate their faith, and yet forget the patience part. We are commanded to imitate their patience. I don't like patience any more than anybody else, but if it is 50% of the inheritance package, then I'm not going to leave it out!

Although this is a book about submission and not healing, my submission journey does intertwine with my healing journey and so I'd like to say one more thing and dedicate this sub-chapter ("It Takes Two, Baby") to those of you who may be in the same boat... waiting to get to the other side. God's promises take faith AND patience, so be encouraged in your patience. Let it be an aggressive warrior patience. Don't just wait for Jesus to wake up though. Lay down next to Him, grab hold of Him, and enjoy Him with worship and adoration in the midst of the storm. It will end. You are a child of God! He has told you in His Word you're going to the other side, so you will! In the meantime, however, do not be discouraged when other people get answers before you. God is not doing the same work in them. God's instruction is not one size fits all. The Bible also seems to differentiate between healings and miracles. In 1 Corinthians 12:28-30, twice Paul makes mention of miracles and healings as separate things. A miracle happens instantly, but the Greek word for healing is "therapeuo" (Strongs #2323) which means "to wait upon, to adore, to relieve, cure, heal or worship". It is where we get the word "therapy" from, which indicates a recovery process. A healing is a recovery. However the Greek word for miracle is "semeion" (Strongs #4592) which means "an indication, miracle, sign, token or wonder". So see? If you pray for healing and see an immediate indication that you are well, that's a miracle. But if you pray and "wait upon" the Lord during a recovery, then that, my dear, is a bona fide healing. No shame involved during the wait! You are right on track! Just make sure that you stay on track and do not waver. That will profit you nothing.

Unfortunately, most of us who believe in healing are often caught implying that everything comes instantly. Name it, claim it. Believe it, receive it. We insinuate that if it doesn't come instantly, there's something wrong with your faith. The truth is, sometimes in Scripture we are told that someone is healed "from that very hour" (Matthew 15:28), and other times we are not. I'm not suggesting Jesus didn't do things instantly, because many times He did, but the truth is we are not always told exactly what happened when the person got home. We know Jesus didn't heal the lepers instantly, but sent them on a journey first. We know of His parable about the widow in Luke 18:1-8 who got her breakthrough only because she kept asking and asking in persistence. We also know Jesus made the Syrian-Pheonecian woman ask thrice and practically beg before He acknowledged her request and cast a demon out of her daughter. In fact, when she came to Him, Matthew 15:23 says, "Jesus did not answer a word." Today we would condemn that sister for not hearing from the Lord, or accuse the brother of not having enough faith to move the hand of God! Listen folks, Jesus did not answer that woman on purpose! He knew what He was doing, and His hush caused her gush of faith!

There are other times in Scripture when the word "healing" is used and yet it *was* instant. In one such example though, Acts 3 & 4 where the lame man at the Gate of Beautiful was healed, it doesn't just say he was healed but that he was "miraculously" healed (Acts 4:22). This is the Greek word "semeion" again. The King James version of Acts 4:22 calls it a "miracle of healing". The man had an indication of his healing right there on the spot. If he had received a healing ("to wait upon") and not a miracle ("an indication, sign or token"), he would have gone home, still been healed in Jesus' name, but waiting for that healing to fully manifest in his body. Still healed, but waiting for his body to line up with the Word of God. So it was the miracle part that made it instant for him, and not necessarily the healing part. Just the same, we can have a financial miracle, or God may wish to stretch it out to teach us intuitive stewardship for something massive we're about to be entrusted with. The same can happen in your marriage too: God may grant you the answer, or He just might give you a new angle instead! Either way, God is up to something good on your behalf.

> *"Does God give you his Spirit and work miracles among you because you observe the law, or because you believe what you heard?" Galatians 3:5*

There have been times I have prayed to be well and seen a little bit of miracle and a little bit of healing mixed together. It's as if God gives you an instant indication to spur on faith, which then keeps you going during the rest of the process. I suppose that is what is happening with me right now. I thank God for doing it this way too, for if He had chosen to do it all at once, I'd have a miracle with a whole lot less character in my life. How much glory would God get out of that?

Sometimes God is after more than just healing your body. There is a sister at my church who was healed instantly of epilepsy years ago around the time I started asking God to heal me too. We were both asking at the same time. He heard us both and responded. However she got a miracle and I got a healing. Interestingly enough though, this sister has struggles in her home and continues to believe God for her husband to be saved, while I sit here with a godly man that I found when I was 17 yrs. old and married right out of school with no waiting involved. How can we remain good friends? Because we both believe that God has heard us and responded, giving us both what we need in the increments we need them. But while many people stop there and believe for no more, this sister and I know that one day we will both have both! Until then, we inspire each other on, like iron sharpening iron. I personally believe that if more people would grab hold of this scriptural differences between miracles and healings, they would feel less condemned in their waitings, and as a result their faith would be increased and we'd see more miracles springing forth all around us like never before in this hour!

THE SUBMISSION REVIVAL

With all that clarified, let me conclude: Out of all the submission stories I could have included in this book, this one of my healing journey was the most important, but the toughest. Toughest because authors like to have an end to the story in mind before they begin! I did not share this chapter with you so you could send me 400 prophetic words about when my healing will spring forth, and so please don't. I am SO enjoying the unveiling of the timing of God that I don't want you to spoil it for me! I am not settling for where I am, nor am I in unbelief. I have seen plenty of immediate miracles flow through my hands including the healing of H.I.V. and cancer. I have *watched* a man's leg grow into my hands and listened to his spine pop and re-align as I sat at his feet praying for it to happen in my pastor's office. But I, like the persistent widow, Namaan, or the ten lepers who were sent on a healing journey before their health was made manifest, am unafraid of perseverance. I have finally learned to be patient, and in my patience I have possessed my soul!

I chose to include this chapter about my frequent tryer

miles because I wanted you to see the depths that God will require you to go in your submission to Him. Not to Him alone, but to others He has strategically placed in your life. There was no other way to prick your hearts with this conviction without laying myself bare and sharing the ways in which submission has literally saved my life. I cling to submission as if my very life depends on it because I know that it does. The height that I want to soar at is the depth that I must be willing to dive to. Submission is my umbrella, my armor, and closer than that, it is the very skin that wraps me up and holds me together each day. I incite you to grasp this! There is a submission revival coming and it is the key to your big doors. It will hasten your promotion. It will expedite your destiny and get you there in one piece! It is not enough to submit directly to God when He is tangling Himself up with others over you whom He wants to direct your journey through. Trust Him! Trust them! Put your money where your mouth is and go for the gold!

THE MISSING KEY

At the very start of this journey I had a dream that I was standing at a large wooden door with Christ. He stared at me with a large keyring full of keys and asked, "What good does it do for Me to have these keys if you will not take them from Me?". Now, all these years later, I had the same exact dream one night and found myself standing at the same wooden door with Jesus. This time I had a key in my hand. I stuck it in the lock and turned it. Nothing happened. Frustrated by many more attempts, I began to kick the door and try to beat it down. I wound up exhausted and fell to my knees on the ground. It was there that I saw a second lock, at the very bottom right corner of the door just above the dirt. I looked at Jesus and He gave me another key. As I put it in the lock, the door swung open as if it had been waiting for years to be freed. There, crying on the ground, I heard God speak: "The key to the top lock is authority. Because the Body of Christ has had so little understanding about the authority I have given them over every circumstance in their life, once that shiny key is discovered many stop there and are satisfied. But doors will not open with authority alone, for I had all authority over all the earth and yet it took humility to save it. Humility is the second key, My daughter. Your submission helped you find it, and you have found it -- and Me -- on your knees." I weep even now just reliving the visitation. I pray to God that part III to this dream reveals what blessings are on the others side of that door. I pray it shows me stepping over the threshold into a permanent residence called authority *with* humility. If not, I pray God keeps me on the outside on my knees until I am ready to move in and call it home.

I believe I am called to stir up bee's nests, even hornets' nests, in prayer. Prophetic intercession precedes every other work of God -- salvations, healings, deliverances -- and serves as the plow that cultivates the soil of lives and regions. Amos 3:7 says, "Surely the Sovereign LORD does nothing without revealing his plan to his servants the prophets". Many of you know you're called to this too. You sense a holy dissatisfaction in your life and you know enough about God to know He can do the impossible. I am not suggesting that submission will entirely remove you from the pangs of warfare as you stir up those things in prayer, because it won't, but it will certainly shield you from all warfare that is not of God. Aren't there enough battles that God allows without us extracting more out of Hell to contend with? Not everything can be reduced to warfare either. I know some Christians who are so proud of their scars that they brag about the constant warfare they're in. Come on people! Just because you are engaged in a battle with the enemy does not mean that God called you into it. Your disobedience and rebellion will eat away at your peace and prevent God's protection if you are constantly running out from under Him. True, just by signing up for God's army you are drafted into battle, but why pick fights that aren't yours? What if you're shouldering another's battle and preventing them from learning to fight? It is time for us to tame our flesh, bridle our wills and submit to the Father of spirits. In doing so, just imagine the army of God that will emerge focused on the tasks God has called them to! A resolute, ardent people so submitted to God that they are invisible to their enemy and thereby able to accomplish each mission without wounding!

"Submit to God and be at peace with him; in this way prosperity will come to you." Job 22:21

SUBMISSION DIGEST (a glance back at all we've learned)

I. The Controversies of Submission
    a. Dry Submarines - Leaving the shore and plunging deeply into humility and submission
    b. Grounds for Submission - Forgiving and learning to trust those in authority over you
    c. Lost Umbrellas - Acknowledging that everyone needs covering by someone

II. The Criteria
    a. Parental Submission - "Children, obey your

parents in everything, Colossians 3:20
b. Marital Submission - "Wives, submit to your husbands as to the Lord." Ephesians 5:22
c. Mutual Submission -"Submit to one another out of reverence for Christ." Ephesians 5:21
d. Occupational Submission- "If your boss is angry with you, don't quit!" Ecclesiastes 10:4
e. Pastoral Submission - "Obey your leaders and submit to their authority." Hebrews 13:17
f. Governmental Submission-""Everyone must submit himself to the governing authorities" Romans 13:1

III. The Counterfeits
    a. Reluctant Submission - Not submission at all but SUBtle rebellion
    b. Pouty-face Submission - Not a submitted tone but a SUBliminal one
    c. Doormat Submission - Not submission at all but SUBhuman

    d. Deceitful Submission - Not submitted but SUBterfuged
    e. Let's Make a Deal Submission - Not submitting but SUBdueing
    f. June Cleaver Submission - Not submission but SUBservience
    g. Sarcastic Submission - Not submission at all but SUBreption
    h. Murmuring Submission - Not submission but SUBstandard

IV. The Clout
    a. Fearless Submission - SUBlime! SUBstantial!

b. Being Worthy To Be Submitted To - "Do not rule over them ruthlessly, but fear your God." Leviticus 25:43 / "Fathers, do not exasperate your children." Ephesians 6:4

c. Frequent Trier Miles - "The Lord will reward everyone for whatever good he does, whether he is slave or free." Ephesians 6:8

As we close out now, I challenge you to pray the following prayer. It is not for the faint-hearted or the wavering. But if you are ready to take a step up by laying your life down, able to fathom how losing your life helps you find it, and willing to trust that submission is the solution to much of the disunity and chaos in your life, then go for it! I double-dog-dare you! Ready? Hold your breath and jump!

"Lord, with the summation of this submission study, I acknowledge to you that I sense your call upon my life -- even if I do not know in full what it is -- and I now understand that I need Your design for protection and covering to fulfill it. I ask you clothe me with humility and courage and help me be at peace when you require a temporary hiddenness from me to protect me. Help me trust Your timing. Help me to submit my will to those you've given the privilege of leading me. I fully forgive all those over and around me who have ever abused my trust, and ask now for a new level of trust as I learn to once again submit to authority. Give me such love for those I pardon that all unforgiveness is washed away and blessings for them well up within me and spring forth from my lips for them. I pray for my leaders now too, the ones you will bring and the ones you've already brought into my life,

and I ask that the wisdom of Solomon be upon them as they pray for me and instruct me with the wisdom of heaven for my life. And God, if Your Spirit does not reside within them may it be done this very hour as I pray this prayer! Be full of God and provoked into relationship with Him by what you see in me! As I submit to them, Lord, may we "submit to one another" and co-labor through the thoroughfares of life. I know this includes my parents, my spouse, my friends, my bosses, my pastor and other church leaders, and even my government leaders. I vow to You today to begin praying for them in a new capacity and ask you for the fresh desire to. May my submission not be reluctant, pouty, doormat-like, deceitful, bargaining, June Cleaverish, sarcastic or murmuring. May I not receive any counterfeit! I prophesy fearless submission over my heart, my memories and my dreams of the future. I declare that there are leaders worth submitting to and that as I submit to them, I myself am becoming a true leader in God's eyes! Make me into your image God, and as I humble myself before you I ask for Your Son, Jesus, to grab hold of my heart and take up full residence there. I acknowledge Him as the One who died for me that I must die to myself for, as the One who was resurrected who will resurrect all my hopes and dreams, and as the Supreme Creator who has created a tailor-made destiny for me that I am about to embrace! I prophesy godspeed to tomorrow, healing to yesterday, and submission to today! Amen and amen!

Submission is possible
Surrender is too
The good news, my friend, is
It's all up to you...

Printed in the United States
123241LV00004B/1-12/A